THE BALANCE OF TOMORROW

Tell me then if I have or have not every rea-
son to be preoccupied with the world's near
future, and tell me whether or not in dealing
with this question I am not dealing with the
real question.

—Donoso Cortes

by Robert Strausz-Hupé

AXIS AMERICA

GEOPOLITICS

THE BALANCE OF TOMORROW

THE BALANCE

OF TOMORROW

POWER AND FOREIGN POLICY IN THE

UNITED STATES

Robert Strausz-Hupé

G. P. PUTNAM'S SONS, NEW YORK

355
S912b

Second Impression

Typography by Robert Josephy

To E. and Joe

ACKNOWLEDGMENTS

My heaviest debt of gratitude is owed my friend, Stephen T. Possony, who assisted patiently in the task of research. His criticism and suggestions, fortified by ever-present knowledge, were invaluable in completing this work.

I wish to thank my colleague Thomas A. Cowan, who read the manuscript and helped to tie up many loose ends in it. Among others to whom I owe a considerable debt are Fawn H. Brodie, William S. Culbertson, Henry Field, Charles A. Micaud, Harold Sprout and Sergius O. Yacobson. James L. Divvins and Walter H. Haas helped in the making of the map and charts. I am grateful to Mary Hoeffel, Elizabeth Mensch, and Yolanda Legnini for the speedy and careful typing of the manuscript.

Robert Strausz-Hupé

PREFACE

THIS book went to press before atomic power was used for the first time in the history of warfare. A source of immense potential energy has now been tapped. The impact of this event on international power cannot be measured as yet. Ultimately, our whole way of life as well as the industrial system as we know it today will be replaced by another way of life and other means of production. This inevitable transformation may be expected to affect international society but slowly—certainly during the crucial years immediately ahead of us with which this book is mainly concerned.

Uranium is a rare element which because of its very rarity cannot form the *sole* basis of industrial production. Therefore the atomic age will really dawn upon us only when uranium is more readily available or when energy imprisoned in some more common element can be set free and can be controlled. In the immediate future, atomic power will be chiefly of military and political significance. The power political implications of atomic fission are as follows:

(1) Uranium has become one of the basic raw materials of state power. Since most pitchblende deposits are situated within the orbit of the three Great Powers, namely the United States, the British Empire, and the Soviet Union, their power relations have not been changed fundamentally—at least as regards their respective raw material positions.

(2) Small industrial powers, like Belgium and Czechoslovakia, controlling uranium deposits, have gained in political and economic importance.

(3) The successful application of atomic fission was the result of close scientific and industrial co-operation between the United States and the British Empire. If these two powers continue to pool their resources, intellectual and material, the security of both will in all likelihood be assured and with it perhaps the peace of the world.

(4) In the military sphere, the accent has been shifted to the offensive—a fact which may not be regarded as conducive to permanent peace.

(5) Despite the immense enhancement of the offensive potential, spacious countries with dispersed industrial areas may still

v

be able to withstand strategic assault if and when driven home with a limited number of atomic bombs; although their security, too, will depend on unflagging vigilance. Accordingly, in the military sphere, the atomic bomb creates a state of permanent and universal emergency in which the maintenance of a passive defense is an essential prerequisite for national security. ·

The history of the invention reinforces the contention advanced in Chapter XII, that brains, industrial organization, and national wealth, as well as the courage to assume calculated risks, are essential if not the most important elements of power. No other country except the United States could in the midst of a deadly war effectively mobilize the material, intellectual, and spiritual resources which went into the development of the atomic bomb. The country which will be able to repeat such an unprecedented performance will emerge as the world's strongest and most potent power.

It is unfortunate that the military demonstration of atomic power during the closing week of World War II will necessarily lead to superficial evaluation of its real importance. The atomic bomb may easily be taken for a *deus ex machina in rebus militaribus,* an implement of war invalidating all other known instruments of power, whereas, in fact, it may in the end merely change them technologically by increasing their destructive efficiency. At the present state of development, and with the information now available in the public domain, it is difficult if not impossible to predict the future of land, sea, and air power in the atomic age.

The immediate danger inherent in the mere existence of the atomic bomb, nay, even in the mere knowledge of its possession, resides in psychological imponderables: a "trigger happiness" induced by anxiety neurosis on an international scale. A ruthless and unscrupulous aggressor will not hesitate to use the new weapon, not to terminate a prolonged war, but to decide the issue by one bold stroke at the very outbreak of hostilities.

The development of the atomic bomb by the great democracies of the West bestows upon them a precious advantage, which they now enjoy on borrowed time. Evidently, the atom bomb may decide a future war. It, like any other weapon, solves none of the problems which make for war. Thus the basic answer to the question of war and peace with which this book is concerned rests now as before in the realm of international morality.

Newton Square, Pa.,
August 20, 1945.

vi

CONTENTS

TABLES

CHARTS

Part One

INTRODUCTION

...Sed quis custodiet ipsos

1. ELEMENTS OF POWER POLITICS

THE ART OF THE POSSIBLE

INITIATIVE in world affairs has been thrust upon the United States. No plans and blueprints for systems of security and peace can alleviate this burden. For security and peace cannot be planned; they have to be won every day. An international system of security may replace old rules by new and better ones, the game may become less hazardous and the players may abide by the rules. But it is the stakes which will determine who can sit in and play at the game of world politics. Seen from this angle, it is not so much the question whether a new system of rules would be better but what the chips in the game are worth. The chips are the country's total resources, human and material. How well the game will be played, how long the rules will hold—to these questions there is no rational answer so long as men are as fallible and imperfect as history has proven them to be. But one thing is certain: No nation can hope to keep on playing that has not counted the chips, does not know what they are worth, and has no clear idea as to how much each player is able to put up.

The horizon of American foreign policy encompasses the political problems of all of mankind. Yet were the statesmen of the ages to descend from the Elysian fields and to walk about in this country, so confident in its power and so matter-of-fact in the execution of its gigantic tasks, they would find a people in anxious search of a foreign policy. They would also think, were they to rummage in libraries and newsstands, that a foreign policy for the United States is a most elusive thing. Then they would recall that never was a statesman able to choose one foreign policy among many kinds of foreign policies; that his own conception had to be made to tally with the means at his disposal; and that, when all was said and done, he never could know whether he *made* policy or accurately and simply; it is not difficult to ascertain what values are to be assigned to them *now*. Likewise, plausible assumptions, allowing for a reasonable margin of error, can be made about the future behavior of certain of these factors. Far more difficult is sizing up the interaction, past, present, and future, of these power factors. This becomes immediately clear when one asks, for example, how future changes in raw material resources will affect the future growth of a given population, or how changes in population and technology will react upon the raw-material position of a state. By intricate manipulation one can introduce other factors, some constant, some variable, some "quantifiable," and obtain equations which are still manageable—on paper. By the time these calculations are completed the result, duly qualified by ifs and buts, lies, all too often, somewhere in the vicinity of a good layman's guess quickly and simply arrived at.

For several important power factors the record of observed data is woefully inadequate. One of these is the industrial potential of nations. The entire history of industrialization is compressed in less than a century and a half; by far the largest part of the world's industrial workers are first or second generation. Therefore a complete set of historical data is lacking from which to generalize on the factor "industrial potential" in future world politics. Generalizations do not become more meaningful simply by being expanded to cover the globe.

The industrialization of the United States and Britain within the setting of representative government and free-market economy are two processes almost coincident in time, and related in character. But they are separated from the industrialization of the Soviet Union by a significant time lag and profound difference in purpose. Not even the most accurate statistics—which, incidentally, are not available for the Soviet Union—can convey a meaningful comparative picture of the "industrial potentials" for war and peace of the United States and Great Britain on the one hand and that of the Soviet Union on the other. Still less can observed data based on actual performance serve as a guide to the future development of the Anglo-American–Russian ratio of indus-

6

page of history. They infiltrate the most perfectly laid plans. Their intervention alone is powerful enough to confuse—even were it not for the inadequacy of available tools of measurement—the most careful calculations as to the consequences which will flow from a given power relationship. They vitiate those precise and permanent arrangements which peoples seek to interpose between themselves and the tide of change.

In exact science, once a formula has been found, it can generally be applied in a routine manner. A practicing engineer or chemist can pursue his trade trusting in a large body of rigorously stated formulas concerning the properties of matter. The practicing statesman lacks such assurances concerning the properties of power. Perhaps an immense advance in statistical techniques and psychology will, a few generations hence, reduce imponderables to accountable quantities. Techniques in gauging public opinion and in conditioning mass responses may point in that general direction. At present, they are just accurate enough within the range of the day after tomorrow, but they are useless for helping to determine foreign policy, which by nature is concerned with intricate, large, and long-range developments. Thus far, situations in world politics have not fitted into an orderly pattern, the experiences of one situation do not apply to another, and each calls anew for the application of creative intelligence. The things which make nations strong or weak cannot be neatly labeled and filed away, available for future reference. Foreign policy remains an art, not a science. And yet, lest undue pessimism prevail, it must be borne in mind that now, more than ever before, the art which is foreign policy is the art of the possible.

GREAT POWERS, SMALL POWERS

"Words are the skin of living thoughts." Such labels as Great Powers, Small Powers, the Big Three or the Big Four, Great Power World, Super Powers, "balance of power," "orbits," and "zones of influence"—culled from the jargon of High Policy—are clichés of things in real life. Actually, the real things behind the labels are willful and elusive—they cannot be standardized. What distinguishes our civilization most markedly from any other is its determined quest to secure by means of mechanical devices assurance against hardships, disease, and death. Felicity-through-machinery, in the *New Yorker's* happy phrase, is one peace aim which, according to advertising pages in national magazines, enjoys unanimous approval. In that philosophy of life the concept of a "machinery" of international security is a perfectly reasonable one. Of course, every efficient mechanism must consist of parts which will retain their shape for a specified period of time. If their consistency is apt to melt away like butter in the midday sun, the mechanism is just a facsimile of one and not a real one. Metaphors applied to global politics are meaningful precisely as long as they are used as metaphors; applied literally they are gross oversimplifications.

What is a Great Power, and what is a Small Power? In the rarefied sphere of global metaphors the answer is quite simple: The United States and the Soviet Union are Great Powers, while the Dominican Republic and the Principality of Monaco are small, very small powers. In the happy world of metaphors the U.S. and U.S.S.R. are elephants, the Dominican Republic and Monaco are squirrels, and it is the merit of realism that it states objectively and unemotionally that the United States and the Soviet Union are much, much stronger than the squirrel states and that the hard realities of power politics are made up of such differentials. Once these "power differentials" are grasped firmly, it is easy to erect a hierarchy of power in which specified privileges, tasks, and rewards can be reserved to Great and Small Powers and penalties can be imposed upon transgressors, heretics, and the like. It is easy to see, too, that in that Dantesque order the principal responsibility of safeguarding the peace, policing aggressors, and promoting community welfare will rest upon the shoulders of the Great Powers who are made of stuff having an atomic weight all its own. These are, briefly stated, the essentials of the Great Power world as viewed by a growingly influential school of thought whose spokesmen take no offense at being called power-political realists. There would be nothing wrong with this world of precise definitions were it not for the corrosive action of change. When are Great Powers truly great, when does a Great Power cease to be great, by what relentless logic of events are Small Powers petrified into smallness? In short, what are the dynamics of power relationships?

Throughout history the test of all power save spiritual power has been force. Men have recognized a power as Great by one mark of distinction only: by the force it could and did use toward the attainment of its own ends. If force is to be the only criterion, it can be shown that throughout history and up to the very present, Great Powers have succeeded in coercing many Small Powers but that some Small Powers have managed successfully and lastingly to thwart the intentions of Great ones. The Napoleonic Wars and World War I blotted out dozens of Small Powers; the subsequent peace settlements returned not only many of those who had fallen victim to the warring Great Powers to their former station, but gave birth to new ones. Some of these new powers came to and retained life in spite, rather than because, of the considered policies of the Great Powers. In recent times Afghanistan, Turkey, and Finland have successfully resisted Great Powers endowed with overwhelmingly superior force. None of these countries owed its survival merely to the mutual jealousies of the Great Powers or to its geographical position as a "buffer state." These small nations survived because the Great Powers, intent upon defeating them, were for a variety of reasons not strong enough to accomplish that end. That the Great Powers in question were not willing to pay the price for so trifling a conquest is an "iffy" argument—for it is precisely the attribute of a Great Power that it can pay any price whenever and wherever it has ventured upon a showdown of force against force.

The fact is that the power of a Great Power may vary most distressingly. What was the standard measure of Russia's power at the Mannerheim Line in the winter of 1940 and at the Vistula in 1944; of Britain's power at Dunkerque and four years later at Caen; of the power of the United States at Pearl Harbor and three years later at Guam, Formosa, and the Philippines? What single frame of reference can accommodate the respective power of imperial Germany in 1914, the Weimar Republic of 1930, and the Third Reich of 1940;

13

the bow-and-arrow power potential of Japan in 1859, and Japanese sea power in 1905? The chips in the game of power politics, it appears, change their value while the game is being played. Nations are not made of the same stuff; no nation is made of the same stuff all the time.

The cycle of Roman history spans nearly seven hundred years. Measured in terms of military power and territorial size, the might of Rome remained less variable in time than that of any empire of more recent times. But there were many Romes, one superimposed on the other, and the continuity of Roman civilization is one of archeology rather than of race and institutions. The Rome of Scipio was the Great Power of the Mediterranean much as the Rome of Diocletian; yet the Romans of Scipio and the Romans of Diocletian were not the same people. The old Romans had given way to peoples of other stocks long before Rome declined, and with them had given way the institutions under which Rome had attained her dominant position. On the other hand, when Japan was accorded the rank of a Great Power her people were of the same stock as were their forefathers a hundred, two hundred, and five hundred years ago. Until the West forced the opening of the "Hermit Empire," the record of the Japanese regarding immixture in international power politics compares with the isolation of the Vatican and Tibet, temporal seats of spiritual power. Yet racially and culturally the isolationist Japanese under the Tokugawas and the expansionist Japanese in the Meiji-Taisho-Showa era were the same people.

Germany—or rather the Germanies—of the eighteenth century consisted of a congeries of small states flanked by the half-Slavic state of Prussia and the German-Slavic-Magyar possessions of the Hapsburgs. The small states were united in nothing but their common aversion to Prussia. Prussia, under Frederick II, became the smallest of Europe's Great Powers. Her greatness, however, had been achieved exclusively at the expense of the other German states, against whom she was supported—at one time or another—by Russia, France, and Great Britain. The transformation of Prussia from the feudal society of Teutonic and Slavic barons and Slavic serfs into an efficient totalitarian state was abetted by the mass im-

14

migration of French Huguenots driven from France by the revocation of the Edict of Nantes. At the beginning of the eighteenth century nearly half the population of Berlin was French. The influx of French Calvinists enriched Prussia not only with the bourgeois element she needed for her commercial development but also with a small group of noblemen of great military and administrative experience. It was this racially indeterminate state which in 1870 wrought German unity, thus setting the stage for the large-scale industrialization of Germany and the rise of German military power. Industrialization created a demand for labor which was met not only by migration from farm to factory but also, up to World War I, by the influx of many hundred thousands of Poles and other Slavic peoples.

For a long time the peoples of the smaller German states, notably the Catholic ones, chafed under the yoke of Prussian predominance. It is none the less true that the Pan-Germanists who, before World War I, advocated an activist German policy in world affairs hailed mostly from the small states of middle and south Germany or were—like Houston Chamberlain—not Germans at all. National Socialism is a product of the Catholic south, and among its founders are south Germans, Austrians, and foreigners, but no Prussians. To this erratic sequence of events must be added two defeats as crushing as any suffered by modern Great Powers, namely the total collapse of Prussia before Napoleon, and Germany's rout in World War I.

Can a common denominator be found to explain the rise to the Great Power status of Prussia, of Germany 1870-1914, and of Germany under Hitler? Obviously, there is no simple answer. No matter what answer is adduced, it will not explain both the continuity of German power and the consistency of German character. By invoking the shibboleths of geographical determinism it is possible to argue that Germany's central position at the crossroads of Europe supplies a strategic leverage which will exert itself in no matter whose hands it comes to lie. By the same token, however, Germany can be shown as open to the cultural influences of all of Europe, which, it is widely held, make for a pacific disposition and hence for restraint in fashioning and using the instruments of power.

No more plausible is the theory that power is primarily conditioned by population. Prussia became a Great Power in the eighteenth century in spite of the fact that she was inferior in manpower to her principal rivals, Austria, Russia, France, and Great Britain. Nor can it be shown that her population had grown more rapidly than that of any other European country of that epoch. Japan's population has increased rapidly ever since she embarked upon the course of Westernization and industrialization. However, Japan won recognition as the first Asiatic Great Power by virtue of her victory over more populous and rapidly growing Russia. Manpower *does* count in the composition of a nation's military and economic potential, and changes in population strength, whether actual or anticipated, shape foreign policy. Dynamic use of population is the most important single phenomenon of modern power politics. This is not to say, however, that population and power stand in a direct cause-and-effect relationship.

The presence of certain important raw materials is an important clue to the nature of state power. Both Germany and Japan were possessed of coal and iron-ore deposits, basis of heavy industry. Yet there were grievous flaws in the raw-material picture of each country, so grievous, indeed, that neither country could have hoped to challenge any of the older Great Powers—had the raw-material factor been exclusively decisive.

Geographical location, manpower, and natural resources, and such qualitative and variable factors as scientific and technical proficiency, national psychology, and political institutions are significant components of a nation's power. Highly perfected methods for the analysis of power factors of all nations are the stock in trade of the political and military intelligence of every modern Great Power. No individual can hope to rival these organizations. But no such collective apparatus has so far charted successfully those deep currents which sweep Small Powers into greatness and erode the foundations of historical grandeur.

It must be assumed that foreign policy, even bad foreign

policy, is made on the strength of information accumulated by agencies whose business is to get it by hook or by crook. There is little to show that a vast accumulation of data has helped a galaxy of international statesmen and military leaders to anticipate, by any sizable margin of time, the rise to power of Germany, Japan, and the Soviet Union. None the less, the power factors were there all the time under everybody's nose; they were much too huge for effective concealment. No one knows whence springs that rare combination of force and circumstance which transforms a state into a Great Power. To reject shallow generalizations on the nature of power is not to cavil at the existence of the thing itself. The greatness of a Great Power is manifest, like liberty and love, through capacity for renewal and reaffirmation.

We have, then, no arbitrary yardstick for deciding whether a power is Great or not. Yet to label correctly is to understand; to understand is to increase one's power, and power is the basis for our entire concern here. As the Chinese say, the whole of philosophy consists in calling things by their right names.

THE BALANCE OF POWER

To recognize the discreet elements of power is not necessarily to know the effects of these elements in action. The favorite device of historians is to assign vague quantitative "weights" to these elements and then to see them in the gross and oversimplified opposition of counterweights. Three, and only three, quantities are recognized: the two counterweights and the balance weight, that small amount of excess avoirdupois necessary to upset a system in balance. Let us examine this primitive allegory of "balance of power."

The matrix of the future general international organization as outlined in the proposals of the Dumbarton Oaks Conference and debated at San Francisco is the condominium of Great Powers. At the moment of this writing many important details of the proposed organization await further clarification. Some features, however, are clearly emerging: The number of Great Powers which are expected to exert global control is smaller than has ever before shared

17

in this control, and the principle of Great Power initiative is to be accepted as the cornerstone of world peace. It may be objected that there is nothing radically new in this proposed arrangement—for has not the modern state system always been dominated by a small group of Great Powers? There are, however, important differences which separate the world-in-blueprint from the world-of-historical-experience.

For one, the state system of the past was loosely knit; the special position of the powers called Great was tacitly accepted by most states most of the time—but in no sense by all states at all times. This looseness of the power hierarchy condoned a measure of anarchy but also allowed for "circulation." Moreover, in major collective actions the Great Powers could not or would not disassociate themselves from the small powers. At the Congress of Vienna the Small Powers quickly invaded the council of the Great—in spite of some attempts to keep them out—and the Great Powers' trusteeship for the *status quo* was from the start extended to include a large number of small states. At Paris in 1919 the influence of France, Great Britain, and the United States—the Big Three—was paramount and the ensuing settlement was the product of Great Power collaboration. It was, however, the characteristic feature of the League of Nations—its virtue or its vice—that it did not formalize the special status of the three Great Powers and, quite to the contrary, diffused their initiative. The repudiation of the Covenant leaves the League forever an unfinished experiment. It is clear, however, that the League was not conceived as a series of constellations revolving around a few Great Power planets.

Similarly, the authors of the Peace of Vienna failed to center their new order upon a Great Power nucleus. That such disenchanted individuals as Talleyrand and Castlereagh may have "failed" quite deliberately is a thesis which cannot be examined in these pages. As matters turned out, that failure allowed for a high degree of "play" between the parts of the international order. The area in which small states could pursue their frequently conflicting interests was large. It was badly policed, but it was broad enough to absorb the pressure of the leading powers which were not immediately brought face to face by every single issue of international politics. It

18

follows that the functioning of so haphazard a system depended to no small extent on the self-restraint of its members.

Indeed, only by the intervention of forces from outside the purlieu of power politics can the subsidence of Great Power conflict be explained. Between 1815 and 1914, Great Britain, France, Austria, Russia, Prussia, Spain, and Italy were at war with one another only three years. In the preceding hundred years, the Great Powers warred upon one another fifty years; in the seventeenth century, seventy-five years. The pacific disposition of the Great Powers toward one another during most of the nineteenth century did not permeate the world at large. The Holy Alliance repressed risings in Spain and Italy; the Great Powers, separately and jointly, intervened against the Ottoman Empire; Prussia fought Hanover, Denmark, and Bavaria; the Balkan peoples rose against Turkish domination, and traded blows with one another; Russian troops crushed the Hungarian rising against the Hapsburgs; and a series of colonial wars carved up Africa and Asia among the colonial empires of the West. However, conflict remained localized. Small wars were isolated by the Great Powers, and the Great Powers isolated themselves against contamination from local conflicts. The danger of collective involvement was met by the collective action of the Great Powers and was averted either by threats of force or by palliatives of compromise. The three wars of the Great Powers, the Crimean War, the seven weeks' Austro-Prussian War of 1866, and the Franco-Prussian War, did not degenerate into general and world-wide conflagrations.

The triumphs, iniquities, and ultimate collapse of this system have been ascribed to the workings of the "balance of power." The balance of power has been a stock device of international politics since ancient times. The scheme is simple: Three or more power units combine in such a manner that the strongest unit among them will be prevented from so increasing its strength as to threaten the independence of the rest. It is a scheme for war and peace. When the strongest state must anticipate that the other power units will behave in accordance with that principle, it will refrain from interfering with the *status quo*; if the strongest state assails the *status quo*, the combined power of the other states will defeat it. This is how the device works for any and all states—under laboratory conditions. To begin with, only Great Powers possess the plenitude of power required for combining that unmistakable excess of strength which will deter or overwhelm a potential aggressor. Secondly, in any state system consisting of many units, confusion, delay, and particularism are apt to stall the workings of the balance of power. Thirdly, states and statesmen are prone to be at variance as to exactly where and when the formula applies. Frederick II thought little of it and said: "The balance is a word that has subdued the whole world . . .; and yet, in truth, it is a bare word, an empty sound."

It is accepted as an axiom of British foreign policy that it must seek to forestall the domination of the European continent by any one power. Any schoolboy knows that at the core of Britain's foreign policy is the balance-of-power doctrine. Strangely enough, what any schoolboy knows, not all British statesmen appear to have perceived. They were, one must presume, agreed on the principle. But obviously it did not mean to Gladstone and Neville Chamberlain what it meant to Palmerston and Winston Churchill. In brief, "balance of power" is one of the many shorthand notations of international politics which mechanistic interpretation just manages to render platitudinous. Defined literally it reduces foreign policy to arithmetic-in-three-easy-lessons, hence to absurdity.

A balance-of-power policy, an up-to-date streamlined model, has been suggested as a sensible American strategy in world politics. The basis of that policy, it has been proposed, is to consist of regional balances in Asia and in Europe while uncommitted United States power is to hold the over-all balance at both ends of Eurasia. This formula points the easiest and cheapest route to United States universal hegemony. It is delightfully simple—which is one among many reasons why it will not work.

On the face of it, there are suggestive similarities between Britain's strategical position in the nineteenth century vis-à-vis the European continent and the position of the United States in relation to Eurasia. These similarities appear even more convincing when allowance is made for shrunken distance in the air age. But the analogy can be pushed no further. By adopting the externals of Britain's foreign policy —the balancing of military and naval power on the Continent —the United States may hope to gain similar strategical advantages and alternatives for future wars. But it has been the essence of British foreign policy that strategical advantages and alternatives be so manipulated that their latent force would serve to restrain potential aggressors and thus keep war a hypothesis. To that end Britain had to rely on a play of forces other than those regulating the strategical balance of power.

Ever since Cardinal Wolsey forged it into an instrument of national policy, the balance of power has shielded Britain against the powerful states of the Continent. To maintain it, Britain formed and dissolved countless alliances and fought many wars. Since 1815 the balance-of-power policy, "an English national institution," has been wedded to a system which functioned as a world-wide institution and—for every practical purpose—as a peace organization of the Great Powers.* English statesmen sought assiduously to identify the balance-of-power policy designed to insure England's military safety with a self-regulating system of the same name as it came to be accepted by all the Great Powers in the nineteenth century.† In this endeavor British diplomacy was supported by British sea power.

It is by no means one of the least important features of sea power that it is of all instruments of force the most discreet. Most Englishmen never laid eyes upon the ships of the line which guarded the approaches of the Channel and the northern water. Few Continentals ever saw them. Of all instruments of power, sea power is psychologically the least oppressive. Britain made such discreet use of her naval power that England's declared interest made other peoples feel less apprehensive of Britain's supremacy than they would have

* A brilliant analysis of British balance-of-power policy as distinguished from an informal balance-of-power system supported not only by British but also by non-British diplomacy is contained in Karl Polanyi's *The Great Transformation*, New York, Farrar and Rinehart, 1944, pp. 259-262.

† In 1853 Count de Garden called the balance of power the "common law of the European peoples."

felt in the face of a predominant protectionist land power. "It has been well said," Sir Eyre Crowe wrote, "that every country if it had the option, would, of course, prefer itself to hold the power of supremacy at sea, but that if this choice be excluded, it would rather see England hold that power than any other state."

The symbiosis of British policy and general interest produced a result which heretofore had not attended the balancing of power: a fair measure of world-wide security instead of incessant world-wide wars. That result could not have been obtained simply by the manipulation of a crude mechanism of power.

The organic structure of nineteenth-century society was far from simple, and the balance of the state power was but one of the many delicate balances which regulated its equilibrium. That structure consisted, in fact, of many interrelated cellular systems; it was informal, and its central controls were shadowy.

The operation of the system—for a system it was, in spite of its informality—depended on several sets of principles whose acceptance by states and ruling social groups was largely voluntary. It was, like any other political system, based on force. But its compensatory features contrived to limit the use of force—largely by making it superfluous or unattractive. One of these features was an intricate code of diplomacy, handed down by the stately functionaries of the eighteenth century to the chancelleries of the nineteenth. "The strict traditions regulating the inquiries, démarches, aide memoires—jointly or separately delivered, in identical or nonidentical terms— were so many means of expressing power situations without bringing them to a head, while opening up new avenues of compromise or, eventually, of joint action, in case negotiations failed." * Even without the benefit of a central institution, close personal contact, identical or similar social background, and uniformity in manners bound the representatives of states into a cosmopolitan community which often brought to heel by mere social pressure offenders who might have resisted military or economic sanctions.

* K. Polanyi, *op. cit.*, p. 262.

No less potent a balancing and pacifying force was the market—the interplay of private economic interest across state frontiers, the influence of international finance over national governments, and the flow of goods as well as labor to wherever they brought the highest returns. The array of these economic interests was not immune to frequent disturbances. The market was racked by cyclic depressions; local wars and revolutions impinged on the orderly processes of international commerce and banking. But the bulk of international transactions remained unaffected. Personal affiliations linked in mutual esteem and profit the international trading community with national governments—as illustrated by such celebrated examples as the international activities of the House of Rothschild, bankers to Great and Small Powers alike, the financial history of the Suez Canal, and the partnership of governments and private capitalists in the exploitation of Middle Eastern oil. While the elaborate diplomatic code supplied the machinery for adjusting world problems of power politics, the gold standard functioned as the mechanism of world economy.

In theory it is easy to draw the line between the sphere of diplomacy and that of economic exchanges. Actually, however, the lines of politics and trade were interwoven in the pattern of international solidarity, which, though it fell short of providing a completely adequate organization for the settlement of the numberless disputes between nations and national and private interests, yet was strong enough to prevent world conflicts which neither the state system nor the system of free trade could have survived. The balance of power and the balance between national and private interests were thus twin expressions of the will to peace, or, more precisely, the will to avoid general war.

Neither the political nor the economic mechanisms of international solidarity were endowed with motive forces of their own. Their simultaneous breakdown within the last thirty years has made it clear whence these forces sprung. Their source was the widely received ethical, religious, and social tenets which had been taken over from earlier periods and continued as a code to govern the conduct of civilized society despite the profound changes wrought by progress in

23

science and technology, by industrialization and urbanization. This common code nourished conservative as well as progressive, reactionary as well as radical, ideologies. The unifying purpose of the Holy Alliance was legitimacy, the defense of throne and church against the revolutionary aspirations of the middle classes and of others committed to national independence. It was to this end that Metternich organized the International of monarchs, aristocracies, and Catholic clergy. Under the Concert of Powers—a more nebulous but no less effective entity than the Holy Alliance, which it replaced after the revolutionary forties and fifties had run their course—the forces of nationalism and industrialism were making over not only Europe but the whole world. Everywhere the middle classes advanced victoriously upon the crumbling defenses of feudalism; the Catholic Church was beset by heresies from within and the assertive hostility of national governments from without. None the less, the advancing ideologies of liberalism and capitalism were themselves rooted in the Christian ethics—Protestant and pietistic —of the middle classes. The ideals of ethics and refinement associated with the feudal, aristocratic way of life were taken over by the middle classes themselves once their economic dominance had been established.

Only the crudest economism can conceive of the nineteenth-century system of world trade as conditioned exclusively by the internal forces of the market. The written and unwritten rules of commerce were rules of gentlemanly conduct translated into the everyday language of business—just as routine diplomacy was transacted by aristocratic conventions, no matter whether its functionaries were heirs to ancient titles or representatives of the middle classes. International integration in that period arose from the fact that the liberal philosophy was dominant in all major trading countries, that a body of ethical maxims commanded universal allegiance, and that the balance of power, especially in its late Victorian and mellow form, offered the basis for the development of international law. It is tempting to fasten upon any one of these devices—free trade, international finance, gold standard, balance-of-power system—and to insist upon its primacy in relation to the others, or to show that it was profits which dictated foreign policy, or that it was power politics which pulled the strings of business. A plausible case can be made for any of these contentions, depending on the choice of one or the other factor as the determining one. But arguments of this kind tend to focus exaggerated attention on specific scenes to the detriment of the whole panorama. That organic whole, let it be repeated, functioned by virtue of many interdependent parts animated throughout by a widely accepted and powerful *esprit de corps*.

The dissolution of international solidarity has been ascribed to as many causes as there are schools of economics, political science, and sociology. Patently, the fragmentation of society and the drying up of vital beliefs and aspirations so characteristic of uprooted industrial-urban existence not only tended to weaken the framework of national life but introduced new tensions to the international scene. Similarly, the unprecedented increase of populations exerted a strain which no society could have withstood without a loosening of its structure. Rather than loosening, however, this structure disintegrated into a formless mass which set the stage for the use of population pressure and mass psychology in pursuit of power-political objectives.

Dislocations within national systems were reflected by an increasing jerkiness of the international system, whose operation, we have seen, depended on a large measure of voluntary team-play and the tacit observance of rules derived from precedent—sum and substance of international law. Political and economic controls had been confined to small groups, and effective public opinion in each country had been exercised by a small educated minority. It is a far cry from the finely chiseled code of nineteenth-century diplomacy to plebiscitary diplomacy, i.e., the marshaling of mass pressure in the conduct of foreign policy. The "dynamic" use of the daily press, the diplomacy of gross cajolery and invective, the going-to-the-people over the heads of a "friendly" government, these and other symptoms of qualitative disintegration signaled the collapse of an international order which was based on compromise.

It has become fashionable nowadays to condemn this whole

system on the basis of its many and flagrant abuses. It was "static"; its decay coincided significantly with sharp changes in international manpower and economic relationships. Its "machinery" was far from perfect; balance-of-power diplomacy and the *"Internationale"* of trading interests did not prevent war and are widely held responsible for World War I. Still worse, the system is now popularly associated, particularly in this country, with class society and high finance, hence with reaction. It is, therefore, not surprising that most contemporary historians—with such notable exceptions as Guglielmo Ferrero—are prone to underrate the breadth of vision of the men who conceived that system and made it work. If sparing use of military force, of human lives, and of economic resources is a test of how well or badly an age settles its power-political problems, then the age fathered by the men of Vienna need not shirk comparison with any other, least of all with the age in which we live. The nation most to benefit by the temperate political climate of the nineteenth-century world was the United States. Only under conditions peculiar to that climate—an unparalleled freedom of movement of persons, goods, and capital—could the United States have attained world rank. In other words, the balances which tended to minimize power changes in Europe favored the growth of extra-European power. Paradoxically, the maintenance of the power balances in Europe caused the balance to shift to America.

In what sense can we say that contemporary arrangements of the Great Powers seek balance? What kind of balanced order do they contemplate? And how do they propose to bring about necessary changes?

POWER, PEACE, AND CHANGE

The Dumbarton Oaks Conference is the result of Great Power initiative; the San Francisco charter seeks to institutionalize that initiative.

The "Proposals for the Establishment of General International Organization" outlined at Dumbarton Oaks are "the results of the exploratory conversations on international organization held in Washington between the representatives

26

of the Governments of the United States, the United Kingdom, the Soviet Union, and China." It is impossible at this moment to say whether these proposals, amplified at Yalta and hammered into the San Francisco agreements, will have crystallized—by the time this book appears in print—into the charter of world organization, duly ratified by the requisite majority of founding nations. To one question Dumbarton Oaks has furnished an unequivocal answer: The future world order will be what the leading world powers make it. These powers are the ones "which have assumed the brunt of the struggle against the aggressor and the main responsibility for its success." [*] This proposition is further clarified by the Russian commentator: "One must admit outright that in this respect the four leading powers are placed by the charter in a special position." We may for the moment postpone discussing the likelihood of France's and China's gathering the necessary military and economic strength to make their voices heard at the table of the policy-making powers. They did not possess that strength when their representatives were sitting in at the Dumbarton Oaks Conference. The enforcement of the security provisions which were formulated at Dumbarton Oaks and which may become the law of the globe is thus made the business of the holders of effective power, the United States, Britain, and the Soviet Union.

It has been observed that the scheme resembles the Holy Alliance, a suggestion which is not meant as praise. The resemblance is only superficial. The Holy Alliance did not include several of the Great Powers of the age. Great Britain, the most powerful country of the time, stayed out; defeated France retained a high degree of initiative together with a considerable measure of power; and in the heyday of the Holy Alliance, its authority did not reach further than it could shoot, i.e., the European continent. The Holy Alliance was created to maintain not only peace but also the established order of society. It was an ideological alliance.

By contrast, the Big Three declare themselves agreed to provide security against aggression. This pragmatic conception leaves suspended ideological issues far graver than those

[*] Embassy of the U.S.S.R., *Information Bulletin*, Washington, D. C., October 13, 1944, p. 2.

dividing nations at any time in the nineteenth century. It is limited in fact to the enforcement of security provisions against potential aggressors from outside the closed circle of the Big Three, China, and France.

It is not proposed here to attribute a metaphysical meaning to what remains thus far a paper constitution of a world police system. But it is obvious that the scheme reflects the measure of those issues which the "leading world powers" anticipate making their common concerns, of those issues which will be left to the competence of Small Powers, and of those issues which will be excluded from joint action of any kind.

It becomes readily apparent by a process of elimination that the area of collaboration is as comprehensive as is the agreement obtaining between the Big Three concerning the future status of a defeated Germany and, by inference, Japan: None of the Small Powers is situated outside the sphere of influence and strategic reach of one of the Big Three; no power, except a Great Power, now boasts of a military potential so large that it cannot be restrained from warring upon its neighbor by regional action initiated by one of the Big Three. It is unlikely that the United States would enlist the aid of the Soviet Union for stemming the aggressive designs of Argentina; that Britain would call upon Russian aid against Egypt; or that Russia would demand Anglo-American intervention against Rumanian expansionism directed, let us say, against Bulgaria. It should go without saying that problems of this kind will never burden whatever security machinery the Big Three may devise.

True, regional guarantees, to wit, regional systems of security presided over by the Great Powers individually, are presumed to be "consistent with the purposes and principles" of the world-wide security system created at San Francisco. But there are no doors opening from one regional system into the other and from each regional system into the new League, which the master key of Great Power veto cannot lock.

International politics consists of concrete cases. A proposition in international politics is as plausible as are the concrete possibilities it envisages. By no stretch of imagination can we conceive of a concrete case of Small Power aggression which one of the Big Three could not settle, or would not insist upon settling, by regional, i.e., unilateral, action. Hence the twofold aspect of the new order:

1) *The indefinite extension of the system of military alliances now binding the three Great Powers—the United States, Russia, and Great Britain—in the war against Germany and Japan.* The common objective of Great Power collaboration, couched in the general language of the Dumbarton Oaks proposals, is security against unnamed aggressors. The principle of harmony and unanimity between the leading powers, "which is the cornerstone of the whole international organization and from which no exception can be made," * precludes the case that any of the contracting Great Powers is to be named as aggressor. Therefore, the only Great Powers left to whom the definition "aggressor" can be applied in the future are Germany and Japan. Since China is being accorded permanent membership and France is to be included, there is no Great Power, actual or potential, against whom the principle of unanimity can be invoked, except Germany and Japan. When Marshal Stalin, in his address on the Anniversary of the Revolution, referred to the decisions of the Dumbarton Oaks Conference, he limited the purpose of the international security organization specifically to preventing aggression on the part of a defeated Germany and, by implication, a defeated Japan.†

2) *The consolidation of Great Power spheres of interest and influence to which the decisions of an international security organization apply only with the consent of the dominant power of the region.* The Dumbarton Oaks proposals explicitly exempt from the jurisdiction of the proposed international security organization disputes arising between states which are parties to existing regional arrangements. This provision tacitly recognizes those facts of life which must be taken for granted in world politics: The Monroe Doctrine, collectivized by Pan-American agreements and sublimated by the Act of Chapultepec, bars intervention in the Western Hemisphere; existing arrangements preclude collective action against aggressors who may threaten the peace of

* Embassy of the U.S.S.R., *ibid.*
† See page 277, Note 1 to Chapter 1.

Africa, the Levant, and the Middle East, except with the express approval of Great Britain; the Soviet Union will not call for the dispatch of international police forces to quell offenders among the "friendly régimes" which are to cohabit the Soviet Union's security sphere in eastern and central Europe and central Asia.

It can easily be shown that by existing treaties, unilateral declarations of the Great Powers, and geographical accident there is no power which does not lie within the sphere of hegemony—or in Mr. Lippmann's term, the "orbit"—of one or the other Great Power, with the exception, perhaps, of Switzerland and the Vatican. Hence, the principle of collective military action against an aggressor is plainly inapplicable against any now existing political unit but Germany and Japan. Thus the area to which the practical collaboration in world security applies shrinks to the control and pacification of Germany and Japan.*

The millions who have been killed and maimed, and the riches of Europe which have been destroyed, were not sacrificed in order to afford Germany another try at domination. Germany must be curbed. She can be curbed by the imposition of a settlement which, to serve the purpose, must be severe and simple. It must be severe lest Germans misunderstand the intention of the victors and harbor the illusion that they can play again at balancing the East against the West. It must be simple, so that it can be enforced. The desired end cannot be attained by carrying our own passion for over-organization in administration, education, and welfare into the defeated country. The solution of the German problem can be solved only by Germans. The solution of the European problem posed by Germany can be solved only by the intimate collaboration of the Allies. It requires no philosophical finesse. There are only two kinds of settlements with finality: One is a Carthaginian peace, to wit, annihilation; the other is large-scale annexation or partition.

The German people will forswear aggression when they are deprived of the means of it. Germany can be deprived of the means by depriving her of the heavy industry which

* See page 277, Note 2 to Chapter 1.

30

powered her war machine. The hard core of Germany's industrial power is the Rhineland with its coal mines and steel mills. Without it Germany cannot fight another war. Its irrevocable annexation by the Western powers as a group will put an end to German power. Security against Germany requires no less; it hardly requires more. Other sanctions will undoubtedly be imposed; they will not modify substantially the strategic picture. Germany will continue to hold the attention of the victors, for only by unrelaxed vigilance can the settlement be enforced until Germany returns to a semblance of civilized government. Therein lies the greatest postwar danger to the Allies: The German settlement, crucial as it is, implies Allied co-operation in a task which is essentially negative.

It must be presumed that the defeat of Germany and Japan involves the destruction of their war potential and that consequently both will cease to be Great Powers in the accepted meaning of that term. Only by drawing upon the resources of other Great Powers were Germany and Japan able in the first place to mount their attacks upon these other Great Powers. Germany, after World War I, could not have restored her industrial plant without the financial aid of the United States and Great Britain, and could not have rearmed without imports of raw materials from the United States, Great Britain, France, and the Soviet Union. Japan was largely beholden for her initial conquests to the access she enjoyed to capital and raw-material markets controlled by the United States and Great Britain. A harmonious co-operation of the Great Powers precludes the possibility that Germany and Japan will again be extended facilities for aggressive preparations (which only these Great Powers can extend and which enabled Germany and Japan to war upon these selfsame Great Powers).

By the same token, such harmonious collaboration reduces positive and, if need be, coercive action to a comparatively modest effort, particularly since Germany and Japan are slated for drastic territorial diminution. It is hardly conceivable that Germany and Japan, smaller in size and less populous, could successfully resume against Great Power collaboration aggressive policies in which they had failed when they were larger in size and more populous and when the opposing Great Powers were still disunited.

The consolidation of Great Power spheres precludes the emergence of new political units which could be large and viable enough to influence the international balance of power. In both World Wars most Small Powers did not prove viable strategic units, and for some Small Powers smallness may have entailed all kinds of political and economic ills. From this and the fact that all Small Powers are situated within the "orbit" of one or another Great Power, it does not follow, however, that the only alternatives facing Small Powers are a choice between inclusion in a Great Power "security sphere" and extinction, nor one between mute acceptance of a system of Great Power collaboration in the enforcement of international security and submissiveness to a single Great Power. There remains, of course, the alternative of Small Powers grouped in independent units well outside the "security spheres" of the Great Powers. An independent east European confederation was favorably viewed by responsible persons in this country and Great Britain, and in 1943 rejected by Russia.* European regional confederations have been proposed by Milan Hodza, Sumner Welles, W. Ivor Jennings, Winston Churchill, and Jan Smuts, and have been opposed by Edward Benes and the Russian magazine *War and the Working Class*. A unified Europe had been advocated long before it was travestied by Adolf Hitler, by Aristide Briand, Count Coudenhove-Kalergi, Winston Churchill, and George Catlin, and was recently proposed by the *London Observer*. The confederation of the Moslem states of the Middle East envisaged by Reza Shah Pahlevi and Kemal Ataturk was opposed by Britain, later expediently sponsored by Germany, and now has been vetoed, too, by the press of the Soviet Union.

The problem of Small Powers is as acute today as it was at the close of World War I. The emphasis of the debate, however, appears to have shifted 180 degrees. Idealization of national smallness has given way to idealization of the Great Power as a protector of the weak. The high mortality rate of Small Powers engaged in disputes with Germany appears

* See page 278, Note 3 to Chapter 1.

to demonstrate the benefits accruing to surviving Small Powers from inclusion in the security spheres of surviving Great Powers. Such a total solution may dispose, once for all, of the problem of Small Powers and suggests favorable analogies with the increase in efficiency allegedly derived from merging small economic units with large ones. Yet it is certain that this total, if not totalitarian, solution will aggravate the problems facing the Great Powers themselves. In the nineteenth century the weakness of small countries provoked aggression on the part of Great Powers who were not peace-loving, and ensuing conflicts invariably threatened to involve other Great Powers. On the other hand, Small Powers insulated the Great Powers against each other geographically and applied their combined weight toward maintaining the international equilibrium, which, rather than the benevolence of any one Great Power, they were prone to identify with their own interests. Without this cushioning effect, the balance of power in the nineteenth century would have jammed quickly and disastrously.

The proceedings at San Francisco, let it be repeated, are not taken here as the last word on future world order. They may have laid the basis for definite agreements, ratified in accordance with the organic law of the founding states, or for no agreements at all. Despite their fragmentary nature, the Dumbarton Oaks proposals put on record minimum goals of Great Power collaboration and are samples of "the art of the possible." * Together with the unilateral actions of the Great Powers, they indicate the main trends which are shaping future world politics and how confidently the Great Powers are anticipating their future relationships. No less indicative is what has been left unsaid: The ranks of the Great Powers, purged by the defeat of Germany and Japan, are not to be opened to new political units which, while not of global stature, could nevertheless act as powerful regional make-weights. The hierarchy of power will consist of the three "Super Powers" of gigantic size and a congeries of small states probably not much larger in size and population than they were before World War I. The Small Powers will, therefore, boast of the same average weight which heretofore

* See page 278, Note 4 to Chapter 1.

33

proved inadequate for righting the international equilibrium against the pressure of Great Powers. In short, while the remaining Great Powers grow immensely stronger, the world of small states ceases to evolve and the individual small states grow proportionately weaker. The military techniques developed in World War II bid fair to compound that proportionate weakening into complete military impotence.

The disparity between the Great Powers and the Small Powers is now so great as to confine collaboration between them to "noncoercive" fields such as cultural exchanges, international relief, narcotics control, and the pooling of scientific information. The increasing concentration of effective power in the hands of the few, and the atrophy of the world state system as a whole, is illustrated poignantly by a comparison with the state system of 1914. The dismemberment in 1919 of the Austro-Hungarian Empire was not compensated for by the creation of new political units of like size; its power potentials were dispersed in the east European "shatter zone." Granted even that both France and Italy will recover speedily from their present low estate, it is none the less obvious that defeat has struck both from the list of Great Powers and that whatever initiative in world politics they may assume in the foreseeable future will depend on what the United States, Great Britain, and Russia choose to do or leave undone. Thus, with the defeat of Germany and Japan the number of Great Powers will have decreased from eight to three within one generation. By contrast, the number of small states will not have been diminished, except for the absorption of Lithuania, Latvia, and Estonia by the Soviet Union—a loss which may be made up by the creation of small sovereignties in Asia.

Perhaps no other issue of contemporary world politics is fraught with more high-minded confusion and deliberate obscuration than the relation of the small to the big nations. Actually the small nation's "problem" exists only in so far as the disequilibrium of power has created it, not because of a specific disease to which only small countries are susceptible. During the last hundred years, some small nations, like Sweden and Portugal, have been peace-loving; others, like Bulgaria, Paraguay, and Hungary, apparently have not been;

a few, like Switzerland and Holland, have set examples in economic management, public welfare, and internal harmony which larger states have thus far failed to duplicate; others, like Ecuador and Ethiopia, have consistently trailed behind in the procession of economic and social progress. On the whole, the small nations have remained the same; the Great Powers have not.

In 1919 the victorious Great Powers, Britain, France, and the United States, exerted a preponderance which virtually amounted to control of the globe. Already then the manifest disparity between surviving Great Powers and small nations, old and new, as well as the vacuum created by the dissolution of the Hapsburg and Ottoman Empires, should have suggested the formation of new political units large and strong enough to play the role of a sturdy "middle class" in world politics.

The might-have-beens of a Danubian and a Balkan federation, the vices and virtues which might have characterized these combinations, and the obstacles which caused these and similar schemes for the integration of small states in larger units to fail are topics beyond the range of this investigation. Let it suffice to point out that a Danubian, a Balkan, and a Scandinavian federation might have acted—inside the League of Nations or out—as effective counterweights to Germany and braced the Great Powers where they needed bracing most, namely, in those issues which became acute outside their immediate spheres of interest. The incoherence of the Small Powers was Germany's most powerful ally in mounting her attack against Great Britain, France, and Russia. If the settlement of World War II does not afford scope for the formation of new autonomous units created by the voluntary association of small nations, it will be the antithesis of a system of balanced power. The issue is not merely an ethical one; it concerns the safety of the Great Powers themselves, and involves a fundamental alternative in world-political strategy. The division of the world into "orbital zones" until no Small Power lies outside the sphere of interest of some Super Power entails the loss of "play," without which not only engine parts but also parts of a state system are exposed to intolerable friction. With the prevailing political and ideological tensions not even a world federation composed of three such sprawling units could function without tumult and rebellions. And this system—if it can be called a system—has the elasticity of cast iron.

Even the concept of the Big Three is of questionable validity. The London *Economist* recently pointed out that Britain is only potentially a world power, that actually she has neither the resources nor the population strength, nor even the strategical position, to justify her claim of equality with the United States and the Soviet Union. The pillars of British power, i.e., leadership of the British Commonwealth of Nations and control of the balance of power, are weakened, the one by the attraction exerted upon the Dominions by new centers of political and economic power, the other by the collapse of the European state system. The Dominions are unlikely to forge closer ties with the mother country and renounce in peacetime all the strategic and economic arrangements which in war have linked their fortunes to the United States. What holds true for the Dominions holds doubly true of India, who will unquestionably press for greater independence. For India's political claims are now backed by large sterling credits, expanding industrial strength, and a rapidly growing population—nearly ten times that of Britain. To these factors must be added the expansion of United States merchant shipping and the increased export capacity of United States industry, which, though friendly agreements may mitigate the intensity of competition, are bound to cut into markets heretofore dominated by Great Britain. Thus Britain can hope to play in world politics and trade only the part of "brilliant second" to the United States. The world system will thus be a bipolar one rather than tripartite.

It is the logic of a bipolar system that it works against the possibility of a future world integration. It tends to crystallize the two world spheres of influence into self-sufficient political and economic blocs. The basis of compromise narrows down to a mutual determination not to interfere in the other power's "orbit." No incentive will exist to dismantle a compact security arrangement fortified by a solid aggregation of client states. Disarmament being impossible, military pre-

36

paredness is the indispensable guarantee of security and hence peace. The danger of conflict will grow as ideological conflicts—now left in abeyance for the sake of wartime collaboration—are resumed. It is both the virtue and the weakness of the agreement between the Allies that ideologies have been made subservient to geopolitics. That this ideological truce can be extended indefinitely is unlikely. Europe has been for some time in a state of undeclared civil war, exacerbated by years of German domination and the strains engendered by large-scale warfare. Among the Big Three it is again Britain who is most exposed to the battering of ideological conflicts. Revolutionary storms have converged upon the traditional outposts of British influence in the Mediterranean. The *Economist* comments on the dilemma confronting Britain in Greece and Italy: "A British policy that was openly and blatantly hostile to the forces of the Left would put this country in the position of a Metternich rather than of a Palmerston—and without any Holy Alliance to support us." The historical analogy may be shaky; but the writer states correctly that for unsupported Britain the choice of alternatives is narrow.

An elaborate system of bilateral military alliances has been created in Europe. It was created before a general system of security was called into being and precludes an international security organization which does not ratify, tacitly or expressly, existing arrangements. It can be argued—and has been—that a system of military alliances created for the express purpose of preventing renewed German and Japanese aggression should be separated from a general system of collective security. For if hard and fast military alliances between the powerful victor nations assure the quiescence of a defeated Germany and Japan, what purpose shall an international security organization serve if it, too, is principally charged with keeping the peace against a defeated Germany and Japan?

If the United States, as Senator Vandenberg suggested, were to join a system of military alliances against Germany, then a peace league could devote its undivided energies to the solutions of that great number of pressing problems which, apart from the pacification of Germany, challenge the

37

collective wisdom of world polity. Senator Vandenberg proposed that the United States conclude a military treaty with its major allies "for keeping the Axis out of piracy for keeps." * "This problem," he added, "stands apart by itself." Once the German menace is isolated by "handling it as the present war is handled," the mortgage of a savage conflict need no longer burden *all* the business an international peace organization must transact. The plaster cast must be applied to the diseased member; it need not enclose and paralyze the whole body of the international community. This conception is not opposed to the principles underlying the Dumbarton Oaks proposals except that it envisions a greater latitude for change than appears to be provided for by the formal unanimity of the Great Powers. The agreement of the Great Powers is born of war. It will make the defeat of Germany a final one, and it may contain the seeds of a lasting peace. But that unanimity cannot blanket the historical formations of the West, freeze the population dynamics of the East, and quell the ideological ferment in Europe and Asia.

At the core of the proposals for the future peace settlement, be they those elaborated at Dumbarton Oaks or discussed at San Francisco, indorsed by Marshal Stalin or amended by Senator Vandenberg, is the idea of military alliances perpetuated long after the termination of the war. The United States will not lay aside its weapons; neither will the other major powers.

The tremendous tensions engendered by two World Wars in brief succession will not easily be relaxed. Huge military forces will stand at the ready for many years to come. They will be at the orders of national governments presiding over nations possessed of vast manpower and industrial strength. None of these nations will abdicate its military power to extra- or supranational agencies. For the first time in the history of man great empires may seek and find common ground in the pursuits of peace. The reality of the present is the concentration of immense power in the hands of a few. The world of the Super Powers is not a clever design, it is an accomplished fact.

* See page 279, Note 5 to Chapter 1.

Part Two

POPULATION AND POWER

There is very little ground, either from reason or observation, to conclude the world eternal or incorruptible. The continual and rapid motion of matter, the violent revolutions with which every part is agitated, the changes remarked in the heavens, the plain traces as well as tradition of a universal deluge, or general convulsion of the elements; all these prove strongly the mortality of this fabric of the world, and its passage, by corruption or dissolution, from one state or order to another.

—David Hume

2. THE BIGGEST BATTALIONS

SIZE and structure of population are datum points from which the modern state must reckon its power-political position. Among states fairly evenly matched in the possession of technological skills, superiority in manpower spells military, hence political, preponderance. Manpower is the basis of military power. The size of population determines the size of the armed forces and the quantity and quality of their weapons.

Sheer numbers of men have counted heavily in the struggles for power throughout history. The science of statistics seems to have been spared the ancients. Yet there is ample evidence to show that Rome disposed of a large reservoir of manpower, recruited large armies and manned large navies. The effectives of the Roman legion (4,000 men) were approximately those of the modern infantry regiment. Several Roman armies, roughly the size of modern army corps, frequently kept the field at the same time. Large armories at home and at outlying bases, and permanent shipyards and storage facilities, serviced the forces operating in Europe, Africa, and Asia. Rome thus marshaled an integrated, well-trained force larger than that of any other power of the ancient world. Conversely, the decrease of Rome's population and subsequent reliance upon foreign mercenaries weakened the fiber of Roman power, and the fall of the empire followed upon a period of protracted population crisis.

Throughout history, decline in population has entailed decline in national power. A sudden preoccupation with population questions on the part of statesmen, scholars, and publicists generally signals crisis. Overpopulation is an economic problem; Malthus was not a demographer but an economist.

In antiquity, once the disastrous consequences of population decline had become apparent, the problem became of grave concern to philosophers and politicians alike. Aristotle observed that "Sparta perished because of a lack of peoples." Polybios held that depopulation of the countryside and emptying cities were the fundamental causes of the decline of Greece. Celibacy and debt, the two great scourges of the ancient world, which always suffered from want of capital and from diminished population in the most prosperous epochs, had brought desolation to the countryside. Large estates worked by slaves replaced prosperous communities of sturdy farmers. "In the towns art languished and morals deteriorated," and birth control and contraceptive practices were rapidly thinning the ranks of urban populations. On the road to slow extinction Rome was only a lap behind her victim, Greece. As early as the year 37 B.C., Marcus Terrentius Varro, senator and landholder, deplored the flight from the land and the shortage of agricultural labor, and examined the general causes of Rome's decay. The case for the return to the land, and for the large family which healthful labor on the soil is said to foster, is as clearly stated in Varro's treatises on agriculture as in the pronouncements of Marshal Pétain's population experts.

The reforms of Augustus were dominated by the awareness of the dangers to which the decline of ancient Roman stock exposed the political institutions of the city and the existence of the empire. The *Lex Julia* is a straightforward population measure. This law made marriage obligatory for all male citizens under the age of fifty. Bachelors were punished by exclusion from festivities and public shows, which at a time when shows and spectacles were a state ministry constituted a serious disability. The law also deprived bachelors of any right to inherit except through persons related to them at most in the sixteenth degree.*

Augustus, far better than the bulk of his countrymen "to whom times and places were vague by reason of distance and who were anxious only for the extension of the empire," knew how thinly Rome's legions were spread over the world. The policing and administration of the empire called, even more urgently than its conquest, for a constant supply of Roman soldiers and functionaries. And Augustus knew, as

* See page 280, Note 1 to Chapter 2.

did every Roman statesman, that as the empire expanded, the pressure upon its frontiers from teeming barbarous tribes grew even greater.

Population decline resembles the slow process of subterranean erosion. The damage is done long before the surface begins to crack. Two generations after Augustus, the decline of Roman manpower had assumed alarming proportions. Imperial policy was henceforth haunted by the specter of an enfeebled race and dwindling legions. Trajan wished to marry every Roman forcibly. A hundred years after Trajan, Caracalla deemed it necessary to grant citizenship to all the freeborn within the empire. In the middle of the fourth century the population of Rome and her Italian dependencies had fallen below 5 million, a drop of approximately one-quarter from Augustus' Golden Age, and a large part of that population consisted of unassimilated immigrants from across the Alps. The "desolation of the countryside" had by then become the stock lament of Roman writers. The barbarians did not overrun the empire; they were sucked into a vacuum.

A similar catastrophe overtook Europe in the Thirty Years' War. Its brunt was borne by Germany. Epidemics and famine took a toll of about two-fifths of Germany's total rural population. In Pomerania, Thuringia, Hesse, Pfalz, and Württemberg about two-thirds of the inhabitants perished, and in Brandenburg, Saxony, Alsace, Bavaria, and Franconia about one-half. The campaigns having been fought mostly on German soil, other European nations were less afflicted. Yet France, the Netherlands, and Scandinavia also lost heavily. Montesquieu meditated a hundred years later upon the significant analogies of European and Roman history, and declared population decline to be the most deadly disease of nations. Indeed, some of the deep scars of that disease, inflicted three hundred years ago, still disfigure the countenance of Germany. The sluggishness of German intellectual and social development throughout the seventeenth and eighteenth centuries may be ascribed to the staggering losses suffered in the Thirty Years War. They explain Germany's lag in Europe's progress toward political unification, her gnawing sense of grievance and protracted political impotence, and some of the dissonances of Germany's national character.

The historic struggles for supremacy were waged by populous states, and victory seems to have favored rising populations.

The struggle for power in fifteenth- and sixteenth-century Italy was mainly waged between the most populous states such as Florence, Venice, Milan, the Papal states, and Naples. The Italian principalities and city republics fell prey in turn to the emergent nation states, Spain and France, whose military and economic might sprang from their more numerous, better-integrated peoples. The supremacy of the Austro-Spanish Empire throughout the sixteenth century was based on a population larger than that of any rival European state.

When France, under the rule of the Bourbon kings, became Europe's most populous country, she also attained military dominance of Europe. The peak of French manpower in relation to the rest of Europe lies somewhere between the conquests of Louis XIV and those of Napoleon. This also was France's bountiful century of great men. In 1800 the population of France was 27 million; every seventh European —Russians included—was a Frenchman. It was Russia, with more than 40 million inhabitants in 1812, which vanquished Napoleon's *Grande Armée* of close to 500,000, the largest force Europe had ever seen marching under a single commander.

The rise of Britain and Germany during the nineteenth century can be traced along the steep curve of increasing populations. When, in 1870, Germany defeated the third Napoleonic Empire, her population had already overtaken that of France. Henceforth French public opinion was never to shake off a profound concern over the nation's waning strength in numbers with respect to the resurrected Reich. The alliance with Russia concluded in 1892 and ratified in 1894 joined 38 million Frenchmen and 92 million Russians in military coalition. This step was not altogether pleasing to Frenchmen sensitive to the crudities of czarist autocracy, but gratified the French general staff. Its apologists were later to extol the benefits which would accrue to France from the "inexhaustible," "unlimited" manpower of Russia in case of another contest with Germany.

In the last decade of the nineteenth century the population of the United Kingdom crossed the 40 million mark, advancing slightly over that of France. The British Isles and the Dominions together accounted for approximately 56 million peoples, and the empire, including all of Britain's possessions and dependencies, for more than 400 million. The geographical distribution exposed the empire even then to strains which, as in the Boer War, severely taxed not only British economic but also manpower resources. However, Britain's might was boosted out of proportion to that of other states by the fact that it was based on sea power. Naval monopoly underwrote British wealth, secured Britain's unique bargaining position, and was the prerequisite for the successful application of the policy of the balance of power. It was the monopolist of power who then, as always, could hope to try his hand successfully at the balancing of power. Naval predominance invested Britain with greater military power than corresponded to her effective strength in men. It is a fact that the crisis of Fashoda in 1898, which brought the long chapter of Anglo-French imperialist rivalries to a close with Britain's bloodless but decisive victory, followed hard upon the heels of Britain's victory in the contest of the cradles. In that contest, France now held fifth place in Europe. Even after the destruction of the Austro-Hungarian monarchy, France stood fifth, facing in growing Italy a new and impetuous rival.

There is no need to labor the plus and minus signs of Europe's numerical relationships; France's European hegemony after World War I, or what passed for it in the chancelleries of Europe, stemmed from the brief unanimity of the victorious Allies and the preconceptions of the past. France purported to do what the history of power and populations showed could not be done for any length of time. While in 1800 one Frenchman had faced six Europeans, in 1930 he faced twelve.

Germany's first bid for world power in 1914 was backed by the combined forces of the Reich, Austria-Hungary, Bulgaria, and Turkey. This coalition, at the height of its fortunes, controlled between 150 and 160 million people. And it took superiority in numbers, ultimately attained by the end of World War I, to enable the Allies and associated powers to defeat the Central Powers. German defeat, then, exactly as twenty-seven years later, was heralded by manpower shortages and impressment of children, women, the crippled, foreigners, the aged, and prisoners of war to free men for front-line duty. Military selection boards called to arms the middle-aged, and did not cavil at pronouncing fit for battle men afflicted with venereal infections, hernia, and heart disease. By contrast, the Allies in 1918, despite Russia's collapse and two million Anglo-French casualties, disposed of not yet fully mobilized reserves equaling two hundred divisions. The manpower of the United States, only part of which had as yet been committed to European battlefields, tipped the scales. True, shipments of American supplies had not yet hit their full stride and large contingents of American troops had not yet seen battle. None the less, the tide was flowing high; the German general staff saw the inevitable, and the worn-out German units were demoralized by the knowledge that fresh troops, eager to fight, were entering the lines of battle. Manpower-in-being, to borrow a term from naval strategy, thus helped to crush the enemy's will to resist.

The history of World War II appears to confirm the saying attributed to Voltaire: "God is always on the side of the biggest battalions." Only against peoples inferior in manpower, such as Poland, Denmark, Norway, Belgium, France, Holland, Jugoslavia, and Greece, could the *Wehrmacht* achieve its spectacular successes, while it was unable to defeat any country equal or superior in numbers. Germany defeated her opponents singly or in batches. However, after the destruction of Poland, Germany's effectives would have been superior to those of her victims even had they chosen to make a united stand. If one considers German technological superiority and interior lines, and also Italy's nuisance value, it is difficult to see how a series of disjointed rear-guard actions could have halted Germany's conquest of Europe.

Whatever the shortcomings of the Red Army in June, 1941, they were compensated for by the quantitative inferiority of the *Wehrmacht*. It was vast military manpower, estimated variously as two or three times greater than the German,

46

which enabled the Soviet high command to maintain strong strategic reserves and repeatedly throw fresh troops into battle. In 1941, 80 million Germans, including Austrians and Sudetenlanders, faced 192 million Russians, including Latvians, Letts, Lithuanians, Poles, Ukrainians, Rumanians, and several Asiatic tribes. However, the ratio of military manpower did not correspond to these figures. Differences in age structure—a larger proportion of younger age groups and a smaller ratio of the aged to the total population—accounted for a Russian superiority in military as well as productive manpower which gross figures fail to reveal. While Germany could muster 13.9 million males between 20 and 45 years of age, Russia could draw upon 34.4 million—without counting her newly acquired territories in the Baltic and in southeastern Europe.

No one knew better than the Germans themselves how greatly Russian human reserves exceeded their own. German demographers, perhaps the most thorough craftsmen in that field of science, have compiled during the past twenty years detailed studies of Russia's changing population. It is highly improbable that their labors were unknown to German military quarters. Why, then, did Germany attack Russia against such heavy numerical odds? Disregarding Hitler's intuitive whimsies, the strategical advantage hoped for from surprise attack, and Germany's trust in tactical mobility and technological superiority, the answer is simple: For Germany, the manpower ratio could only turn from bad to worse. In spite of frantic efforts toward stimulating the birth rate, no German expert seriously expected that the population of the Reich would grow substantially in the future. Even at the height of Hitler's drive for babies—which was, indeed, attended by a measure of success—the population of the Reich failed to reproduce itself.

A net reproduction rate shows the net increase or decrease of a population within one generation. It was clear when Hitler came to power that were the German rate maintained at the 1933 level throughout one generation, Germany's population would decline by more than one-quarter. By 1939, improved economic conditions and the Nazi government's natality policies had raised it to 0.98, or 2 per cent less than

47

the rate required for maintaining the population at a station
ary level. Russia's net rate of reproduction is estimated at
approximately 1.60. Both rates (the German is possibly padded by Nazi statisticians) serve to forecast roughly the future
population status of both nations: Had the German general
staff chosen to postpone war to 1950, 82 million Germans
would have stood against 203 million Russians. The slight
increase in the German population would be due to the survival of the older age groups, a carryover from the higher
fertility of preceding generations. By 1970 the surplus of the
past would have been consumed and absolute decline would
have set in: 79 million Germans would be facing 250 million
Russians.

These figures, like all projections of future population
growth, are based on a number of assumptions, chief among
them being that the rate of change remains constant and that
political frontiers remain unaltered. Migration, social and
economic changes, and a host of other variables may also
modify projected lines of growth. Nevertheless, some likely
errors tend to cancel out each other, and forecasts based on
observed data thus "afford a valuable frame of reference with
which to analyze the prospects of future change." * In political and military strategy, just as in economic life, "expectation" enters into the formation of policy. Once Germany had
decided to wage war with Soviet Russia, the sooner she entered it the better were her chances of winning. Germany's
assault upon Russia, from the demographical point of view,
was a "preventive" war. Even in 1941, Germany's fortunes
had to be staked heavily on whatever edge technological superiority, strategy, and mobility would give the *Wehrmacht*
against Russia's superior numbers.

Crude manpower is of little military significance. No matter how large their populations, backward countries do not
make power-political history but must suffer it. Without
developed industries and natural resources a large population
is a source of military weakness. This holds particularly true

* Frank H. Notestein, "Population and Power in Postwar Europe," *Foreign Affairs*, Vol. XXII, No. 3, April, 1944.

for countries, like India or China, where food requirements exceed agricultural production.

- Malthus held that man's sex passion and material needs were in everlasting conflict, and that there would always be more people born than could be provided for. "Population is necessarily limited by the means of subsistence." * The last hundred years' boom in pessimistic social philosophies favored the wide dissemination of Malthus' doctrines. Malthus expressed his ideas mathematically: Population tended to increase in geometrical ratio, while subsistence tended to increase in arithmetical ratio only. Malthus hedged his theories with cautious qualifications, and his ideas were imprisoned by the predominantly agricultural society in which he lived. Yet Malthusianism permeates modern thinking on all kinds of economic, political, and military problems. It is generally expressed in terms of "too many people" or "too many goods." "Mature economy," "oversaving," and "underinvestment" are essentially Malthusian concepts in modern economics. Similarly, "too many soldiers" and *"l'armée de métier"* are Malthusian adaptations to military policy. The restrictive practices of organized labor, discrimination against aliens and racial groups, and bars to immigration—"too many people for too few jobs"—are examples of modern Malthusianism in action. This "sophisticated" Malthusianism is not based on a correct understanding of the dynamics of modern industrial society. In its original and simpler form the theory of Malthus *does* apply to present-day conditions in China and India.

In China, crop failures and a poor system of distribution have resulted frequently even in peacetime in famines affecting many millions. Approximately 80 per cent of China's 350 to 450 million inhabitants are engaged directly in agriculture. Yet China has imported food for a number of years. While these imports were small compared to total consumption, they were increasing in the 1920's and 1930's. And if one concedes that the Chinese standard of living "for fully 90 per cent of the population is subhuman as compared only to the standard of an English unemployed worker on relief

* Warren S. Thompson, *Population Problems*, New York, 1942, pp. 21-23.

(in 1937)" * and that this observation puts the matter rather mildly, then indeed the Malthusian formulation applies to the case of China.

Japanese aggression wrought havoc with China's food supply. Japan's "rice strategy" converted some of China's most fertile regions, such as the Lake Tungting area, into battlegrounds. A nominal 3 to 1 numerical superiority in manpower has not enabled China to expel unaided her Japanese foe.† At best, Chinese manpower and geographical space were weapons of delaying action. True, it was a large force of men armed with light weapons who fought that long and valiant delaying action, "selling space for time." Hundreds of thousands of coolies, armed with picks and dirt baskets, dug hundreds of miles of roads, leveled airfields, and improvised fortifications. Yet it is precisely this dissipation of manpower on tasks modern technology accomplishes with machines which reduced agricultural output and thus sharpened China's ever-present dearth of food.

The Chinese soldier has given proof of remarkable valor and endurance. Yet widespread illiteracy and lack of adequate facilities for occupational training have proved formidable obstacles to technical education, hence to the manufacture, servicing, and use of many types of modern weapons. It follows that in war China's huge population partially compensated for technical backwardness but also magnified to the breaking point the strains of a system which barely satisfied the requirements of minimum subsistence.

India, next to China, is the most populous country of the globe. The Indian census of 1941 reports a population of 389 million and a ten-year increase of more than 50 million, *i.e.*, a number larger than the total population of the United Kingdom. Indisputably, the military strength of India, in terms of fighters as well as producers, stands in no relationship to her huge reservoir of manpower. In length of mileage, India's railways stand first in Asia. Unlike China, India pos-

* W. Burton, "Natural Resources of the Far East: A Qualitative Summary," *Asiatic Review*, Vol. 33, October 1937, p. 791.

† The Japanese Empire, including Manchuria (42 million inhabitants), Formosa (5.5 million), Korea (25 million), and Kwantung Province (1.8 million), contained in 1935 approximately 150 million people.

sesses a nucleus of heavy industry and large proven deposits of strategic raw materials. Yet her population problem, like that of China, fits Malthus' formula—albeit complicated by a different set of circumstances. The Indian population, unlike the Chinese, has been growing rapidly. It has doubled within less than a hundred years and had increased from 300 million in 1921 to nearly 400 million in 1945.

Neither emigration, land reclamation, nor the introduction of better farming methods into certain agricultural regions was able to align food production with rising requirements. While the output of the Indian agricultural worker is estimated as substantially higher than that of the Chinese,* India nevertheless imported large quantities of foodstuffs, particularly rice from Burma, for consumption in the densely populated Bengal province. When, in 1942, Japanese occupation of Burma coincided with crop failure in the Ganges valley, catastrophe overtook millions of Indians. The figure for the toll in lives taken by the famine has not been published. Nevertheless, it is a fair guess that the calamity entailed serious military consequences. India's growing population had turned into a liability; the Malthusian "limit of subsistence" effectively limited India's military power.

Population pressure and technological backwardness do not suffice to explain the weakness of China and India. China and India are really geographical expressions rather than political units. Each represents a collective term for what are in fact aggregations of independent and semi-independent states; these states attained unity only at rare moments of history, and then nearly always under foreign rule. In most "foreign wars," the foreign enemy enjoyed the support of native forces. China lacks even that measure of administrative unity that British rule imposed upon India.

One test of effective administration is the ability to take a census; the Romans observed the principle of counting those peoples they expected to rule permanently. By that token, British rule of India is tighter than appears from formal del-

* Colin Clark, *The Economics of 1960*, London, 1943, p. 36. See also Professor Rao's figures for Indian food production and consumption in *Sankhya*, Vol. 4, Part 2.

egation of that rule to native legislatures and the princes. India's decennial population count is thought by experts to be accurate within the fraction of 1 per cent. China's population, by contrast, has been variously estimated at from 350 million to 500 million, the best guess being that the actual figure lies somewhere in the middle.* The government of China can only guess the number of people over whom it claims sovereignty; it has never been able to conduct a nation-wide population count.

Concerning the present military usefulness of Chinese manpower a keen observer writes as follows: "Figures for the total number of front-line and reserve troops mobilized for the war against Japan vary from 4,000,000 to 15,000,000. Actual combat troops provided with the simplest arms probably do not number more than 3,000,000 men. But this number reflects not available manpower, but technological backwardness." † The same author concludes that ". . . mechanized troops must combine discipline with individual initiative under combat condition. . . . [Chinese] social values . . . are the product of historical causations quite different from those of Europe and America. . . . Indoctrination in mechanical precision and discipline is but one aspect of a general process of changing the place of the individual in Chinese society." ‡ This shrewd diagnosis of Chinese facts-not-fancies could, with slight modifications, be broadened to include the present-day military usefulness of Indian manpower. However, there has been little remarkable foresight recorded anywhere about the nature or extent of "general processes" of change, to wit, social revolution; least about the scope of the Russian experiment.

At the core of twenty-five years of Soviet economic and strategic policies is a revolutionary redistribution of man-

* According to an estimate of the Chinese Ministry of the Interior the population was, in 1940, 459,339,764; Chinese Ministry of Information, *China Handbook, 1937-1943*. Professor George B. Cressey estimated the population of all of China including Manchuria at 473,992,369; *Asia's Land and Peoples*, New York, 1944, p. 44.

† David Nelson Rowe, *China Among the Powers*, New York, Harcourt, Brace, 1945, p. 26.

‡ *Ibid*, pp. 29-30.

power. In 1913, 85 per cent of the Russian population lived in villages and only 15 per cent in towns. Twice as many people were employed in village handicraft industries as in factories. In 1939, urban population amounted to 33 per cent of the whole. Between 1913 and 1939 the Russian people increased from 130 million to 170 million, despite World War I losses in lives and territory.* Thus, proportionate increase in urban population is all the more impressive when converted to absolute figures: Between 1913 and 1939 the population of the towns more than trebled, having risen from 18 million to 56 million.

Increase went hand in hand with qualitative change. Expanding industry recruited labor from the ranks of the peasantry and the female population of the towns. During the first Five Year Plan industrial labor increased by 12.5 million, of whom 4 million came from the cities and 8.5 million from the villages. The third Five Year Plan depended for its completion upon the annual addition of 1 million workers to the national labor force. More critical than the problem of drafting illiterate peasants and housewives into factory work was that of turning them into skilled workers. Soviet leadership allowed little scope for individual initiative and wage incentives. It determined how many hands were to stay on the collective farm, who could be spared for factory work, and who were to be trained as skilled workers. It established hundreds of trade schools which were to train workers in six-month to two-year courses, and decreed that trainees were to be drafted not only from towns but also, at the rate of 4 per cent, from the collective farms.

From 1926 to 1939 more than 3 million people moved from the densely populated district of European Russia to the Urals, Siberia, and the Soviet Far East. The purely industrial character of this migration is borne out by the fabulous growth of cities in Siberia and the far east. While the population of these grew to thrice its 1926 size, farm population increased by only 17.5 per cent.

* Russia lost, as a result of World War I, territories containing approximately 30 million inhabitants. The population of Russia was estimated at 160 million in 1910. It had increased threefold in the last hundred years of czarist rule.

Regarded from the long-range point of view, Soviet policy on the industrial and agricultural fronts stacks up to a gigantic struggle for a mobile reserve of manpower. The goal of Soviet agricultural policy was the freeing of men for factory work and the army; that of Soviet migration policy the filling up of the eastern areas where industry would be beyond the reach of potential enemy powers, and of distant borderlands where armies were to be raised from and supplied by local populations.

Strategically, these vastly conceived policies were put to the test in the war against Germany. Because their application, while obtaining tremendous results, fell short of a complete utilization of Russian manpower, Russia was able to draw upon unused reserves long after Germany had reached the peak of her manpower utilization. It was Russia's hidden reserves—the millions from the collective farms—which pressed upon the Germans when victory over Russian armies in the field seemed to have put final victory within their grasp. Paradoxically, the very incompleteness of Russia's mobilization of manpower may have been one reason why Russia was able to sustain terrible defeats and to fall with new vigor upon the enemy.

Germany's attack upon Russia was most probably synchronized with the attainment of maximum efficiency in the utilization of manpower, military and industrial, domestic and foreign, this being, indeed, the sole rational basis for calculated risk. As German *Blitzkrieg* petered out in the eastern plains, Russia was building up her productive and military strength from her immobilized, potential power.

Neither Russia nor Germany—unlike the United States—published the strength of its military effectives in this war. Private estimates are notoriously wide of the mark; the actual figures are closely guarded military secrets. However, some recently published estimates may serve to illustrate the order of magnitudes: The Red Army is reported to have disposed of 500 divisions at the beginning of 1943, and its effectives, including replacements, garrison troops, and supply forces, are said to have totaled 17 million. The strength of the *Wehrmacht* is believed to have been, in 1941, 300 divisions and its total strength 8 million; the number of all

Germans fit for military duty is estimated to have been 14 million.* Another estimate allows for a 1941-1944 toll of 2 million dead and 5 million wounded.† Out of a total of 21 million men between the ages of 18 and 50 this would leave no more than 14 million, of whom 3.5 million are between 40 and 50, and 4 million (i.e., 20 per cent, and probably much too low a figure) unfit for military service. By the end of 1944 there would have remained no more than 6.5 million Germans who by any conjuration could be classified as military manpower in 1944. These figures, be it repeated, are based mostly on conjecture. However, they correspond roughly to the size of each country's military age group, and accord reasonably well with World War I estimates of the costs in dead and wounded of large-scale land warfare. In the light of the Red Army's steady progress in the summer of 1944 and the sudden appearance at the front, at the height of the offensive, of new army groups, a 2.6 to 1 ratio in Russia's favor appears a conservative estimate.

It was manpower which cushioned Russia's early reverses and supplied the surplus strength for the final follow-through. Without vast excess reserves of labor Stalin's declaration in 1941, "We must start from the beginning. . . . We keep on the defensive and carry the offensive into the factory," could not have called forth so prodigious an effort as, for example, the reconstruction from scratch of Soviet aviation industry and the mass manufacture of new tanks and antitank weapons. Without it the grandiose program for the reconstruction of liberated areas, while the military offensive rolled on with undiminished force, would have remained a vain gesture. The goal of this program, providing for the rehabilitation of a war-torn area 272,150 square miles in size, is reported to have been exceeded.‡ It is doubtful that any Western power could have mustered in the midst of the most massive offensive recorded in the history of war the labor required for executing a huge program of peacetime reconstruction.

* A. Reithinger, *Why France Lost the War*, New York, 1941, pp. 22-4.
† Hanson W. Baldwin, "Germans Still Intact," *New York Times*, August 15, 1944.
‡ E. C. Ropes, "Russia Restores Reoccupied Areas," *Foreign Commerce Weekly*, Vol. XV, No. 4, April 22, 1944, p. 3.

Because she succumbed to the same power Russia vanquished, the case of France invites comparison. It is now fashionable to ascribe France's defeat to the corruption of her political system and Russia's victory to the perfection of Soviet institutions.

The Soviet "system" in June, 1941, had probably fully as many shortcomings as the French in May, 1940. Real wages were low, economic planning had bogged down in a good many sectors, most notably in that of transportation, and the performance of the Red Army in Finland reflected neither glory upon itself nor the efficiency of Soviet war industry. The Soviet press decried abuses and mismanagement in this or that plant with considerable candor, ascribing them now to misdirected zeal, now to the activities of "wreckers." It appears from the Red Army's disasters in 1941, in White Russia and the Black Sea region, that Russia, notwithstanding the lessons of the Finnish War and the warning example of Allied defeats in the West, was no better prepared for war than France. Yet Russia could retrieve herself, even after she had made the very military mistakes which had sealed the fate of France. From that fate Russia was saved by space and population. Russia lost entire armies; she set up new ones. She lost her best agricultural districts; she created new ones in the East. The low quality of Russian weapons was partly compensated for by their quantity, because Russia was able to maintain heavy production. The Russians, unlike France, could accept heavy losses yet afford repairing their mistakes. They were able, in the dark hours of 1941, to change radically their production methods. When the *Luftwaffe* had destroyed the obsolescent French air force, France lost not only the domination of her sky but also her aviation factories. In 1941, Russia lost her air fleet of 10,000 planes, outclassed by the *Luftwaffe's* latest models. Yet Stalin could say in December, 1941: "It is silly to sacrifice our pilots in old crates. We will mount a new air offensive in our aviation plants." Soviet aviation industry accomplished in the midst of war two tasks: the transfer of factories and the production of better planes. At Teheran, Stalin stated that Russia produced 3,000 planes per month, approximately as many as Britain.

As regards men fit for military service, the German-French

manpower ratio was, in 1940, 3 to 1; to wit, approximately 15 million against 5 million. Germany in the 20 to 30 age class, which is most fit in the active prosecution of war, could muster almost as many soldiers as France in all age classes from 20 to 50 combined. French war plans provided for the mobilization of at least 5 million men, or the withdrawal of approximately 40 per cent of all the employed male population from its previous occupation. It is estimated that Germany, before the war, employed in armament industries 3.5 times as many workers as France; the mobilization of 5 million men in each country is calculated to have increased that ratio to 5 to 1 in Germany's favor.* In short, France went to war close to the limit of her capacity, while Germany possessed a comfortable margin. Significantly, the manpower relationship of Germany to France is approximately the same as that of Russia to Germany, namely 3 to 1, and the ultimate realities of the two military situations did not lie far apart. Germany was able to conquer France; she was defeated by Russia.

Large armies can be raised only from large populations, and a large army is still the main condition of victory. The larger the population, the greater the quantity and variety of weapons it can produce. Strenuous effort and higher quality weigh heavily against mere numerical superiority. Yet as the spread of technological proficiency rapidly turns quantity into quality, larger numbers are transformed into greater military power. The more populous a country is, the larger the industrial plant it can man. If it is geared to mass production, the old and rigid difference between skilled and unskilled labor all but vanishes. The problem of marshaling the labor force is transferred to the level of job planning and occupational schooling. The training of the fighting man, who, too, is made increasingly to handle precision tools, resembles closely the "processing" of skilled workers. Just as war and farming in the advanced countries have become mechanized, so the technician-soldier is replacing the peasant-horseman-soldier who for centuries was the backbone of military power.

* A. Reithinger, *op. cit.*, p. 23.

As the production engineer succeeded in breaking down manufacturing processes into a great number of single operations, it became possible to convert, in a comparatively short period of time, a nation's potential of manpower into an effective force of "skilled" workers. However, the bulk of these recruits to skilled labor are skilled in single operations only. It is this distribution of the productive process over a great many single operations which enables industry to integrate the potential of crude manpower rapidly and smoothly. There is no "average" man or woman who cannot be trained to one or another of these thousands of single operations. The monopoly of crafts and the bottlenecks of skills are made to yield to a multiplicity of separate functions performed by different workers; i.e., to numbers.

One of the most serious bottlenecks to develop in United States war production was, for example, that of skills in the optical industry. The making of an expert lens grinder required an apprenticeship of four to five years. The United States had heretofore relied heavily on the importation of optical instruments from abroad, particularly from Germany, and the domestic supply of craftsmen fell short of wartime demand. The production experts of the War Manpower Commission succeeded in breaking down the job of lens grinding into fourteen separate operations, in which workers could be schooled within training periods ranging from a few weeks to three months, no previous experience being required. A similar dilution of jobs that formerly were the domain of craftsmen risen from long and exacting apprenticeships enabled such industries as shipbuilding, aircraft production, and manufacture of electronic devices to employ as many housewives, waitresses, salesmen, lawyers, and cosmeticians as cared to take the proffered jobs. No less important was the shortening of the training periods required for learning the simpler kinds of multiple operations. More workers could be trained without increasing the number of instructors, and the "unskilled" adult's aversion to lengthy schooling could thus be overcome. By these and similar methods has been accomplished a phenomenal mobility of manpower; virtually the entire able-bodied population not already engaged in war industries now forms a mobile labor reserve, available for productive use upon short notice.* The bars to full utilization are socio-economic, not technological, problems.

Advances in the division of labor and in automatic operations have greatly enhanced the importance to war industry of woman-power reserves. The rapid transformation of the housewife into an efficient industrial worker is perhaps the greatest single achievement in the saga of the expansion of labor forces under wartime conditions in the United States and Great Britain. In 1944, 6.6 million women, nearly 40 per cent of the total female population, were employed in British industry. Three-fifths of the jobs in the munitions industries were filled by women.†

The mobilization of woman-power played a key role in prolonged German resistance after the terrible losses in men suffered by the *Wehrmacht* on the Russian front in the winter of 1942-43. By July, 1944, 16 million women, 76 per cent of the Reich's total female population between the ages of 15 and 55, were gainfully employed. Approximately 12 million were engaged in industrial work. In 1943 approximately 1.5 million women entered the Reich labor force. This number is approximately equal to the number of new recruits gained that year by the *Wehrmacht*, as calculated by a Soviet Russian authority.‡

In peacetime, industries are rarely operated at capacity. Each modern war creates its own new devices, requiring unforeseen changes in established industries and the development of new ones. Manpower, too, is never put to maximum productive use in peacetime. The smooth meshing of surplus man- and machine-power in rapid response to the exigencies of war is a basic condition of military power.

A large population can afford high standards of selection. The greater the numerical superiority a nation enjoys, the higher can it set the physical standards of its army. In 1939

* See Walter Dietz, "Training within Industry," *Factory Management and Maintenance,* October, 1943, and releases of the War Manpower Commission, "Job Instruction Aids to Industry," March, 1944.
† Statistics Relating to the War Effort of the United Kingdom, pp. 3-4.
‡ Eugene Varga, "The Results of Total Mobilization in Germany," *Pravda,* July 22, 1943.

the average age of the French soldier was 26; in the American army it was, in 1942, somewhat above 21. The age of the average trainee of the U.S. air force was 20 and the upper age limit was 26; in Great Britain, Canada, and France a comparatively large number of men in their late twenties and early thirties were admitted to military aviation training. In 1944, when Germany was putting men in their sixties into uniform, the U.S. Selective Service set the upper age limit at 26. In 1943 and 1944, from half a million to 1 million German 17-year-olds had been called to labor service and a large number had been mustered into combat units. In the United States the lower age limit stood unchanged at 18, and training periods were not shortened materially.

In 1940-41, the average army selectee in the United States was 68.5 inches tall and weighed 152 pounds; the same figures for the *Wehrmacht* in 1939 were 66 inches and 146 pounds. While in 1940-41 the combined rejection rate of all registrants was 52.8 per cent,* the rate for men between the ages of 30 and 37 was 76 per cent. In France, about 65 per cent of all men in the latter age group had been called to arms by September, 1939. According to a study prepared by the Selective Service, the principal causes of rejection in more than 42 per cent of all cases examined in 1940-41 were defective teeth and eyes, nervous and mental disorders, and educational deficiency. That in Germany, France, and Italy rejections on these counts averaged only a combined total of 15 per cent does not indicate, of course, that these nations are endowed with better teeth, eyesight, and emotional stability; they were compelled to set lower standards in order to fill up their cadres—a fact conveniently overlooked by those who deplore the "low" health standards of the United States compared to those allegedly attained in totalitarian countries.

The United States military establishment in 1944, with approximately 12 million men, was the largest on earth next

---

* The average rejection rate up to February 1, 1944, was 45 per cent as compared with a figure of 30 per cent in World War I. G. St. J. Perrot, "Findings of Selective Service Examinations," *The Milbank Memorial Quarterly*, Vol. 22, No. 4.

to Russia, and probably equal to the combined effectives of Germany and Japan.

The line of demarcation separating, in various countries, military from civilian manpower is not clearly drawn. Not only do large numbers of civilians man the United States Merchant Marine, but many are also directly employed by the Army and Navy. The United States Army Air Force alone employed, in 1944, 500,000 civilians, from unskilled laborer to scientist. Domestic transportation, shipping, and the garrisoning of bases and outposts absorb a far larger portion of American military effectives than are similarly employed, for example, by Russia. On the other hand, in the United States, home defense and air-raid precautions require less personnel than, for example, in Great Britain. In the sector of industrial manpower, a larger working force is kept militarily neutral in the United States than in any other major belligerent country. Numerical strength acquires strategic value only with reference to the military situation: The requirements of sea, land, and triphibian warfare are not the same either as regards quantity or quality of effectives. Nevertheless, these special cases are far from supporting the case for military Malthusianism: i.e., a small, highly trained army of professionals.

Long training periods are inadequate substitutes for a broad range of selection. A populous country can afford to select only those best fit for military service and may shorten training periods, as only the best human material need be taken. Three times within seventy years France tried unsuccessfully to overcome the handicap of numerical inferiority by extending the period of military service and creating elite formations of highly trained professionals.

Historically, the idea of the "small but highly trained and exceptionally mobile professional force," *l'armée de métier*, took root in those countries where either political conditions or lack of manpower, or both, stood in the way of the mobilization of a large national army. After World War I, Germany was not permitted to have a large standing army; the British public thought it did not need one; and France feared that she would soon lack the recruits to keep up a strong one. The theories of Generals von Seeckt, Fuller, and de Gaulle, each a proponent of a small hard-hitting force of professionals, proposed to solve the insoluble problem: how to be strong without being strong in numbers. The military ideologies to which their teachings gave rise were most readily accepted by peoples permeated by neo-Malthusian doctrines, namely, the Western democracies.

Von Seeckt, Fuller, and de Gaulle believed that their élite armies of the future would restore mobility to warfare. As proponents of mechanization and mobility they focused military thought upon a practical escape from the horrible dilemma of trench warfare. It is not that part of their teachings, however, which attracted general attention. They also believed that economic costs and the difficulty of the new techniques would prove the limiting factor; the professional force would have to be backed by a huge industrial and labor force, but only a small band of men would do the actual fighting. It is that which the public wanted. It was thought that the rationalization of warfare would have the effect of shifting the weight of manpower from the battlefield into the factory, an alternative which Malthusian economies with a large excess capacity of production in terms of machines and labor could have contemplated with equanimity.

It has been variously estimated by experts writing in the 1930's that one soldier would need the support of from 7 to 21 civilians. Had these estimates proven correct, the United States armed forces in 1944 would have needed the backing of from 80 to 240 million workers—patently an absurdity. Hanson W. Baldwin wrote: "In World War I whatever statistics are available indicate that the ratio of workers in war industries . . . to men in uniform was less than one to one . . . the ratio has increased [in World War II] probably to between 1.3 to 1 to 2.5 to 1." The operations of lend-lease placed an added burden upon American industrial and farm manpower. Baldwin concluded "that on the basis of 10,-000,000 men in the armed forces, about 55,000,000 other workers will be required in war and civilian industry, lend-lease manufacturing, transportation and communication, farms, shipbuilding, and other jobs, from domestics to clerical positions. We have no such number today; the problem is to increase the number of workers, to increase the man hours available. In essence, this is the basic problem of victory." The task before the American strategists was to make *masses* mobile, and for this additional masses were needed. United States logistics were based on manpower.

In summary, there is no way of dodging the weight of numbers either on the battlefield or on the home front. Ever since the United States entered world politics as a Great Power, i.e., since the Spanish-American War in 1898, it has ranked as the most populous among Western nations. Even before World War I it numbered more inhabitants than Great Britain and France combined, then the strongest powers in Europe. In 1944 the United States Army Air Force was numerically larger than the German army which in 1939 was launched against Poland. The American navy exceeded in 1944 the combatant strength of the French army of 1940. The ground forces were larger than the combined German *Wehrmacht*—army, navy, and *Luftwaffe*. The War and Navy Departments were staffed, in Washington alone, by more officers and men than served in the army of the Austrian Republic. These are crude figures of manpower relationships. Power contests are a crude business in which accounts are settled in numbers of men.

3. TOMORROW'S POPULATIONS

IN THE past the United States, remote from the battlefields of the Old World, could choose its course in war and peace. History no longer pivots upon Europe. By the time World War II has ended, all belligerent nations based upon the European continent, except Russia, will have been defeated. Those who will have regained their sovereign status will have done so by virtue of the intervention of non-European powers. With the dissolution of the European system the United States is confronted with a fundamental change in the realities underlying its foreign policy. No settlement in Europe can in itself furnish guarantees of United States security. United States security depends no longer upon the width of oceans or on traditional alignments, but upon American strength and therefore upon manpower.

What will be the situation of the United States twenty-five years from now? No one can hope to predict accurately the growth of population. However, it is possible, given the current trends of birth and death rates, to estimate future population within a margin of error not exceeding, on the basis of the most divergent estimates, 12 per cent over the next twenty-five years, and more likely amounting to less than 4 per cent.* From these estimates of growth it is possible to deduce, within a similar range of probability, the place the United States will hold by, let us say, 1970, in the international line-up of manpower.

Assuming "medium" fertility and "medium" mortality, i.e., continuation of trends prevailing throughout the last two decades, and net immigration of 100,000 annually, the population of the United States will rise to 155 million in

* Population forecasts are based on various techniques. Their efficacy is discussed exhaustively by A. M. Carr-Saunders in his *World Population, Past Growth and Present Trends*, Oxford, 1936, and Warren S. Thompson, in his *Population Problems*, New York and London, 1942. For methodological refinements see also Frank W. Notestein and others, *The Future Population of Europe and the Soviet Union*, League of Nations, Geneva, 1944, pp. 183-198.

64

1970, an increase of 24 million over 1940.* Large as will be this over-all gain in population, it reflects a declining rate of increase due to the fact "that the same general downward movement of natural increase which we have observed in much of Europe is present in this country." † The rate of natural increase (ratio of children to women) in the United States has been falling steadily since 1930. The birth rate has reached in some states of the Union such a low level that a future over-all decline of the population is deemed probable by some experts. However, these pessimistic estimates, even were they to prove correct, are of small importance for gauging the population of 1970, the largest portion of which is now alive. Only a catastrophic increase in the death rate and decline in births, contrary to anything experienced in this or any other Western country, could entail actual population decline within the lifetime of this generation. Rejecting decline and stagnation in the near future as unlikely, we may assume that the population of the United States will have increased by one-fifth between 1940 and 1970. Is American manpower, though increasing, growing in proportion to the growth of other peoples and the growing stake of the United States in world politics?

The United States, compared with other Western nations, still holds a privileged position. Forecasts for Great Britain envisage an outright decline of 10 to 20 per cent between 1945 and 1970; Britain's population will probably decrease from 47 to between 42 and 38 million. Natural increase declined steadily in England from 405,000 a year in 1900 to 120,000 a year in 1935, although the total population increased by one-fifth. The age composition favorable to births, unfavorable to death, was passing, and at the same time the population was failing to avail itself of the favorable age

* Warren S. Thompson, *op. cit.*, p. 282. This estimate was prepared by the Scripps Foundation for the National Resources Committee; "Population Statistics, National Data," Government Printing Office, Washington, 1937. A second estimate prepared in 1943 by Warren S. Thompson and P. K. Whelpton, for the National Resources Planning Board, exceeds the figure computed previously by approximately 4 per cent.

† *Ibid.*

composition to replenish its lower age groups. The general shape of the future structure is therefore clear. During the present generation the largest part of the population will move into the upper age groups, and deaths will increase; the heavily populated younger middle-age groups will pass into the upper middle-age ranks, but because of the fall of the birth rate in the past generation their places cannot be filled, since too few children have been born. The younger middle-age groups will be numerically weaker than their predecessors.* Thus the production of a future population of the present size would demand a very considerable rise in the birth rate, that is, a decided increase in the average family. It is very doubtful whether this can be achieved soon enough to counterbalance the increase of deaths which must take place in the immediate future. Thus the population of England is entering a period in which age composition will be unfavorable to births, favorable to deaths, and marked by a *natural decrease* instead of continued growth.

The population of Canada,† South Africa, Australia, and New Zealand is still increasing and might keep, during the next generation, the white population of the British Empire as a whole at about the present level, i.e., 70 million.

It seems unlikely that the decline of French manpower can be halted. The population of France, 42 million in 1938, is estimated for 1970 at only 35 to 37 million, and this forecast does not allow for losses sustained in World War II. It is far too early to assess the inroads on French population growth of war, enemy occupation, malnutrition, dearth of medical supplies, and forced migration of French workers to Germany. With each man killed in battle two births are

* W. D. Forsyth, *The Myth of Open Spaces*, Melbourne and London, 1942, pp. 122-4.

† The population of Canada, 10.4 million in 1931, will increase, according to various estimates, to between 14.5 and 15.6 million. During the last generation Canada's population has grown as much by dint of immigration as by natural increase. Trends of fertility resemble those of the United States, except for the high birth rate of French-Catholic Quebec, supplying one-third of the nation's annual increase out of a population of 2.8 million (1931).— Steven Cartwright, "Population, Canada's Problem," *Contemporary Affairs*, Toronto, pp. 10-11.

lost.* Preliminary reports indicate that during the five-year period 1939-1943 the French birth rate averaged 14 for each thousand of inhabitants and deaths exceeded births by more than 500,000. Some experts, therefore, hold that France faces drastic depopulation and that by 1970 her people will have shrunk to 30 million. This view may prove too gloomy. The French birth rate in the years immediately preceding World War II has shown a tendency to rise slightly but perceptibly, and the number of French births in 1943 was exactly what it had been in 1939, namely 442,000.

A very sharp increase in births may be expected after the end of the war. After World War I the French birth rate rose to a higher level than it had attained in the twenty-five years preceding it, while the death rate dropped.† The rate of increase, which had steadily declined since 1850, was for 1920-25 considerably higher than between 1890 and 1913, and only after 1926 did it fall below the level attained in 1881-90. This resiliency of a people which many experts had condemned to slow extinction is all the more remarkable for the fact that war had cost the lives of 1.5 million Frenchmen and potential fathers. Long-range trends indicate that French manpower *will* decline; they do not point to a diminishment, by 1970, much larger than one-tenth of the present population.

Up to World War I, Italy lagged behind the average increase of European population. Only after 1918 did the Italian population increase more quickly than that of other European countries (with the exception of the Slavic group). It was a high death rate, 21 per thousand inhabitants in 1903-12, which weighed heavily against the comparatively large number of births, 32 per thousand in the same period. The slowing up of population increase in other European countries, more than any factor inherent in Italian population growth, enabled Italy to draw abreast of France and the

* L. Hirsch, "Demographic Effects of Modern Warfare," *What Would Be the Character of a New War*, New York, 1933. See also Horst Mendershausen's discussion of the "Hollow Age Classes" in his *Economics of War*, New York, 1943, pp. 321-3.

† M. Huber and others, *La population de la France*, Paris, 1937, pp. 67-71. J. J. Spengler, *France Faces Depopulation*, Durham, 1938, p. 53.

United Kingdom. Italian statistical data do not indicate a vitality more exuberant than that of other European peoples, as has been so frequently and boisterously alleged by Fascist propaganda. Only if the Italian population is compared with the French, as was frequently done by Italian demographers, can one speak with some justification of Italy as a "young people." It is largely the high fertility of the peasants in southern Italy, Sicily, and Sardinia which appears to justify expectation of a net gain.* In Italy, as elsewhere, urban populations have low birth rates. Increase of the total population is due to the high fecundity of the rural south. As a result, the racial composition of the Italian people is undergoing a slow change; the southerners are not only gaining proportionately but are spreading to the north and to urban-industrial centers. There is, even during World War II, a surplus of births over deaths, and it is estimated that by 1970 the Italian people will have grown to 50 or 53 million. This forecast does not take emigration into account, although this factor has played a considerable role in Italian population movements.

The number of Italians or descendants of Italian emigrants living outside Italy is estimated at 9.5 million, of whom almost 4 million live in the United States and 1 million in France. Italian emigration reached its peak in 1913, when nearly twice as many Italians left their country as were born into it; between 1890 and 1915 the number of emigrants totaled approximately half the number of births.† However, after 1921 there began a slow repatriation of one-time emigrants. In 1939 the number of *rimpatri* actually exceeded that of the *espatri*.

Italy is an overpopulated country—as long as she cannot increase industrialization—although this fact is not convincingly demonstrated by figures alone. The population density of Italy equals that of Germany; it is lower than that of Great Britain and Holland. More than half of Italy's people are peasants; a large part of the other half live in small rural towns. Italy's area of cultivable soil is, next to Poland, the

* "Present and Post-War Population Problems of Italy," *Population Index*, Vol. IX, July, 1943, p. 146.
† Robert Michels, *Italien von Heute*, Zurich, 1930, p. 250.

68

most densely settled in Europe. Thus poverty, exacerbated by defeat, will drive many Italians to seek their livelihood abroad—if bars to immigration the world over are lifted. As this will depend on changes in political and economic policies over which the Italian people have no control, no estimate of Italy's future manpower can hope to gauge accurately the effects of that most problematic and unstable factor of population change, to wit, migration.

Spain's population, like that of Italy, is growing, and is slated to increase from 25 million in 1940 to 33 million in 1970.* Spain, too, was until recently a country of emigration; in 1930, 2.5 million Spaniards, or 10 per cent of the homeland's population, lived outside the country while maintaining Spanish citizenship. However, Spain is far richer in industrial raw materials, and is only half as densely settled in relation to arable soil as is Italy. Thus, industrialization and land reclamation could absorb population increase more readily in Spain than in Italy.

By 1970 the combined population of the "Latin bloc"—France, Italy, and Spain—will have increased, if the above estimates prove correct, to 120-125 million from 112.5 million in 1940, in spite of the assumed decline of French population. This fact is, at present, of small political importance. It acquires significance only within the frame of reference of European regionalism and the supranational ideas of Latinity and Catholicism. This affinity of race, language, and religion is generally stated in cultural terms. Nevertheless, it will continue to evoke in many minds—in spite of, or perhaps because of, the many divisions of the Latin world—visions of a political community of interests. The formation of extra-European power blocs cannot but arouse the Latin peoples to the contemplation of their own world-political future. While most of the thinking done on that topic has so far been confined to intellectual, and mainly reactionary, circles in Europe as well as in Latin America, its influence may prove a far from negligible factor in world politics, particularly in United States foreign policy.

* *Boletin de Estadística*, Madrid, October-December, 1941, p. 127.

Available estimates of Germany's future population disagree widely. All estimates given in these pages are based on the unrealistic assumption that rate of population change will in the future continue to be what it has been in the base periods chosen. The projections, therefore, do not allow for the effects of war, future territorial change and migration, and a host of other factors impinging on the "orderly unfolding of past trends." Their value lies in the rough model they provide for testing performance under real conditions. In the case of Germany it is particularly difficult to maintain this fiction of normal development—useful though it is for setting up a model.

Estimates vary because experts disagree as to which period is the one most representative of Germany's recent fertility trends. There is the question, too, of the expansion of Ger-

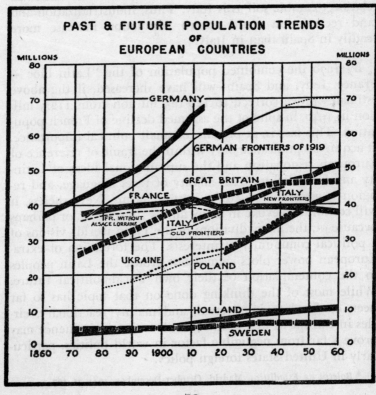

PAST & FUTURE POPULATION TRENDS
OF
EUROPEAN COUNTRIES

man territory during the last ten years. Territorial change was accompanied by large-scale two-way migrations about which little accurate information is available, and appears to have affected the vital trends of the *Altreich*, i.e., Germany within her 1936 boundaries.

If fertility levels of 1937-39 are assumed to be typical, the German population within the 1936 borders will have risen from 69.5 million in 1940 to 71.8 million by 1960, and declined to 69.8 million by 1970.* This recent American estimate agrees substantially with several forecasts made before World War II by the German statisticians F. Burgdoerfer and A. Reithinger.† It is easy to draw from these estimates significant conclusions as regards a "middle run" improvement of Germany's power-political position in the fifties. In 1935 Friederich Burgdoerfer, leading German population expert and member of the Geopolitical Institute, published the following estimate of European manpower relationships:

TABLE I

DEVELOPMENT OF THE POPULATION
OF MILITARY AGE IN EUROPE, 1925 TO 1960

(in thousands)

COUNTRY	1925	1930	1940	1950	1960
Males aged 20 to 45					
Germany	11,378	12,438	13,107	12,981	11,707
France	6,760	6,977	6,715	6,790	6,558
Great Britain	7,692	8,083	8,691	8,721	8,030
Italy	8,347	7,098	7,959	9,412	9,458
Poland	4,415	5,222	6,230	7,773	8,184
Males aged 20 to 25					
Germany	3,065	3,211	1,898	2,546	2,458
France	1,680	1,647	889	1,554	1,409
Great Britain	1,871	2,000	1,710	1,626	1,605
Italy	1,859	1,948	1,474	2,023	2,021
Poland	1,318	1,641	1,089	1,789	1,831

* Notestein and others, *op. cit.*, p. 56.
† A. Reithinger, *Das wirtschaftliche Gesicht Europas*, Stuttgart, 1936, p. 16.

71

The year 1940 was thus the critical year of German manpower, and German preponderance in Europe will be maintained, according to this estimate, until 1950. In 1940, Burgdoerfer modified this earlier forecast in view of the sharp increase of the German birth rate of 1937-39—a phenomenon generally ascribed to "full employment" and the Nazi government's drive for babies. He now predicted that the coming of age of these "Hitler babies" would assure Germany of a rising supply of military manpower up to and even after 1970. This eventuality is rendered doubly ominous by the absolute decline of the population of western and northwestern Europe expected for just that time. Moreover, such a swelling of Germany's military contingents might coincide with a relaxation of the controls imposed by the victors of World War II and subsidence of international vigilance. Thus, it is argued, an unregenerate Germany might indulge, in the sixties, in the same mathematical calculations which her leaders may well, in the thirties, have made the basis of military action. Assuming even that history repeats itself—which it does surprisingly often but not indefinitely—there are some flaws in this argument.

Up to 1910, Germany's birth rate was still the highest in northwestern and central Europe. In 1933 it was one of the lowest in Europe, and fell short, by one-quarter, of the rate required for keeping the population stationary. If an estimate of German population in 1970 were to be based on the low fertility levels of 1925-33, it would hardly exceed 60 million. It is generally admitted by German as well as foreign experts that subsidies and honors to large families, stringent laws against abortion, and official benevolence toward procreation out of wedlock met with limited success. The German birth rate rose upon Hitler's accession to power because general conditions improved—or because the German people believed they did.

In 1943 the birth rate, which according to Nazi statistics had stood at 20.3 in 1939, had fallen to 14 per thousand inhabitants, lower even than the French of the same year. It seems all was not well with general conditions as judged by the man in the street.

In France and Britain population increase has been declining for several generations, but has declined more slowly as birth rates became smaller. By contrast, German population change has been more abrupt—a consequence of abrupt social and economic changes. Are the years 1925-33, a phase of postwar reconstruction and of economic and social crisis, or the years 1933-39, a phase of re-employment through militarization, the most suitable base period for projecting future German growth? The hard fact of Germany's renewed defeat appears to answer this question. Moreover, fertility is not spread evenly over Germany. The territorial concessions she will forced to make will probably most substantially reduce her holdings in the west and east; i.e., in the predominantly Catholic Rhineland and the provinces of Silesia, East and West Prussia, and Pomerania, with their more or less recently assimilated Slavic population elements. It is these regions which had the largest birth rates in the Reich. Middle Germany had the lowest, and middle Germany's population will make up by far the largest portion of that remaining within the Reich.

Urbanization, in Germany as elsewhere, was associated with a falling birth rate; the cities grew by virtue of the pull they exercised upon the rural areas. Burgdoerfer showed * that the population of Berlin, for example, would decline, were it cut off from immigration, from 4 million in 1935 to 3 million in 1955 and to 1.5 million in 1985. The local birth rate was far below that needed for Berlin's population to reproduce itself. It was precisely migration from the rural east—Prussia east of the Oder—which had transformed Berlin from a petty capital of Prussian kings into Europe's second largest city. Vienna after the dismemberment of the Austro-Hungarian Empire is an example of a city which lost the "hinterland" upon which it had fed for its bigness. It is not a metaphor to say that Vienna with a birth rate of 9 per thousand (the lowest in Europe), and bereft of the attraction she once exerted upon the Danubian basin, was a dying city.

Were Germany's frontiers pushed back to the Rhine and Oder rivers, her remaining territories would be composed mainly of urban and industrial areas, except for the southern

* *Volk ohne Jugend*, Berlin-Grunewald, 1932, pp. 71, 72.

part of Bavaria and Württemberg. They will continue to be areas of concentration. The de-industrialization and de-urbanization of residual Germany is precluded by the density of its population, even were such a process considered desirable by Germany's neighbors, who at least for some time to come will look to German industry for war indemnities in kind. The employment of millions of able-bodied Germans in the rehabilitation of European devastated areas, as Mr. Varga suggests, will not relieve the population pressure of rump-Germany, for the repatriation of Germans from areas relinquished by Germany will largely offset outgoing German labor.*

At the moment of this writing, future mass exchanges of populations appear probable. Because of its mechanical simplicity this device will be extensively used in the settlement of such problems of national minorities as the Sudetenland, Transylvania, the Baltic states, and western Poland with its probable extensions to former German territory. The balance of these exchanges will be heavily in favor of Germany, hence will add to the population of the urban-industrial residue. These developments are foreshadowed by many authoritative statements issuing from Allied quarters; they are the logical consequence of total war waged within the framework of mass society. They certainly do not favor German population growth and promise to exacerbate the fundamentally Malthusian tendencies of the German people.

The Red Army alone claims to have inflicted 9.1 million casualties on the Germans and the German General Staff's preliminary figure is 3.5-4 million German soldiers and civilians killed in battle and by air bombing.† Even disregarding war losses and psychological factors, it is difficult

---

* It has been suggested that the victorious Allies should encourage and support German birth control. Such a proposal was anticipated poetically by Gilbert K. Chesterton:

> "Abu Ben Adem,
> May his tribe decrease
> Through the cautious use of birth control,
> And die in peace."

† "German War Losses at Least 3,500,000," cable by Drew Middleton from Paris, *New York Times*, May 25, 1945. p. 5.

to see why German population growth after World War II should be governed by factors more favorable than those operating during the aftermath of World War I. If that period is assumed as "typical," and this assumption appears optimistic, then the population of a diminished Germany will be below 60 million in 1970 and will never have exceeded that figure in the meanwhile.

If German manpower proves in the future a power-political threat to the European *status quo,* it will do so for reasons not inherent in its own make-up. That threat could present itself only as a consequence of realignments of power wrought by hands other than German. Was this not the situation created after World War I by the disintegration of the system established by Allied victory? The analogy is false. Between 1918 and today another stage in the world-wide redistribution of population strength and productive capacity has been completed. This process, of which World War II is but a climax, closes with considerable finality Germany's brief career as a super power. Like Malthusian France, Malthusian Germany will retain manpower sufficient for the exercise of what is politely called "regional" power—which is, world-politically, no power at all.

During a brief historical period, shorter than Western man's expectancy of life, the military effectives of Germany held the balance of power upon the European continent. It was that concentration of human force which pressed upon the rest of Europe, worked the expanding German plant, and energized the latent strategic possibilities of a central geographical position. For a recrudescence of that power, international trends would have to run backward, like a film being run off the wrong way around. These trends point, for the middle and long run, to new centers of population growth and political power to the east and away from Germany. By the end of this decade, the quantitative point of gravity of European population will have shifted to beyond the twentieth degree of longitude, i.e., the Warsaw-Belgrade line.

It is estimated that the population of the Soviet Union within its 1939 borders will have increased from 174 million in 1940 to 251 million in 1970, an increase greater than the entire German population now existing or ever likely to exist.* If this projection comes close to what Russia's population will be in fact, then there will be in 1970 more Russians than all western and central Europeans combined, including Germany, Great Britain, and France, the Great Powers of the nineteenth century. Though also in Russia the average size of the family is declining and war losses will total several million, there are so many more families that the number of births will remain high. Moreover, the number of children and young people now living will, for another generation at least, form a solid base for growth. Thus the age composition is favorable to births, and as the old-age group is proportionately small, deaths will be proportionately few. It is precisely this condition which obtained in western Europe up to thirty years ago, i.e., during the period of large natural increase. If Russia were to follow the western pattern (which is also that of the United States), her population would become stationary or decline within another two generations. This possibility is, from a political point of view, of small interest; the Soviet Union will remain the most populous country in Europe. Russia is the only large European country with the prospect of substantial population growth.

The security zone of Russia, or zone of Russian influence or whatever one cares to call the region of Soviet hegemony, includes the smaller Slavic states of Europe. The differences in natural increase between European peoples can be represented by two slopes, a minor one rising from northern Europe toward the Mediterranean, and a major one rising from the English Channel toward the Baltic plains. Except for industrial Czechoslovakia, the Slavic states between the Bosphorus and the Baltic enjoy the best prospects of growth in non-Russian Europe. As a group they will increase from 65 million in 1940 to 85 million in 1970, if estimates are realized. The Slavic bloc would thus unite a population as large as that of the rest of Europe (335 million against 334 million). The bloc's productive and military age groups 20-34 will be one-fifth larger than those of all other European countries combined (84.5 against 72 million).

* Notestein and others, *op. cit.*, p. 56.

In 1939, 38 million Soviet citizens lived in Asia. The development of industries in the shelter of the Urals, beyond the reach of hostile European powers, and the strengthening of the Asiatic border regions, have dominated the strategic thinking of the Soviet regime since its earliest days. Industrialization and mechanization of agriculture in Russian Asia set in motion mass migration not only from the land to the towns but also from densely settled rural regions of Russian Europe. When the Red Army fell back before the German invader, it shielded the withdrawal of many war-important industries. Whole plants, together with their skilled personnel, were moved to Asia. In addition, millions of peoples uprooted by the war, villagers with their livestock, skilled workers, Jews from the border regions, and the forcibly evacuated Volga Germans streamed eastward. Only a part of these masses will return to the areas across which the war has been fought. Many of the transferred factories will remain where they are now. Mass migration has created new markets; the output of raw materials in Soviet Asia has made giant strides, and hundreds of thousands of war refugees will prefer staying in their new homes, however bare of comfort, to returning to the devastated war zones whence they came. Strategically, plant and people are where Soviet planning intended them to be even before dire emergency speeded the movement. Thus the process of transforming the empire of the czars into a highly industrialized and urbanized base of Soviet power, which within a capitalist society might have required many decades of organic growth, is being compressed into less than half a generation.

Soviet planning and the impact of war stirred mightily the melting pot of Russian Asia. Already under the czars there was a distinct Siberian nation in the making, "Russian in the core, but modified also by the influx of foreign blood." * The opening of the Russian east, unlike the American west, with which it is so often and loosely compared, extended Russian domination not only to sparsely settled regions but also over a large part of the tribal society of central Asia, composed of Turco-Islamic peoples. In 1931 these peoples

* Eric Fischer, *The Passing of the European Age*, Cambridge, Massachusetts, 1943, p. 129.

totaled approximately 9 million—about one-quarter of Soviet Asia's population. Under Soviet rule the individual groups, Uzbeks, Kazakhs, Turkmens, Tadzhiks, Kirghiz, Buriat-Mongols, and lesser tribes, were subject to policies of assimilation which, infinitely more subtle than the bludgeoning tactics of czarist officials, were accomplishing what mere force could not have wrought, namely, Russification.

The substitution of the paraphernalia of Soviet civilization, "the multinational state on a socialist foundation," for those of a feudal society under Islam, and mass immigration of Russian settlers, are rapidly fusing a new Asiatic-Russian people. The Soviet encouraged linguistic and cultural autonomies. Soviet sponsorship of local speech and custom, by removing the sense of racial inequality, removed the bars to the circulation of races, intermarriage, and assimilation. On the other hand, communist society is Russian-dominated society. For Russian is the language of modern education, technology, and, on an interregional level, of Communist Party affairs. "The Soviets win the youths of these Central Asian peoples first for communism, secondly for a common future, and thirdly . . . for assimilation." * The crucible of this racial amalgamation is the Russian element. Nevertheless, the product, the Asiatic Russian, is a distinct and vigorous personality. He is bound to play an increasing role in the future development of the Soviet Union as a whole, of Soviet Europe, and of Asia. In the future, the Asiatic Soviet republics will demonstrate in full view of all the peoples of Asia, Soviet methods in the production of wealth and racial equality. Already czarist Russia knew that to hold her possessions in the east was to settle them; the Soviets have succeeded in creating a vast reservoir of Russian manpower in the heart of Asia. If prewar rates of natural increase and immigration continue, the population of Soviet Asia will have risen in 1970 to over 70 million.

The "frontier" to the east will, for decades to come, mitigate whatever Malthusian tendencies may assert themselves in the social pattern of the Soviet Union. With the tasks be-

* Eric Fischer, *op. cit.,* p. 131.

78

fore it of rehabilitating the devastated areas in Europe and building its empire in Asia, the Soviet Union does not suffer from "population pressure" but from a lack of labor. "Full employment" is no problem in the Soviet Union; neither is the "social capillarity" of the upper classes which in a capitalist society tends to restrict births because of the high costs of "keeping up with the Joneses" and of education. The increasing austerity in private morals likewise strengthens the position of the family in Soviet life. Age structure, "frontier," and pyschological climate thus appear to favor a rapid growth of the Soviet population.

The cycle from "youthfulness" to "aging" is, thus far, a characteristic of Western peoples in their passage from industrial revolution to "mature" economy. There is a basis for the belief that Russia will follow the same course, but this hypothesis does not affect the high probabilities of 1970 pointing to a population of 250 million within Russia's 1939 borders, and of 285 million if the boundaries of 1941 are restored.

Japan borrowed the mechanics of Western progress, not its inwardness. She began to acquire the former when the West forced her gates in the 1850's, and to transform, with the Meiji restoration in 1868, a feudal agrarian regime into an industrial state. Changes in population growth and structure followed the general lines of the Western pattern. Japan's population increased from 27 million in 1852 to 73 million in 1940. Because the geography of insular Japan resembles broadly that of England, and because Japan has led in the industrialization of the East as England has led in that of Europe, the development of the two countries is often compared. Indeed, the rate of Japan's population increase throughout the last eighty years was about the same (only slightly lower) as that of England from 1810 to 1890, and Japan's present population structure closely resembles that of England in the 1890's. Urbanization, which went hand in hand with the industrialization of Japan, was even more rapid than in the West, and declines in the death and birth rates accompanied the economic transformation just as they had done earlier in western European countries. Just as in the West, the decline in death rates preceded that in births, the time lag priming the sudden forward surge which within fifty years doubled Japan's population.

In 1940 half of the population lived in towns, one-fifth in the six great cities Tokyo, Osaka, Yokohama, Nagoya, Kyoto, and Kobe. It is in these cities that birth rates have declined most rapidly. Were the past trends—industrialization and migration from land to city—to continue, decline in births would overtake decline in deaths, and Japan, like England today, would be faced with real population decline.

The transformation of Japan was wrought by the impact of Western civilization; Japan, however, has not absorbed all of it. Population increase is slackening, but the Western cliché will not fit Japanese conditions as long as habits of life and thought formed in the age of Japan's secluded feudalism retain their hold on the masses. The fertility of the industrial areas *has* been declining, chiefly, some experts believe, because of the increasing age of marriage, which in turn is due to young women's employment as factory labor and the long periods of military service for men.* But in Japan, factories and cities, patriarchal family and medieval village exist side by side. The state stimulated and directed the development of industry; it is the state which guards the traditional structure of a feudal-military society. Neither is wholly assimilated to the other. Hence the contradictions of modern Japan; hence also the doubtful value of analogies derived from the experience of Western peoples.

In 1935 male life expectancy was 47 years, which by Western standards leaves considerable room for improvement. Yet were it even to remain the same, and were rural fertility to decline at the same rate as urban (for which assumption, thus far, conclusive evidence is lacking), Japan's population in 1970 would still be 93 million, which estimate, like each foregoing one, projects past trends into the future and does not pretend to foretell what that future will be.

War losses will cut deeply into Japan's military age groups.

* In 1935, the rate of net reproduction was for towns what it had been in 1920, namely 1.2; for rural Japan it had risen from 1.8 to 1.9.—Irene B. Taeuber and Edwin G. Beal, "The Dynamics of Population in Japan," *The Milbank Memorial Fund Quarterly*, Vol. XXII, No. 3, July, 1944.

That they have done so already may be deduced from the suppression since 1935 of significant data by the Statistical Bureau of the Cabinet. However, neither much greater losses nor crushing defeat will, in the near future, substantially alter the trends of Japanese population growth as they have evolved from the past.

Many Japanese and Western students have argued that population pressure generated the expansionist tendencies that turned Japan to foreign conquest. Yet population increase has not increased materially the pressure on the land; per capita production of rice has slightly increased; and economic transformation has permitted the absorption of natural increase in the developing industries and service occupations of the growing urban areas. The problem is thus one of expanding markets and consumer purchasing power rather than of expanding space. On the other hand, the demolition of the Japanese Empire, alone, need not affect the situation which thus far has made for the population increase of the home islands, for up until now only a fraction of that increase has been diverted to the conquered territories, or for that matter, to any other areas overseas. In 1938 only 1.5 million Japanese resided in Japan's overseas possessions, and of these a goodly number were officials. Barriers to Oriental immigration had closed, before World War II, Australia, North America, and many Latin American states, except Brazil and Peru, to Japanese would-be settlers. But it is by no means clear that they would have settled abroad as readily as Japanese propagandists claimed they would have, had Western countries relaxed their discriminatory policies. Prospects of future Japanese population growth are determined by the economic future of the Japanese homeland with its askew Oriental-Western, agrarian-urban, medieval-industrial countenance.

If the population of China were to increase after World War II at the same rate as the Japanese from 1870 to 1900, it would be 800 to 900 million in 1970. At that time the population of India, were it to grow as rapidly, would be around 600 million.* Whether the populations of China or India

* Indian experts predict a population of 750 million in the year 2000.—
Indian Information, Vol. XV, No. 149, p. 122.

will actually attain these levels will depend on circumstances that will be different from those which confronted the Japan of the Meiji restoration, if for no other reason than that the rise of Japan more than any other factor has served Asia as an object lesson in Westernization. This, however, can be said confidently: Japanese history does not warrant the belief that increase of the Chinese or Indian peoples will halt in the near future, nor that all such increase must necessarily remain fallow industrially and militarily.

From the first Tokugawa census count in 1721 to the last in 1850 the Japanese population remained stationary, fluctuating between 27 and 30 million.* This stability was not due to human foresight and birth control but to the action of famines and diseases, i.e., the regulating factors of orthodox Malthusian theory. This situation is precisely that in which large parts of India and China still find themselves today. Yet the Japanese people so perilously close to the subsistence level were transformed within less than one generation into the industrial and military manpower which defeated first China and then the Russian Empire.

It can be argued that whatever gains are being scored by backward peoples through better sanitation, transportation, and administration are quickly absorbed by additonal growth, and that hence the large populations of colonial and semicolonial Asia are being stifled by the very "improvements" bestowed upon them by the West. Yet Japan waxed strong in the face of the very Malthusian controls, famine and disease, which curbed the growth of its population and now still curb the preindustrial societies of China and India. It was the balance of power in eastern Asia—as the rivalries of the Western powers had shaped it—which afforded Japan the opportunity of becoming the first modern Asiatic power. For taking advantage of this opportunity, Japan's indigenous civilization—a feudal-agrarian society, its vital growth controlled by famine and disease—was neither better nor worse suited than are the present civilizations of China, India, Java, or Korea.

In summary, in 1970 the numerical strength of the Western peoples will probably be what it is now; increases in

* Taeuber and Beal, *op. cit.*

82

North America and southern Europe will have counterbalanced declines in western Europe. The Slavic group is slated for an increase of approximately two-fifths. The populations of China and India may not increase as rapidly as the Japanese in the era of Westernization. Although they may grow at a slower rate, additional hundreds of millions will crowd into regions which are now the most densely populated on earth. Will these massive movements remain of purely regional significance? This question may prove to contain the world-political problem of the future. It has been shelved by World War II. It may not become acute before 1970. It will then still confront the majority of Americans now living.

4. POPULATION TRENDS AND POWER

STABILITY and security will be the watchwords of the stationary and declining peoples of western and central Europe, of whom none will possess the manpower potential required for war as a modern World Power must be able to wage it. Germany is taking her place among the aging peoples—because of her defeat, probably two decades sooner than if she had turned her energies to the pursuits of peace. The international morals of declining peoples may be no better than those of growing ones. However, declining populations are, as a rule, not war-making nations. Malthusians are pacifists.

If our reading of the manpower realities of Asia is correct, there are being added to the two major centers of growing populations possessed of advanced technological skills—namely Russia-in-Asia and Japan, each slated to exceed in numbers the largest European nation—two new cores of skilled manpower, namely India and China. Their populations are slated for substantial increases.

The size of Asiatic populations dwarfs that of the peoples of the Western Hemisphere. At present, the population of the Americas is approximately 275 million. By 1970 it should have increased to 350 million, a figure substantially lower than that for India's population of today.* By that date the population of the Soviet Union will have increased to 250 million within the 1939 borders, and to a much higher figure if territorial gains in eastern Europe are to be included. Estimates of the future populations of India and China are fraught with so many difficulties that any figure given represents a mere guess. In all likelihood their combined populations will, in 1970, have crossed the billion mark. By contrast, the combined populations of western Europe, Britain, France, Belgium, and Holland will hardly exceed 100 million.

* See page 281, Note 1 to Chapter 4.

By 1970 far-reaching changes in the distribution of the world's population will have taken place. The altered balance of manpower will result in an altered balance of political power, no matter what provisions are now being made for damming the human tide of Asia and resuscitating the flagging vital energies of the Western peoples. In Table II the population of the United States is considered as a constant and the relative changes of the other powers are shown in percentages of U.S. population, present and estimated.

TABLE II

DEMOGRAPHIC RANK OF WORLD POWERS

(All Age Groups; U.S. = 100)

	1940	1970
U.S.S.R.	130	160-180
United States	100	100
Japanese Empire	92	140
Japan Proper	50	64
Germany	62	38
British Empire (white population only)	50	42
Great Britain	35	25
Italy	33	38
France	30	23

Total population figures give only an incomplete picture of manpower relationships. If the probabilities of 1970 are measured exclusively in terms of military age groups, the position of the United States is even less favorable. The peoples of the United States and Europe, except the Slavic group, are aging. The United States as well as western Europe will contain in 1970 a high percentage of older persons, while such nations as, for example, Russia, Japan, India, and China, which today have only a small proportion of old people, will show increased contingents in the productive-military ages.

Between 1945 and 1970 the total population of the United States is expected to increase by 18-20 per cent; however, the age group between 20 and 40 years will not increase by more than 9 per cent, namely from 50.5 to 55 million. In Table III the productive-military age group of the population of the United States is considered as a constant, and the relative changes of the other powers are shown in percentages of the United States.

TABLE III

DEMOGRAPHIC RANK OF WORLD POWERS *

(Military Age Groups 20-34; U.S. = 100)

	1940	1970
U.S.S.R.	123	155
United States	100	100
Japanese Empire	67	157
Japan Proper	47	98
Germany	57	44
British Empire (white population only)	48	42
Great Britain	36	31
Italy	32	34
France	32	26

In 1970 there will be no power in Europe, except the Soviet Union, much more than one-third as populous as the United States. The Big Three of Eurasia—the Soviet Union, China, and India—will contain three-fifths of all mankind. Japan, in spite of defeat in World War II, will be more populous than any European power except Russia. By contrast, the traditional allies of the United States in Europe will have declined to the status of secondary powers.

Our estimates place the white populations of the United States and the British Commonwealth at a total of approximately 220 millions in 1970. Their combined reserves of manpower weigh heavily against the crude manpower reserves of Eurasia. Yet the balance is becoming increasingly precarious. The forces set free by the demographical revolution which began a hundred and fifty years ago in western Europe and now encompasses the whole globe are far from spent. The United States is faced by growing population pressure upon the landlocked areas of Eurasia as well as the Asiatic rim lands drained by the Indian and Pacific Oceans

* See page 282, Note 2 to Chapter 4.

(IN VARIOUS COUNTRIES)

YEAR

MALES OF AGES 20-34 IN MILLIONS

(000,000 OMITTED)

INDIA

RUSSIA

UNITED STATES

GERMANY

JAPAN

GREAT BRITAIN

FRANCE

ITALY

and by stagnation and decline in Europe-on-the-Atlantic. Is not this shift of highs and lows bound to make the weather of international politics?

From a humanitarian point of view gradual and uniform growth is far more desirable than sweeping change. Yet it is in the latter form that progress has come to Asia.

The population dynamics of Asia confront the Western powers with an insoluble dilemma. Can the industrial development of these densely settled regions proceed rapidly enough to provide a living for increased populations? Will accelerated industrial development not in turn improve living standards, hence reduce mortality and thus annul whatever temporary relief it affords from population pressure? Granted even that industrialization will reform the social milieu and that Indian and Chinese peasants-become-wage-earners will adjust with docility and speed their habits of procreation to an urban-industrial environment, fertility will not be reduced in advance of mortality.

The Malthusian concept "too many people" has found its way into the vocabulary of the average man of the West. Because it has been for a long time part and parcel of his mental baggage, it determines his behavior—a behavior which is far from simple or natural. There is as yet no counterpart in the East for this set pattern which rules Western man down to his procreative instincts. It cannot be reproduced in any and all climates by packaging industrialization—particularly when superimposed on ancient civilization—in educational programs. Perhaps Western technology will produce the identical effects wherever it spreads, independent of indigenous culture. The Japanese experiment is far from furnishing a clear answer. For that matter, even under the apparent uniformity of the European pattern are hidden puzzling contradictions.

It is doubtful that the demographical impact of industrialization can be cushioned by planning or persuasion, especially when it is foreigners who do the planning and persuading. The consequences of industrialization in the East will, beyond the shadow of a doubt, be cataclysmic. The current rate of growth precludes all gradualness of transition; prevailing political and social tensions are making certain that it will be convulsive. If solicitous aids, advisory and financial, extended by foreigners to an industrializing Asiatic country are guarantees of its peaceable evolution, then Japan should have been the most peaceful country in Asia.

Amid a host of imponderables only one near-certainty emerges. It has the concreteness, at least, of a sound military estimate. The introduction of Western techniques will within two or three decades make Asiatic manpower effective; to be sure, not in every country and not all of it in any country. But a fraction, only, of so large a mass will weigh heavily in the scales of world power.

5. NOT TOO MANY, NOT TOO FEW

AN ATTEMPT has been made in the preceding pages to plot future shifts in the world's balance of manpower. Our estimates prophesy nothing; whatever truth they contain is that of a crude diagram. The workings of a host of variables will make certain that future realities will not conform neatly with our assumption, namely, that observed rates of change will be continuous. The accuracy of population forecasts, like that of the course plotted by even the ablest pilot, depends on continual observation and many revisions. However, no particular finesse is needed to discern the general direction in which the manpower center of gravity is being displaced. We are crossing a divide which separates the great era of Western population growth from one of stagnation, perhaps contraction; the peoples of Asia are expanding, while the powers of Europe, except Russia, and the United States are not. No measure of complacency can obscure power-political implications of a cruder sort: Among peoples fairly matched in technological "know-how," political supremacy has been attained invariably in the wake of superiority in numbers. It is surprising that while the effects upon the national economy exerted by population decline are widely debated, the phenomenon is rarely viewed as intrinsic to the broad process that is changing the international balance of power.

Adam Smith regarded growth of population as the driving force of progress. Increasing division of labor, he declared, spurs productivity, hence increases income and the demand for labor, and thus creates economic conditions favorable to population growth. A growing population stimulates inventiveness and enterprise, wellsprings of national wealth and power. It is not to Smith, but to the pessimist Malthus that nineteenth-century economists have turned for an analysis of the interaction of progress and population growth. "Schooled in the traditions of the Malthusian theory,"

Alvin Hansen writes, "economists, thinking in static terms, have typically placed an optimistic interpretation upon the cessation of population growth. This indeed is also the interpretation suggested by the National Resources Committee which recently has issued an exhaustive statistical inquiry into current and prospective changes in population growth." * Hansen holds this conclusion to be "in a fundamental sense . . . thoroughly sound" because growth of population at the rate experienced throughout the nineteenth century would rapidly present insoluble problems.

The 1930's were not only the decade of economic malaise but also the first in which the United States experienced a large-scale slackening of population growth. The population which in the preceding decade had increased by 16 million was adding only half that number. The economic consequences of this trend, which in western Europe appears to have asserted itself about half a generation earlier than in the United States, are obscured by wartime developments. They may or may not be already upon us; the political consequences certainly are. The politics of an aging people are not those of a young one. Age demands security; youth, action.

Social protectionism is the dominant issue of the internal politics of all nations of slowing population growth and an increasing proportion of old people. It can be argued that this is a mere coincidence, an insignificant aspect of the great transition from a "market economy" to a managed society governed by a noneconomic ethos. It can also be argued that in a "mature" economy job opportunities are limited and that as living standards rise, so rises the premium of security. It can also be argued—but why continue? The common frame of reference for these and a host of other explanations is Malthusian pessimism, antithesis of the dynamic outlook of Adam Smith. Can it not also be averred that the late stickiness of Western national economies is fatally connected with slackening population growth and the increasing influence of older age groups upon politics, economics, and national psychology?

* Alvin H. Hansen, "Progress and Declining Population," *American Economic Review*, Vol. 29, No. 1, pp. 1-15.

Much has been written in recent years concerning optimum populations for the different countries of the world. The notion is seductive. If the population of a given area is too small to make effective use of its resources, or if it is too large to be supported, there must surely be a mean that is "just right." At that level the economy attains the highest well-being, or—in technical language—net output per head is maximum. Thus a population is "just right" at that level at which, with given resources, agricultural or mineral, industries or foreign trade, the addition or subtraction of one person will result in a diminution of output per head. This defines rigorously what is the critical level—on paper. For no one has been able to state anything which more than remotely resembles it for any particular country in actuality. The reason for this is simple. The output of a society is not easily defined. It is compounded of an immense variety of goods and services. No method has been found for reducing that variety to a common denominator.

If population increases, some goods may become more plentiful, others harder to get. The shift from one to the other may or may not increase average well-being. If the shift is a substantial one, it may become possible to determine whether a country is overpopulated or underpopulated. However, the population of any given area is not merely a function of its physical productivity and natural resources, but also of its techniques, economic organization, and cultural values. The optimum of that area will vary with these variables, none of which is easily defined. The Germany of 1932 was, according to many German and foreign economists, an overpopulated country with several million unemployed and several hundred thousands of would-be emigrants. In 1938 in spite of the acquisition of large portions of other peoples' *Lebensraum*, she introduced thousands of foreign workers and repatriated Germans living abroad, and still suffered a shortage of labor. Was she then an underpopulated country?

An optimum population, such as the National Resources Committee seems to have contemplated for the United States, implies stability. It can only be defined for the conditions of technique, organization, and age structure as they are at present. Although technological progress has tended to increase the optimum population of all Western countries, it need not do so under all conditions. If it occurs without a corresponding increase in production, it will merely displace workers and decrease the optimum population. Thus the advantages from an increased division of labor may be cancelled out by the workings of the law of diminishing returns.

An optimum population is undoubtedly a convenient concept for a sovereign planner. It would nail down at least one of the slippery variables which mess up his blueprints. It would, for example, greatly facilitate a static solution of the problem of full employment. However, it takes time to adjust a population to the optimum; and in that time technological progress may have intervened to shift the optimum to some other point. To preserve an optimum population, the right age structure must be preserved, lest too many or too few nonproducers—the too young or the too old—alter the right proportion of the productive population. However, in the process of adjusting the size of the population, the age distribution must be changed. For an optimum once attained must be kept so by an orderly renewal of the population.

Evidently, the notion of optimum population is not very helpful. It would be hardly worth discussing were it not, stated more or less coherently, the essence of modern Malthusian thought which permeates contemporary political ideologies. It is closely associated with economic and social protectionism of all kinds. The arguments it is called upon to fortify are more important than the theory itself.

There can be no doubt that there exists a broad range within which the size of population stands in plausible relationship to the most advantageous utilization of a country's resources, and, more important, beyond which contraction or expansion becomes an urgent economic and political issue. Siberia, in this sense, before Russia's eastward expansion was, and is perhaps still today, an underpopulated country. Present-day China is an overpopulated country. These observations, however, are meaningful only as long as we conceive of populations as states of movement rather than as static masses. The rhythm of that movement, and not so much the mass upon which it acts, determines the true potential force of a people.

93

In 1940, France, in spite of her arrested growth, was still a populous country. It was a stagnant one, technologically and industrially. The Chinese population, endowed with so much inventiveness and skill, has remained in about the same state of techniques for several centuries, in spite of overpopulation, perhaps because of it. Neither France nor China need be fated to inertia in perpetuity.

Adam Smith's dynamic approach drives to the pith of the problem not only of economic welfare but also of competition between nations. It can be argued plausibly that neither Germany nor Japan is overpopulated and that their craving for more vital space was whetted by noneconomic motives. Indeed, had these countries turned their energies upon trade, their peoples could have enjoyed a comparatively high standard of living. No one insists that Russia, with a population one-fourth again as large as the United States', and with twice as large a rate of natural increase, is an overpopulated country. Perhaps Russia's natural resources in minerals and water power are greater than those of the United States; that this is so is yet far from proven. Her cultivable area is probably not much larger than that of the United States; in neither country is the cultivable area worked anywhere near as intensively as it is in Europe. Why then is population growth in Russia considered symptomatic of national vigor and beneficial to the national economy, whereas a stationary population in the United States is considered "optimum"? Either conclusion may be false; they cannot both be right in the same context. Nevertheless, both are frequently advanced by the same people.

It is a necessary corollary of any theory which postulates a stable population as essential for insuring the greatest well-being per head, that there are two different optima: one internal, the other in relation to other powers. In other words, one for peace, the other for war.

From the military point of view the largest population is the best, provided its food requirements can be met. The larger the military-productive age groups, the greater is a nation's military strength. For the groups under or over military-productive age are consumers, hence a drag upon military efficiency. By the same token, for future wars, let us

94

say in ten or twenty years, large groups of young people and proportionally smaller numbers in the older military age classes will supply the basis for *anticipated* manpower requirements. Few military men and almost no statesmen will put the military case thus crudely. However, for a so-called stable population, the case is real enough and cannot be disregarded without courting military risks. It is of no importance for a growing population, unless growth is far too rapid —a danger hardly faced by any Western nation.

6. POWER AND POPULATION POLICY

THE United States alone among the major Western powers has not espoused a positive population policy. The lead in making procreation a matter of public policy was taken by the principal land powers of Europe.

Italy and Nazi Germany introduced elaborate legislation penalizing common practices of birth control, and subsidizing large families. These practical measures were inflated with a generous dose of racial metaphysics and not-so-subtle hints at patriotic fulfillment to be found in perpetuating the fatherland. The Third Republic's timid attempts at subsidizing large families and motherhood were enlarged by the gerontic rule of Vichy into a gushing, tragicomic campaign for national rejuvenation by way of legislated fertility. Decrees promulgated by the Supreme Soviet providing state aid for large families and honors for mother heroines do not greatly differ from those enacted by fascist and nonfascist governments.*

Prime Minister Winston Churchill, in his speech on March 22, 1944, dwelt on the plenitude of rural life and the preservation of the race. He said: "One of the most somber anxieties which beset those who look thirty, or forty, or fifty years ahead, and in this field one can see ahead only too clearly, is the dwindling birth-rate. In thirty years, unless present trends alter, a smaller working and fighting population will have to support and protect nearly twice as many old people; in fifty years the position will be worse still. If this country

* The Supreme Soviet, in a series of decrees of July 9, 1944, made divorces much more difficult to obtain, and granted financial aid for large families, ranging up to a lump sum of 5,000 rubles or $950 at birth of an eleventh child, plus a monthly payment of 300 rubles or $57. The decree also created honors for mothers, the highest one "mother heroine" for women rearing 10 or more children, and revised family taxes to encourage births. The new decrees also put additional emphasis on big families by enacting new taxes for both the man and wife who have fewer than three children. Childless citizens must pay 6 per cent of their yearly income; citizens with only one child, 1 per cent; citizens with two or three children, ½ of 1 per cent.

is to keep its high place in the leadership of the world, and to survive as a great power that can hold its own against external pressures, our people must be encouraged by every means to have larger families. . . . I hope to see a healthy revival of vigorous country life on the basis of higher wages and improved housing." *

Sir William Beveridge proposed that every woman should be entitled to receive a marriage grant of from £1 to £10 and 13 weeks' maternity benefits.† On March 2, 1944, the Prime Minister announced that a Royal Commission on Population had been set up. It was "to examine the facts relating to the present population trends in Great Britain; to investigate the causes of these trends and to consider their probable consequences; to consider what measures, if any, should be taken in the national interest to influence the future trends of population; and to make recommendations."

So contradictory are the reports on the concrete results of populationist experiments in the past that probably no one will ever know in what measure they succeeded, or would have succeeded had there been more time. Available data tend to foster the suspicion that they "succeeded" in good times—when public confidence was high, business prospered, and national fortunes in peace or war seemed bright; "failed" in bad times—when unemployment or protracted military conflict, real or anticipated, dampened men's spirits. However, measures designed to maintain population increase in the face of trends which, were they indefinitely continued, would lead to the extinction of the race will in all likelihood become an important part of the public policy of the Western countries.

The extension of life meets with biological limits more rigid than those which govern fertility. On the other hand, policies directed at increasing birth are fraught with many difficulties and dangers. If state intervention is to be effective, it must be energetic. For it must overcome the powerful drift of urban-industrial society to smaller family units. If asso-

* Prime Minister Winston Churchill, in "A Four-Years' Plan for Britain," a broadcast speech, March 22, 1943.

† Sir William Beveridge, *Social Insurance and Allied Services*, New York, 1942, p. 132.

ciated with programs of social security, intervention runs the risk of accentuating those forces which have brought about decline in the past—the dilemma of paternalism in general. Moreover, it conflicts with the mores of countries steeped in liberal-individualist traditions. The economic advantage from larger families is by no means self-evident to modern man; the military—"cannon-fodder"—argument is abhorrent. In the United States neither argument stands a chance against the rooted convictions of the public.

If action on neither death nor birth can engender a reversal of Western population trends, there remains only one other method: immigration. It is the least expensive; it yields the quickest results. Yet it is being universally rejected. The objection which is being most frequently opposed to its manifest advantages are twofold: It destroys the cultural and political homogeneity of the receiving country; it sharpens the competition for jobs and adds needlessly to the social charges of the community.

It is not proposed here to review the pros and cons of this hotly debated issue. The broader question whether immigration enhances or diminishes the military strength of the receiving country can be examined on the basis of abundant historical evidence at hand.

Athens and Rome admitted large numbers of foreigners to citizenship. The emperors of Rome accorded citizens' rights first to the inhabitants of Gaul, then to ever larger contingents of foreigners. For centuries these "barbarians," Romans-by-assimilation, defended the empire against the onslaughts of the barbarians-from-outside.

The princes of the Middle Ages called foreigners to provinces depopulated by plague or famine, employed foreign warriors in their military establishments, and invited foreigners to settle in backward regions and mount the defense of remote borders. The rulers of northern Europe welcomed Flemish weavers and Dutch shipwrights to their lands. The Huguenots, driven from France by religious discrimination culminating in the revocation of the Edict of Nantes, brought their skills to Prussia, an inestimable contribution to the power of that barren, predominantly Slavic principality. German gold- and silversmiths, glass blowers and ironmongers plied their trades in England and Russia. From among the émigrés from revolutionary France, not all of whom were nobles, the receiving countries drew some of their most celebrated public servants, scholars, and soldiers. After Catherine the Great took the Crimea, the expansion of Russia's population was speeded by wholesale assimilation of alien populations. From the amalgamation of diverse European elements arose the largest nation of European stock, the United States. Yet modern migration is not exclusively bound up with the filling up of vast, thinly settled regions overseas, nor is the melting pot a specifically American institution.

European nationalism is based on the theory that it is possible to define ethnic identities and that a language seals those who speak it into one nationality. There are many other and more complicated definitions, but these matter little. In practical politics the touchstone of nationalism is speech. For language supplies the simplest and crudest denominator of unification. In the eighteenth century, public opinion in Europe was public only insofar as it reflected a cosmopolite consensus; it was multilingual.

Modern nationalism is based on the assumption that speech distinguishes the individual as a member of a nation and that anyone unable or unwilling to speak the "national language" is excluded from the nation. Yet a language can be learned by adults as well as infants. Thus one dilemma of modern nationalism arises from the question, At what point does acquired linguistic proficiency qualify an other-national for admission to the nationality the speech of which he has made his own? If admission is to be refused, on what grounds of otherness is he to be barred? If he chooses to remain outside by his own volition, yet the nationality whose speech he has acquired now claims him as its own, which language—the one he spoke first or the one he acquired subsequently—is to be the criterion of his true nationality? This may seem an oversimplified interpretation of the nationality problem. Yet all nationalist conflicts in Europe have revolved around these two questions.

The issue of nationality thus hinges largely on the interpretation of the prior claims the linguistic community has over the individual and the group. The matter is not made simpler by the question of who is to arbitrate these claims. Even were it possible to define such authority, it would be necessary to establish standards—a typical nationality—by which individual cases can be judged. Yet this typical, homogeneous nationality does not exist—at least not in Europe. Its existence would presuppose a measure of isolation which was not afforded any people in the history of European civilization. That history, to the contrary, is characterized by a continuous mixing-up of peoples.

Continental movements were far larger than migrations to extra-European destinations, excepting the mass movements to North America. They were larger not only in the dim past but also in most recent times.* It is generally conceded that Irish immigration throughout the nineteenth century contributed substantially to the rapid increase of England's population. It is a much less well-known fact that Germany was able to increase her population from 41 million in 1870 to 67 million in 1914 only because of massive east European, particularly Polish, immigration. So completely were strong foreign elements assimilated into the German element that this phenomenon has virtually escaped the notice of the outside world. Germany's superiority in manpower vis-à-vis western Europe is to a large degree due to the contribution of Poland. German population increase reached its peak in the 1880's, i.e., before the 50 million point had been reached. Even then the largest increase had not occurred in those territories which had been inhabited by Germans since Roman times. The regions of highest fertility were those of the east. They were originally inhabited by Slavic peoples whose speech survives to this day in place names and in the names of many Prussian nobles. Their racial and psychological characteristics are well preserved in the make-up of the average German living in the territories east of the rivers Saale and Elbe.

Decline of German fertility in the 1880's was accompanied by a remarkable change in trends of migration. German emi-

* W. D. Forsyth, *The Myth of the Open Spaces*, Melbourne and London, 1942, p. 13.

gration to overseas countries stopped abruptly; Germany now became a receiving country. Booming cities sprang up in the rapidly industrializing areas in western and central Germany. Labor in the coal mines and steel foundries of the Ruhr was recruited to a large extent from foreigners because too few Germans were willing to work under conditions which Polish and other Slavic immigrants found acceptable. On the other hand, agricultural production in eastern Prussia, hard hit by the "flight from the land," was maintained by the introduction of Polish day laborers. The "Polish question" became a major issue of German politics. The nationalists opposed Polish immigration; the government, fully aware of its prime importance to the country's economic development and military strength, seemingly bowed to nationalist pressure. Actually, immigration flowed unhindered. Since 1886 no statistics have been published regarding naturalization of immigrants and "Germanization" of foreign names.

Official figures on the ethnic composition of the German population vary absurdly from census report to census report. The number of Poles living in Prussia is given for 1861 as 2.4 million. The birth rate of the Polish population was higher than that of the German population, and it is obvious that the last published figure—4.1 million in 1910—does not reflect either the true natural increase of the older Polish element or the true size of immigration, which for the period 1890 to 1910 alone is estimated at an average of 60,000 per year.* If the vital statistics of Germany's Polish-born and -descended citizens are corrected and allowance is made for migration, then the Polish element in Germany's racial composition, even after the loss to Poland in 1919 of the province of Posen with 1.8 million inhabitants, must be reckoned as at least around 7 million. In other words: Every tenth German can claim, or be claimed by, Polish nationality.

The recapitulation of these facts is of interest not only because of the light they cast—or fail to cast—upon the "values" of nationalism and nationality, but also because of their very

* *Encyclopédie polonaise*, Vol. 2. "Territoire et population de la Pologne," Fribourg and Lausanne, 1920, p. 116; and A. and E. Kulischer, *Kriegs- und Wanderzüge, Weltgeschichte als Völkerbewegung*, Berlin and Leipzig, 1932, pp. 195-210.

real significance as regards European migratory movements *in the most recent past.* In 1919, Clemenceau commented on the arithmetic of European peace as follows: "There are in Europe 20 million people too many. They are Germans." This was the Tiger's way of saying that France was too weak to resist another German assault. In 1939, Daladier promised the French people that in the forthcoming operations against the German army he would be *"avare du sang français"* (sparing of French blood). In 1940, Pétain complained that France had been defeated because she had "too few children, too few allies." Already in 1907, when deaths exceeded births by 29,000, the public had become fully alive to the decline of French manpower. No one could fail to recognize the challenge—least of all throughout the uneasy years between the Agadir crisis and the outbreak of World War I. In 1911, Colonel, later General, Mangin published his celebrated book *La force noire,* in which he called the attention of his countrymen to the manpower reserves of the French Empire. His advice was at first not taken seriously. However, the realities of war, and the terrible losses with which France had to pay for the incompetence of the general staff in 1914, forced the government to draw on the supply of colonial manpower. The African and the Asiatic made their appearance in army and factory.

France lost during World War I close to 2 million people. By 1918 her population was reduced to 37.5 million. Only the recovery of Alsace-Lorraine closed this enormous gap. However, French losses had been heaviest in the younger male groups. France, in order to restore her economic productivity and repair war damages, had recourse to immigrant labor. The 2 million Frenchmen killed or disabled during the war were replaced by 2 million foreigners. Moreover, the deficit from declining birth rates was made up by the higher fertility of aliens. Immigration was thus a means of warding off outright population decline. It could not increase the population; it succeeded at least in preserving it. Without it France would have declined to 35 million. Thus France "survived only with the help of aliens." *

* Georges Mauco, *Les étrangers en France,* Paris, 1932, p. 182.

When France succumbed in 1940, her sole hope was then, as in 1914, that a more populous country, hence a more powerful one, would come to her rescue. Yet, do empty cradles really explain French inferiority in manpower with respect to Germany? Frenchmen are broadly agreed that they do and that this explanation extenuates the rapid failure of France's military resistance. This version of French defeat is based on the tacit assumption that it was the inexorable destiny of Germany to become more populous than France by one-half.

Just before the outbreak of the Franco-Prussian War in 1870, both France and Germany were superior in manpower to the United States. Since then, French population has increased by 4 million while the German increased by 27 million. In the same period the United States grew by 100 million. Yet, had this country been closed to immigration, the present population of the United States would hardly exceed that of France. There can be no doubt that France was in a position to receive far larger contingents of immigrants than she allowed to enter. Actually, between 1932 and 1934 she lost more than half a million of her immigrant population.

France after World War I suffered from a chronic shortage of labor. The problem of French political economy was not how to combat unemployment. It was, on the contrary, how to expand industrial production, particularly production of weapons France needed in the inevitable showdown with Germany. To increase production, French industry had to rely on an ever larger supply of foreign labor. In the mining, building, and machine-tool industries, foreigners made up in 1929 nearly one-half, and in the steel industry, one-third, of the total labor force. To expand these industries additional labor was needed, and the bulk of it had to come from across the French frontiers. Why it did not come, and why "too-little-and-too-late" hamstrung whatever measures were taken to employ foreign manpower productively, is a riddle whose answer must be sought in the maze of Malthusian fears and racial prejudices in which France—not alone among Western nations—had lost the bearings of national policy.

The most important overland migration of the last fifty years has been the movement of 30 million Chinese to Manchuria and Inner Mongolia. Mass immigration to Manchuria began in 1878 when the official bars to immigration imposed by the Manchus were removed. Chinese from Shantung, Hopei, and Shansi were attracted by the relatively high wages in mining and construction and by the natural fertility of Manchuria's soil. The bulk of these migrants were seasonal workers; only a few stayed to settle. In 1926, however, a marked change occurred in the nature of Chinese immigration; the seasonal worker was being replaced by the permanent settler. Until 1931, immigration exceeded 1 million annually; less than one-third, only, returned to China proper. In the year 1931 the number of Chinese immigrants decreased sharply. Yet in 1933, one year after the establishment of Japan's puppet state Manchukuo, Chinese immigration was again resumed. Japan exercised strict control. However, she did not seek to halt the flow of Chinese immigration, which within sixty years had completely altered the population balance of Manchuria. Without this continued influx of Chinese manpower, Japan's conquest of northeastern China would have remained bare of all but geographical significance.

The adoption by Manchukuo in 1937 of the Japanese-inspired Five Year Industrialization Plan created an increased demand for Chinese and Korean labor. The Japanese themselves, like Westerners in the same stage of economic development, have turned to the cities. When they have gone abroad, they have done so as entrepreneurs, exploiters, and overseers, not as settlers.* Statistics as late as 1940 indicate that the plans of the Japanese government for the mass colonization of Manchuria were attended with exceedingly slim results. In spite of huge government subsidies, only 50,000 Japanese colonists were settled between 1932 and 1940. It was Chinese immigration, unaided by government subventions or ideological incentives, which wrought the transformation of Manchurian population and economy. The Japanese were undoubtedly the gainers, and their policy of the open door to immigration goes to show that they knew it. For it is chiefly Chinese immigrants who supplied the labor in the grand

* Owen Lattimore, *Manchuria, Cradle of Conflict*, New York, 1935, p. 236.

Japanese design for turning Manchuria into a self-supporting base of the Kwantung Army and a source of agricultural produce for the Japanese homeland. The Chinese immigrant contributed mightily to Japan's military effort.

Paradoxically, Manchuria under Japanese tutelage is becoming more Chinese than it ever was under Chinese rule. The Chinese immigrants who have swarmed across the border of the puppet state have greatly strengthened the claims of the Chinese national government to Manchuria. By ethnic affinities, Manchuria is an integral part of China, for 95 per cent of its inhabitants are Chinese. Chinese immigration has activated the latent wealth of Manchuria and has, incidentally, made it a far greater prize in the power-political struggles of the Far East than it was under either Chinese or Russian rule. Incidentally, not only Japan but also Russia has freely drawn on China's reserve of manpower. Chinese immigrants have helped to develop her far eastern and maritime provinces, and Chinese as well as Korean workers have been observed as far west as Kazakhstan and western Siberia.

Indian immigration has stimulated the economic development of Britain's Asiatic and African possessions. Indian traders, craftsmen, and laborers have played an important role in mobilizing the wealth of the Malay States and Burma, and thriving Indian communities exist in nearly every one of Britain's crown colonies in Africa.

Thus far no Japanese or Russian official has argued that gains in manpower through immigration have been other than beneficial to their respective economies. Russia, as has been noted, intends to supplement her domestic labor force by helping herself generously to whatever foreign, i.e., German, labor she can get. Polish manpower has helped to make Germany strong. France, "surviving with the help of aliens," would have been stronger than she was in 1940 had she pursued a systematic policy of tapping the surplus of south and east European manpower which could have been hers for the asking.

Indeed, mass immigration raises serious problems, yet none that cannot be solved within the framework of a vigorous economic and political system. That immigrant manpower is a liability, not added wealth, is a new doctrine. That doctrine is a nice blend of Malthusian thought in economics, and arguments of cultural (racial) exclusionism. Its gist is that the historical receiving countries of America and Europe are justified in reversing their past liberal policies by restricting immigration or suspending it altogether either because they are "filled up" or because the right kind of immigrant stock is not available. Let us examine these assertions:

1) *Immigration causes unemployment.* The breakdown of the world economic system after World War I resulted in mass unemployment not only in the older industrial states but also in the younger overseas countries. "The resiliency of the employment market has disappeared." It could endure, in the conditions of *laissez faire,* only as long as there existed a "frontier" the opening of which was profitable enough to warrant the introduction of pioneer workers. With the end of the era of frontier development, capital and workers should be diverted to projects which will raise the standard of living, stimulate the demand for goods, and thus create employment. These projects do not call for immigration and hence are tailored to existing productive capacities. Perhaps the ablest exposition of the case against immigration is to be found in the recently published book of the Australian economist W. D. Forsyth, which bears the meaningful title *The Myth of the Open Spaces.* Forsyth views the problem of overpopulation as insoluble in the traditional manner, to wit, by emigration, and advocates the industrial development of overpopulated regions, if need be by "organized international cooperation in such matters as capital supply." These and related arguments, as for example the one that the admission of foreigners will add to the state's expenditure for social services, are being advanced by many labor leaders, politicians, and economists who have joined in fighting the menace of the immigrant.

2) *Immigration impairs the racial and cultural homogeneity of the receiving country.* More important than consideration of population growth and economic development is the preservation of the ethnic identity of a people. The argument need not be further elaborated. It reduces to the

familiar equation, race = language = nationality = culture.

Both arguments are open to serious objections. It is a fact that the most prolonged and severest crisis of unemployment overtook the classical immigration countries of the West *after* they had enacted, in the 1920's, a series of measures designed to restrict immigration or to halt it altogether. Under conditions of high social protectionism it is pertinent not only to ask how many persons are unemployed but what kinds of jobs they seek. In France, for example, 84 per cent of all immigrant workers were employed in industry, in spite of the fact that the shortage of manpower was greatest in agriculture. This apparent contradiction is explained by the fact that foreigners took those places in industry which, because of their low wages and attendant risks, did not attract French workers, employed or unemployed. These were jobs in construction and road building, in brick factories and in the coal and iron mines.

Even in times of widespread unemployment a broad range of jobs offered does not necessarily find ready "takers." Crude figures for employment and unemployment tell us nothing as to the very real demand for skills and crafts the domestic "employment market" fails to meet. Even widespread unemployment is not an airtight argument against the admission of certain classes of immigrants. No economist will argue that work performed by immigrant labor, which would not be performed by domestic workers because these are not qualified or willing, does not create new wealth and hence new job opportunities. If this qualitative point of view is sustained by considerations of peacetime economics, it applies doubly to the economics of war and its unpredictable range of demands for manpower and skills. However, the argument that immigration "causes" unemployment implicitly accepts the Malthusian premise, to wit, "too many people and too few jobs." Once this premise is rejected it is difficult to see why the introduction of potential producers into an economic system should weaken it because these are foreigners. The only other possible explanation of the alleged harmfulness to a receiving country of gains in manpower by immigration would be that a dichotomy exists between a nation's economic strength in peace and its economic strength in war. Adam Smith, for one, held that it does not.*

As regards the "cultural" argument against the admission of foreigners to the national community, its validity depends on a satisfactory definition of national "culture." Needless to say, there is no such definition commanding universal agreement. Culture, in all its expressions, is a highly personal matter. A national culture, too, is the creation of individuals, solitary individuals at that, and no poems, symphonies, philosophical systems, or scientific theories have originated from group effort. Therefore the assimilation in a national culture of foreign elements should not present a more formidable problem than, let us say, the education of the native populace in the appreciation of that culture. Were there indeed a fundamental difference, it could be explained only by a special dispensation accorded by the mere fact of birth upon the cultural soil—which is what Nazi anthropologists assert. All peoples of European stock have shared in the same broad historical experience. The cultures of individual nations possess distinctiveness only by the degree of their acceptance or denial of the common heritage. The rich experience of the United States furnishes no concrete data showing that this or that element of European stock has proven in the course of time more or less recalcitrant to the workings of the "melting pot." The names on the casualty lists and list of recipients of military honors of two World Wars are the family names of all of Europe.

The United States is the most powerful nation of European stock; it is a congeries of all the races of Europe. Their innate characteristics as well as those developed in the process of adjustment to the new environment have gone into the new solution, the American character. One catalyst was language—which caused Bismarck to observe that the most important fact in modern world politics was that Americans spoke English. No less important was a broad tolerance of, and capacity for absorbing, an unlimited number of races,

* That Adam Smith conceived of military power as being directly related to a country's economic organization in peacetime is trenchantly argued by Edward Mead Earle in *Makers of Modern Strategy*, Princeton, 1943, pp. 121-2.

religions, and folkways. So trite is this statement that it should not require emphasis beyond the primer stage. Yet it contains a fundamental truth, no less fundamental because it is obvious. To dismiss it as a mere historical incident, is to miss the essence of American power past, present, and future. Had immigration ceased after the Civil War, the population of the United States would hardly now exceed that of the larger European states and would probably have fallen behind that of Germany. The cumulative effect of immigration upon the growth of the United States is shown by the following table:

TABLE IV

SHARE OF IMMIGRATION IN AMERICAN POPULATION GROWTH

Period	Per cent
1830-40	13.5
1840-50	26.5
1850-60	34.7
1860-70	28.0
1870-80	28.5
1880-90	42.9
1890-1900	31.5
1900-10	41.8
1910-20	17.0
1920-30	21.6

It is unlikely that the population of the United States faces prospects of substantial growth within the next generation if there is no immigration. This holds particularly true for the white component of the population.

The decreasing rate of immigration to the United States within the last twenty years is not due to the goal's having become less attractive. It is due to a political decision. The Immigration Act of 1924 not only set a maximum limit considerably below the average of the preceding period but reduced each nation's yearly quota to 2 per cent of the number of its emigrants resident in the United States as determined by the U.S. census of 1890. It thus reduced total immigration from southern and eastern Europe to one-fifth of that from northern and western Europe, whereas still in 1914 the former had been six times as large as the latter. This is not the place to examine the formal considerations and "felt necessities of the times" which prompted the enactment of the law of 1924. European population dynamics of 1924 were not those of 1890. The act favored those nations whose population growth was declining, and restricted immigration from those nations who in the intervening thirty years had experienced an accelerated rate of growth. Since then, divergent regional trends have become further accentuated, and the Immigration Act of 1924 holds the fair promise of restricting immigration far more effectively than its framers may have intended.

A book might well be written on the far-reaching consequences of this legislation as regards American and European history between two World Wars, and as regards the development of the British dominions and Latin American republics who, in the wake of the United States' change of policy, enacted similar restrictive measures of their own.

The drying up of world trade in the desert of protectionism parallels closely the stagnation of international migration induced by legislation. Yet the migratory urges of Europe had not subsided; they had shifted. "It is an apparent coincidence," W. D. Forsyth writes, "that the overseas countries should have lost their capacity to absorb vast masses of immigrants in the very generation in which Europeon population growth had declined. Some underlying unity may still be traced between these two phenomena." The coincidence is indeed only apparent. For only western, northern, and central Europe, i.e., the principal sources of European immigration up until the last decade of the nineteenth century, are faced with population decline. The Latin south and Slavic east is not. "Overpopulation" is an ambiguous term. None the less, it does apply to certain geographical regions and economic conditions, and it is meaningless to argue that under modern technological conditions there is no visible limit to population densities.

If four to five acres of land per head of agricultural population are required—as the foremost experts agree—in order to provide a living, then Greece, Bulgaria, Poland, Italy,

Czechoslovakia, Hungary, Rumania, and Spain, all of them predominantly agricultural countries, are overpopulated and must expect, due to their relatively high birth rates, a further deterioration of the man-land ratio in the future. Industrialization and better utilization of the soil may, in the course of time, somewhat relieve that pressure. Yet none of these countries, except Czechoslovakia and perhaps Spain, possesses the raw-material base for large-scale industrialization; none disposes of abundant capital. Their respective peasantries are no novices at obtaining the highest possible return from their labor, and it is far from certain, glib generalization to the contrary, that "mechanization," increased application of chemical fertilizers, and soil reclamation will yield substantially higher returns in the near future or even in the middle run. If four to five acres per head constitutes an existence minimum, the excess population of southern and eastern Europe in 1940 can be estimated at from 18 to 33 million. Part of it may be absorbed by industrialization and increase of agricultural yield, but certainly not all of it.

Careful estimates place the figure of peoples driven from their homes by the twin scourges of racism and war as lying between 10 and 20 million. Already in October, 1939, President Roosevelt suggested that as many would be under the necessity of emigrating from Europe after the war. The need for manpower to assist in the reconstruction and rehabilitation of national economies will undoubtedly favor the repatriation of many of these uprooted millions. It is "even conceivable," George Warren surmises, "that the smaller nations in their political concern for security after the war may encourage repatriation of their nationals not only from Europe but also from overseas in order to replace manpower lost during the war or to build up population strength at home." The countries of western Europe, it is anticipated, may also seek to keep their citizens at home, be it by direct prohibition or by the indirect method of granting generous social benefits. Yet this still leaves millions of uprooted peoples and fails to solve the problem of overpopulation in southern and eastern Europe. No amount of clever argument designed to show why it behooves these millions on economic, cultural, and ethnic grounds to stay where they are or to go where they do not wish to go can obscure the fact that the decision as to where they will go in fact is one of the principal issues confronting American foreign policy. The phrasing "foreign policy" is advisedly chosen, for the disposal of this problem will determine decisively the manpower balance, hence the political balance of power in Europe, and will—to the extent that the United States chooses to transform this European excess into an accretion of its own manpower—determine its future military strength.

Only by restoring the circulatory system of Europe's population can the demographical balance of the Continent be restored. It is patently in the interest of the United States as well as of Britain to restore to France, if not her past grandeur, a least her regional power. On this point there is fair agreement no matter how large are current differences in opinion on the ultimate disposal of the globe and how large or small is to be the role France is to play in world politics. Europe's demographical center of gravity is inexorably moving eastward, and the relative strength of the German language group will never be as great as it was in World War II. It is none the less true that the manpower preponderance of Germany vis-à-vis western Europe will not have been affected immediately by this war. Directed migration, we may agree, is indispensable in order to reduce Germany's demographical lead and to arrest French population decline.

It will be far more difficult to obtain agreement on a positive United States immigration policy. At the moment of this writing, let it be admitted, the chances that it will be obtained are slim indeed. Yet without it a positive manpower policy is confined to pro-natalist measures of dubious efficacy. Without it, too, the influence of the United States upon Europe will be smaller. The principle of selective immigration is so widely accepted that no revision of the Immigration Act of 1924 could become law without retaining that principle. Indeed, the sponsors of the Immigration Act professed that they did not seek to limit or prevent immigration but to improve its quality. The act favors not only certain "nationalities" (which are in fact determined by the place of birth of the individual) but also persons intending to and qualified for working on the land. Yet the flight from the land is a phenomenon common both to the old industrial and the younger overseas countries. Moreover, in Isaiah Bowman's words, "most of the pioneer lands that remain are 'marginal' in climate, fertility and transport." Soviet colonization policy, in its single-minded concentration upon expanding the national economy as a whole, conceives of agriculture as the handmaiden of industry and of rural population as a reserve industrial labor force. In the Soviet Union "farming as a way of life" is not endowed with the prestige values it possesses in the United States.

In the United States the outflow of labor from agriculture has been accompanied by an increase of agricultural production. In the last thirty years agricultural labor increased by one-quarter (3 million), but productivity per head rose 40 per cent. That trend is here to stay; not only does the United States need no large number of foreign agricultural laborers (except perhaps seasonal workers), but a large number of its own agricultural population will flow to the towns. Thus agricultural work will provide employment for only a comparatively small number of immigrants, although such intensified forms of farming as, for example, cheese making, vineries, and truck gardening may offer rewarding scope to foreign workers without ill effect upon the competitive position of older establishments. If the United States were to admit approximately 300,000 immigrants a year—which is far below the 1880-1930 average—the large majority will have to be absorbed in secondary and tertiary industries.

The selection of immigrants capable of hard work and adjustment to a new environment will necessitate a careful screening. Immigrants possessing special skills will naturally be in demand. Those not so endowed, but physically and psychologically fit, should be taught new trades and skills or undergo occupational retraining. It is in this manner that the United States can increase its manpower and enrich its economy.

Migration thus becomes one crucially important field of American foreign policy—both as regards Europe and the United States' own strength. The decision has to be made now. If the nations of the West do not accept the free gift of manpower, the Soviet Union will. This would only further

113

displace Europe's population equilibrium and accentuate the physical and psychological division between a dynamic-growing East and a static-stagnant West.

The preceding chapters attempted to survey the broad trends which are reshaping the population distribution of the globe. Manpower, we observed, is but one among the many factors of power. It is the one which supplies the animate force transforming all the elements of power into political realities. Contemporary power relationships, unlike the stabler, more predictable conditions a hundred years ago, cannot be frozen, because manpower relationships will not stay put. Strength in numbers becomes, by virtue of modern production and training methods, increasingly synonymous with military power. Malthusian ideas—a "stable" population, a "stable" economy—beget, inexorably, static foreign and military policies. Yet strategic bases, weapons-in-being, stockpiles of raw materials, and the world's most colossal wealth in inanimate assets cannot assure the future power of the United States. The security of the United States rests upon the growth, creativeness, and stamina of its people, not upon Maginot Lines, be they fashioned of concrete and steel or the figments of the Malthusian mind. Readiness to change, to build and advance anew and to assimilate races and ideas, are the dominant characteristics of the American people. Therein lie strength and weakness. The virtues as well as the vices of a people go into the making of its power. The power of the United States is not a thing of unalloyed genius; neither was the greatness of Rome nor the preponderance of Britain. The United States has thus far not surrendered to the pessimistic philosophies which gained ascendancy in Europe. The United States finds itself today in the exceptional position of alone preserving the general political concepts which it inherited from the nineteenth century. Americans still profess adherence to the principle that not only goods but men and ideas must be able to move freely across political boundaries. By rejecting this principle they can obtain that kind of security which protects them against hardships and discomforts, some real, some imaginary, but not against the great and dangerous responsibilities which two World Wars have thrust upon them. The dangers of population decline were upon the nations of Europe before they were recognized. The United States has fair warning, and the remedy lies at hand in its own tradition.

Part Three

RAW MATERIALS AND POWER

All struggles for power involve the control of scarce resources.

—Lionel Robbins

7. THE HIERARCHY OF RAW MATERIALS

POLITICAL and military power is largely based on industrial power. Industrialism calls for an unlimited supply of raw materials, chiefly minerals. In early times the essential raw materials of political and military power were ores, fuel for transforming them into metal, gold and silver, and the tools for fashioning precious metals into coins and trinkets. Today there is hardly one among the host of raw materials modern man extracts and consumes which is not used for making tools of war. Hence the attainment of power involves the control of raw materials. All other things being equal, those countries are the most powerful which possess an adequate supply of all "essential," "strategic," and "critical" materials or which are able, by virtue of their mastery over transportation routes, to import, in time of war, materials inadequately supplied at home.

None of the Great Powers, including those most abundantly supplied with natural resources, namely, the United States and Russia, is completely self-sufficient. Yet self-sufficiency in all respects is not of paramount importance. If it were, no country, and surely not such poorly endowed countries as Japan and Italy and, to a lesser degree, Germany, could ever have risked war. It is now clear that countries at war can manage surprisingly well without a number of valuable raw materials.

Coal is the chief reducer and energizer of modern times. It is needed for virtually all kinds of industrial production. To recount its manifold uses would be as tedious as it is unnecessary. It is the power mainstay of heavy industry, the chief raw material of chemical industries, and the main producer of heat, light, and electric motive force. In most of its uses coal cannot be replaced by any other commodity. On the contrary, it is coal which serves as the chief raw material for most substitutes. As a source of energy it may partially be replaced by water power, oil, or wood. Neither the water power, the wood resources, nor the oil reserves in any industrial country are sufficient to make up for the loss of even one-third of the coal production. The importance of coal has increased lately because countries deficient in oil are forced to rely for their liquid-fuel needs on the liquefaction of coal.

Ranking in importance with coal in modern economy are iron and steel, the basic materials of almost all weapons and durable civilian goods. It is an axiom, none the less true for being perfectly obvious, that without steel and iron neither the prosecution of large-scale warfare nor the maintenance of a vast heavy industrial production is possible. Without ample domestic supplies of both coal and iron a nation may develop prosperous industries of variegated kinds; it cannot fight major wars. No great power can survive without them.

There are minerals for which substitution is possible only in exceptional cases and which themselves are essential for the functioning of a large-scale substitute or *ersatz* economy. Among these, coal and iron ore are by far the most important. Coal and iron are the basic minerals of machine civilization, which, in a crude, "paleotechnic" form, could keep going on them alone.

There are also many raw materials for which substitutes can be used, either synthetic ones or other available materials. Chilean saltpeter was replaced by synthetically produced nitrogen; oil can be extracted from coal; rubber can be produced from coal, oil, and a variety of plants. Automobiles can be run on gas generated by wood burners. Aluminum instead of copper can be used in the making of electrical wire.

Finally, there are raw materials the lack of which entails shortages in the civilian economy, but which are not indispensable for the conduct of war. In this category are many foodstuffs, clothing, and luxury goods. Rationing can stretch available provisions which thus are made to last for several years. A large supply of foodstuffs is an important military and political weapon. However—glib assertions to the contrary—food does not win modern wars.

The German statistician Ferdinand Friedensburg * as-

* *Die mineralischen Bodenschätze als weltpolitische und militärische Machtfaktoren,* Stuttgart, 1936, p. 175.

120

signed indices to minerals according to their military importance: coal, 40; oil, 20; iron, 15; copper, lead, manganese, sulphur, 4 each; zinc, aluminum, nickel, 2 each; tin, 1; and other alloys, 1. Coal and iron combined are thus computed as representing more than one-half of a country's raw-material potential. Needless to say, an advanced technology is unthinkable without a long list of other materials, since only the most perfect tools and weapons can meet the exacting standards set by international competition. But there are many ways of making up for deficiencies in minerals—except, on the whole, for those in coal and iron.

8. GEOGRAPHY OF COAL AND IRON

COAL and iron have remained the bedrock of military power in World War II. As regards materials, perhaps the most significant difference between the two World Wars lies not in new devices used but in the greater amount of steel required to make the older devices effective. In World War II the weight of armor is heavier, fire power greater and more generously supplied to individual fighting units than in any war of history or, for that matter, in all wars of history combined. Steel is the material of war making; coal is the essential precondition of steel making.

New discoveries may put an end to coal-iron-steel supremacy. Laymen will be chary of predicting the changes to be wrought in the future in world distribution of industrial potentials by harnessing solar and atomic energy and ocean tides. Strangely enough, research in these fields was begun and seems to have progressed furthest in countries rich in coal and iron.

It is still reasonably safe to predict that in the near future the coal-iron complex will not relinquish its supremacy in the realm of strategic raw materials. Hence only those countries will retain Great Power status which either possess ample deposits of iron and coal, or are richly endowed with one and enjoy strategic access to the other.

Nature's distribution of coal and iron riches is most uneven. There are only a few countries which possess both in quantities so great that they are able to wage major wars. The United States is the world's largest producer of coal and possesses probably the largest coal deposits. In peacetime the United States averaged approximately 40 per cent of world coal production. Its deposits are so large that coal production could be expanded to meet even the most extravagant needs. In the United States, peacetime consumption per head averaged about five tons and was the highest on earth. The railroads took one-quarter of the annual output, which was likewise the largest tonnage of coal any nation consumed in overland transportation.

The other three leading producers of coal are Britain, Germany, and Russia. These four countries alone account for four-fifths of total world production. These same countries also account for most of the world's coke production. Russia stands in fourth place among the great coal producers. Yet she is continuously increasing her production and it is probable that within a comparatively short period of time her production will exceed that of Germany and Britain.

The last published official figure put Russia's coal production at close to 150 million metric tons per year. This quantity is not much smaller than German coal production in an average peace year, although it still trails considerably behind that of Britain and the United States, being one-half of Britain's and less than one-third of American production. After World War II a great expansion of Russian coal output is virtually certain, while no substantial increase elsewhere is in sight. In 1937 the International Congress of Geologists at Moscow estimated Russia's coal resources at the stupendous figure of 1,000 billion tons, of which 93 per cent were assumed to be located in Asiatic Russia. Large reserves are situated in the Soviet north, notably in Petshora Basin and along the lower reaches of the Yenisei. The coal deposits of the Donets and Kuznetsk basins alone would place Russia permanently in the front rank of coal producers, and possibly of coal exporters. Russian coal is of high quality, and a considerable portion of known deposits consists of excellent coking coal.

What are the coal resources of the East? Much has been written about the mineral resources of the Pacific regions, particularly those adjacent to the Yellow Sea. The Japanese have not been bashful about the industrial might of their empire; there is a veritable deluge of books and articles on the bright future of an industrialized China. Yet it is surprising how small a body of established facts is obtainable from the bulk of this literature, obviously intended for Western consumption. Its motto: *Épater le bourgeois.*

It is, however, generally conceded that the East is comparatively poor in coal deposits. China alone possesses large known reserves of coal, although recent estimates are far more modest than the enthusiastic and still widely accepted estimates of the German geographer Richthofen. Indeed, large reserves exist in Hunan, Szechwan, Shensi, Yünnan, and Kweichow. Almost all of China's developed coal fields are in Manchuria and north China. Although there is much high-grade hard coal, reserves of coking coal are small.*

Many contradictory statements have been made about coal deposits in Manchuria, and the truth must be sought amid a tangled web of evidence. This country possesses two of the most profitable coal mines of the world. Undoubtedly, Manchurian coal could serve as the basis of an expanding industry. Still, available facts do not encourage the opinion that Manchurian industry could compete in the foreseeable future with the industrial centers of the West. The coal fields of Japan proper have for many years been insufficient to supply the requirements of her heavy industry. Total reserves are estimated at 6.2 billion tons, less than 1 to 2.5 per cent of the amount credited to China. In quality, most of the coal is mediocre.†

India possesses coal deposits large enough to support a first-class industry. She has reserves of a size exceeded only by those of the United States, Russia, central Europe, England, and Canada; and, more important even than that, her coal is of good quality. There is an adequate supply of good coking coal.

From a strategic point of view coal resources of other countries are negligible, although a small coal supply may some-

* The total coal output of China in 1940 was estimated at 18 million tons—3.7 per cent of U.S. production. The production of coal mines controlled by the China national government was 5.7 million tons. See T. S. Lovering, *Minerals and World Affairs*, New York, 1943, p. 130.

† The following statements may serve as samples of the utter confusion which is the essence of Far Eastern statistics: "The latest estimate for Manchukuo is 15 billion tons."—Schumpeter, Allan, Gordon, and Penrose, *The Industrialization of Japan and Manchukuo 1930-1940*, New York, 1940, p. 424. "The coal deposits of the country are estimated at 11,437,265,000 tons . . ."—*Japan-Manchukuo Yearbook 1940*, p. 752. "Chinese coal deposits are admittedly rich and widespread, though estimates of the total quantity vary. Minimum figures are 234 billion metric tons; maximum, 997 billion tons; and it has recently been suggested that estimates of the reserve in Manchuria should be raised another 10 billion tons."—C. H. Behre, Jr., and Kung-ping Wang, "China's Mineral Wealth," *Foreign Affairs*, Vol. XXIII, No. 1, October, 1944.

times assume tactical importance (Indo-China, Australia). South America and Africa are almost devoid of coal, as are the countries of southern Europe and the Middle East. On the western European continent coal is concentrated in the Ruhr valley, Saar basin, Holland, Luxembourg, Belgium, and northern France, i.e., within an area only one-twentieth the size of Europe. Large coal fields, second only in importance to the Ruhr, are mined in German, Polish, and Czechoslovak Silesia. The seams are thick; coking and steam coals of high grade are found in this region.* If one single power were to control the production of coal between the Channel and the Vistula, it would rank as the world's second largest coal producer. It must be remembered that Germany briefly contrived to do so from 1940 to 1944.

In the three years preceding the outbreak of World War II, world production of iron ore exceeded 200 million tons annually. The United States led with a share of one-third of the total (74 million tons); France was next with approximately 16 per cent; Russia, Germany, and England followed with 14, 7, and 6.5 per cent respectively.

In 1942, U.S. production was 93 million tons. The Mesabi range in the Lake Superior district alone contributed 70 millions, or 75 per cent of the total. Its open-pit ores are the most easily mined among world ore resources. It was this unique circumstance which, perhaps more than any other single material factor, made possible the colossal expansion of U.S. steel production for war in general, and the rapid increase of U.S. naval tonnage after Pearl Harbor in particular.

The ore reserves of the Lake Superior district are estimated at 2.5 billion tons containing approximately 50 per cent iron. Only 300 million tons, however, can be worked by open-pit methods. According to estimates based on various assumptions as regards future war requirements and peacetime consumption, these reserves will be exhausted within from fifteen to thirty years. In the United States, most iron blast furnaces are geared to the handling of high-grade ore low in

* T. S. Lovering, *Minerals in World Affairs*, New York, 1943, p. 128.

125

phosphorus and sulphur content, which qualities are most happily combined in the Lake Superior product.

The United States possesses vast reserves of iron-bearing materials of a lesser grade. At Birmingham, Alabama, low-grade ore carrying only 35 per cent iron is used, and the steel industry of the south has managed to operate successfully with this marginal material. However, the bulk of production is concentrated in the north.

Blast furnaces are about the least mobile of industrial equipment. Some steel men therefore believe that unless measures are taken for strengthening the position of the United States in raw materials underlying the manufacture of steel, the capacity of the industry cannot be maintained and the United States will not be prepared to fight another war. Whether this alarmist view can be substantiated by the available technical and geological evidence cannot be examined in these pages. Reason does dictate, however, consideration of the fact that most steel making outside the United States is carried on profitably by the use of processes for smelting low-grade magnetite and phosphorus ores.

On balance the United States is an importer of iron ore. These imports, while amounting to only 5 per cent of total consumption, exceed in weight and value imports of all other ores. Large deposits of high-grade ore are available in the Western Hemisphere. The reserves of Wabana ores of the Belle Isle district in Newfoundland are estimated at 2.5 billion tons, are close to a good harbor, and carry 52 per cent iron. They are, however, high in phosphorus and are chiefly in demand by Canadian and English steel plants employing the Thomas process. Plants equipped to handle this type of ore are relatively few in the United States. Nevertheless, the Wabana ores may prove a far from negligible "second line of defense" in the raw-material position of the United States, if for no other reason than that American naval and air controls supply a secure cover for Atlantic seaboard coastal shipping.

Extensive iron-ore deposits, estimated at 3 billion tons, occur near the eastern end of Cuba. A small amount of chromium and nickel is present. The ores contain only 40 per cent iron and are little worked. More important, because of their high iron and low phosphorus and silicate content, are the vast ore deposits in the state of Minas Geraes, Brazil. They are estimated at 7 billion tons. One drawback is their remoteness from the coast. In 1942 the U.S. Export-Import Bank provided the Brazilian government with funds for the construction of railroad and dock facilities. American loans also helped to build a modern steel plant. As Brazil lacks suitable facilities for smelting ore, a substantial expansion of Brazilian steel making appears unlikely for many years to come, and the bulk of iron-ore production, approximately 1.5 million tons annually, will move overseas.

It is obvious that, should exhaustion indeed threaten domestic ore reserves, and should conversion of existing plants for blasting lower grades involve the diversion of excessively large resources in manpower and capital, Brazil, Newfoundland, and Cuba are areas of "special interest" for the United States in its strategy of raw materials. What makes this special interest particularly acute in the case of Brazil is her possession of the famous high-grade manganese deposits in the province of Minas Geraes, estimated at 10 million tons.

Manganese is the single basic commodity which affects all steel making. It is the best all-around material for procuring strength and deoxidization. Manganese does not occur in large commercially available quantities in the United States. This deficiency is considered the Achilles' heel of the steel industry. The United States imported in peacetime approximately 750,000 tons of the ore, of which 60 per cent was supplied by the Soviet Union, the Gold Coast, and British India, the remainder being shipped by the Union of South Africa, Brazil, Cuba, and the Philippine Islands.* Brazil's production, it appears, can be expanded to cover possible stoppages in imports from other continents. Increased production from domestic ores, notably those of the Cuyana range in Minnesota, remains a costly, but militarily important alternative. Moreover, manganese, unlike bulky iron ore, can be stocked in quantities large enough to meet military requirements in excess of domestic resources for several years.

Many kinds of steel are made for many purposes. In the making of these steels, alloys other than manganese are as es-

---

* C. K. Leith, J. W. Furness, Cleona Lewis, *World Minerals and World Peace*, the Brookings Institution, Washington, 1943, p. 73.

sential as the steel itself. Tungsten, vanadium, molybdenum, chromium, and nickel are valued for special properties they impart, such as hardness, tensile strength, and resistance. All of these alloy metals, except nickel—of which neighboring Canada accounts for 85 per cent of the world supply—are produced in commercial quantities within the borders of the United States, and the import requirements of some can be met by intrahemisphere production. Some of these alloy metals can be substituted for one another; stock piles of these and similarly strategical and critical materials present no overwhelming technical or financial problems. In sum, the raw-material position of the American steel industry is strong enough when measured by the exacting standards of national self-sufficiency and strategic "accessibility." Because of some real and larger anticipated shortages, it is not ideal, but neither is that of any other Great Power as now constituted.

In 1939 none of the three Great Powers of Europe proper, Great Britain, France, and Germany, entered the war possessing even remotely the near-perfect balance of the American coal and iron-ore combination. Britain and Germany produced about one-third more coal than each needed for domestic purposes, and were dependent, the former for 30 per cent, the latter for 70 per cent, on iron-ore imports. France produced more than twice the iron ore she processed and less than two-thirds of the coal she consumed. Consolidations of British-French and French-German coal and iron-ore resources would have roughly complemented each other. In fact, considerations which were of a political and military, rather than strictly economic and technical, nature have barred this road to functional integration.

A history of the European diplomacy of steel, far more discreet than, for example, that of oil, still remains to be written. It might cast an interesting light on the influence, or lack of influence, on Franco-German relations exerted by such German and French steel masters as the Roechlings, Thyssens, de Wendels, and Schneiders. As yet undisclosed information, one suspects, will hardly sustain the thesis of the primacy of private over national interests. There is ample evidence that steel and the geography of steel have figured in European strategic thought virtually since steel masters began to make their product. But it was governments and general staffs, not steel makers, who dominated the growth of the European steel industry almost from the start.

In 1871, Bismarck forced France to hand over the easily mined, high-grade deposits of Lorraine but failed to annex near-by deposits of high phosphorus ores. When techniques had been developed for mining these ores, and processes for their use had been invented, France steadily increased her share in European production while continued mining was depleting Germany's reserves. After France regained Lorraine, she became the largest iron-ore producer in Europe. France also was, both before and after Hitler, Germany's most important purveyor of iron ore.

German strategic planning for World War I contemplated the speedy conquest of the French mining regions close to the borders of Luxembourg and Belgium, especially the Briey basin. Germany, preparing for World War II, apparently entertained no such hopes for speedy consolidation of Westphalian coal and Lorraine iron, for the Herman Göring plant for the extraction and processing of low-grade ores at Salzgitter in the Harz Mountains was built at tremendous cost in money and labor. It was designed to make Germany independent of foreign imports. As soon as France had been conquered, the plant was temporarily shut down, a monument to misdirected resources.* However, German plans for war *did* provide for gaining speedy control of the Baltic Sea and thus of the shipping lanes which link German ports with Sweden's rich high-grade ore deposits at Kiruna. From 1940 to September, 1944, Sweden's output, approximately 15 million tons yearly, went mostly to Germany, a far from minor contribution to Germany's war economy. Its importance is attested not only by German policies with regard to the Scandinavian powers but also by the tenacity of German resistance in the Baltic states down to the last months of 1944.

Swedish ore shipments, traveling across the Baltic Sea, transhipped at Stettin, and borne along inland waterways, supplied the heavy industry of Silesia. The importance to Germany of this rich industrial and mining area was greatly

* Horst Mendershausen, *The Economics of War*, New York, 1943, p. 48.

increased by the conquest of Czechoslovakia and Polish Silesia, uniting all the resources of the region under German management, and by its relative remoteness from the bases of Allied air power.

The extent to which Britain's dependence on the iron ore of northern Spain has shaped Hispano-British relations is a matter of conjecture; it is certain that Spanish deliveries were no item of indifference to Britain once her other European sources of ore imports, namely France and Sweden, had fallen under the sway of German power.

Perhaps the most authoritative information on the scope of Soviet heavy industry which has recently come to hand is a statement by Marshal Stalin that it was planned "to boost the Soviet Union's steel production from the current and pre-war 22 million ton capacity to an annual output of 60 million tons." Incidentally, this figure given by Stalin would represent two-thirds of the United States' actual capacity, and half of its capacity per head of population.

In 1937, Russia was third in world production of iron ores as well as of steel ingots and castings. In Europe her heavy industry is based on the Donets basin; in Asia, on the Magnitogorsk-Kuznetsk combine. Until the Asiatic centers were developed, the Donets basin supplied the bulk of Russian steel. The modernization of mining and of steel-making facilities, which had been much impaired by the ravages of war and revolution, was carried out between 1924 and 1935 with the aid of American and German technicians and equipment. The juxtaposition of coal beds north of the Sea of Azov, iron ores in the Dnepropetrovsk district, and manganese deposits near Nicopol affords an ideal setting for steel making in the Donets basin. The ores carry 50 to 60 per cent iron, and reserves are estimated at several billion tons.

Strategical necessities, and the migration of millions of peoples and hundreds of plants to eastern Russia, have speeded the creation of a vast autonomous industrial system in Russian Asia, "half-way between Poland and the Pacific." Its pillars are the iron-ore mines of Sverdlovsk and Chelyabinsk, the steel town of Magnitogorsk, in the Urals, and the coal deposits of the Kuznetsk basin on the slopes of the Altai Mountains. There are rich deposits of coal, notably coking coal, in the Urals, while the Kuznetsk basin boasts of iron-ore deposits relatively small in size but rich in metal. The close integration of both regions was announced as an official goal of the Second Five Year Plan, and visitors report that great progress was made in this direction. W. H. Lawrence, who in July, 1944, visited the Magnitogorsk, writes as follows:

"Some factories we saw in this area were modeled after American production units, notably the Magnitogorsk steel mill, which resembles the Carnegie Illinois plant at Gary, Ind., and when completed it is designed to outproduce the Gary plant. Some plants had a large percentage of American tools. Others were predominantly Soviet machine-equipped. But there was a certain amount of pleasure also in watching heavy German-made equipment fashioning implements of war that we knew in a few weeks would be smashing Germany. . . . In the Magnitogorsk Iron and Steel Combine iron ore from a magnetic hill less than two miles away joins with coal from the Kuznetsk combine, 1,200 miles distant, to more than double the total steel production of pre-revolutionary Russia.* It employs a score of thousand workers, including 45 per cent women, in six blast furnaces, eight rolling and two blooming mills and a great many construction workers are rushing additional units into production."†

No exact figures of the capacity and output of the combine have as yet been released. It has been described in several books by American, British, French, and German authors. The Soviet government has made available photographs, facts, and figures descriptive of individual plants and townships. But when these data are compared with the detailed information available for American or British economic activities of all kinds, the striking fact is brought home how little concrete knowledge the outside world possesses about a development designed on so gigantic a scale. The picture of the *whole* development is far from complete.

Goals and attainments for individual projects can be gleaned from the published decrees of the Council of People's Commissars of the U.S.S.R. and the Central Committee of the Communist Party, and from directives of local party leaders.

* Russian steel production was 3.9 million tons in 1916.
† *The New York Times*, July 13, 1944.

From Stalin's remark and the goals officially set by the Five Year Plans it can be inferred that steel capacity east of the Urals is 5 to 6 million tons. This figure must be taken as a shot in the dark rather than an estimate.

It is clear, however, that Russian heavy industry in Asia is no hothouse product and has all the prerequisites for phenomenal expansion. Russia has lavished prodigious energies upon her arsenal of military power in eastern Asia, thus activating the potentials of that region which in Sir Halford Mackinder's prophetic metaphor is the "heartland" of Asia and the "pivot of world history."

Up to the 1930's, northeastern China and Japan were almost unanimously considered to be only modestly endowed with resources of iron. Since then new estimates have been circulated which contradict earlier, more cautious ones. They are being constantly revised upward by the Japanese. Enthusiastic reports issued by Japanese-controlled sources are gems of inconsistency, and betray the clumsy hand of Japanese propaganda. Japanese sources assert that only now has it become possible to explore the mineral resources of Korea, Manchuria, and north China and that vast wealth has been discovered. The reliability of Japanese statistics must be assayed in the light of a regulation promulgated by the Japanese authorities in June, 1939, which prohibits "the giving of information to Japanese or foreigners as to the quantity . . . of certain strategic articles produced in Japan, the colonies, and Kwantung Leased Territory." *

Japan has hardly had the time to prepare detailed geological surveys of her recent acquisitions. Chinese surveys prepared for territories now occupied by Japan are either incomplete or inaccurate. Moreover, discoveries of new mineral resources frequently give rise to gross exaggerations, an occurrence by no means confined to Japan.

Paradoxically, it is Japanese "disclosures" which have fostered abroad the belief that the Yellow Sea region is rich in those mineral resources which form the basis of heavy industry, and that their recapture after the defeat of Japan will speed mightily the economic transformation of China. This

* Schumpeter, op.cit., p. 367.

optimism is widely shared in this country. The facts from which it derives were largely manufactured in Japan.

The steel industry of Japan proper depends on coking coal imported from Formosa and north China. In 1936 only 13 per cent of Japan's iron-ore requirements were met from domestic sources. In that year she imported 3.4 million tons of iron ore from British Malaya, China, Australia, and the Philippines; 1.7 million tons of scrap from the United States; and 1 million tons of crude iron from Manchuria and India. For the same year the total steel production of Japan, Korea, and Manchuria is given as 5.7 million tons,* 11 per cent of U.S. production. It is by this order of magnitudes that later Japanese claims should be gauged.

Japan, too, has followed the fashion of "X Year Plans." In 1935 a five-year schedule was set for the expansion of iron-ore production in Manchuria; the goal for 1937 was 6 million tons. Since then high hopes have been placed on the development of Manchurian, Chinese, and Korean production. The ores at Anshan and in Tung-pien-tao in Manchuria, at Lung-yen, Pailingmiao, Likuo, and Wu-an in north China, and at Musan in Korea were to supply the bulk of Japan's requirements.† Since then reports of ever larger discoveries of mineral reserves and ever increasing pig-iron production have kept Japanese statistics boiling.

In 1934, estimates placed the coal deposits of south Manchuria at 4.8 billion tons and iron-ore deposits at 800 million —mostly low-grade ores too high in silica content. In 1939 the coal deposits were reported as 15 billion and the ore deposits as 2.5 billion tons which now suddenly contained a large proportion of high-grade ore.‡ In 1944 the estimate of the iron-ore deposits had risen to 4 billion.§ Japanese newspapers also revealed the discovery of iron-ore deposits—estimated at 80 million tons—in the Chitaokou district of Tung-pien-tao province near the Korean border, carrying from 60 to

* G. H. Smith and Dorothy Good, *Japan, a Geographical View*, American Geographical Society, 1943, p. 44.

† *Far Eastern Review*, British Ministry of Information, Ser. 254, April 25, 1944.

‡ *Japan-Manchukuo Year Book 1940*, pp. 752-5.

§ *Asahi Shimbun*, January 9, 1944, quoted in the *Far Eastern Review*, April 25, 1944.

75 per cent iron. Output for 1941 was given at 1.5 million tons. In 1944, however, a Japanese source admitted that "the development of the iron mines in Tung-pien-tao is not progressing according to plan. As long as Showa Steel Works has no possible means of blasting poorer quality ores in unlimited quantities, it is indispensable to increase the import of better quality ores from Northern China."

According to an official Chinese estimate, the total deposits of north China are 175 million tons, or more than half the estimate for the whole of China, which is 323 million. The experts of the North China Development Company, a Japanese concern in charge of mining operations in north China, did not see fit to raise the old estimate which, incidentally, is the equivalent of less than two years' U.S. ore production in wartime.

Manifestly, nothing can be learned from the jungle of Japanese statistics as regards the *real* production of Japanese mining and heavy industry. It is likely that the Japanese themselves do not know what it is. It seems, however, that there have been in late years no material improvements as far as the raw-material position of heavy industry in the Yellow Sea region is concerned. It appears to be as dependent as formerly on overseas supplies of high-grade iron ores—besides certain alloy metals, such as chromium and copper, which occur neither in Japan, Korea, nor China. If the estimates the Japanese themselves issued as late as 1939 are accepted as trustworthy (and there is every reason to believe that they, too, are padded), the iron-ore reserves of Manchuria and Korea are in the neighborhood of 1,200 million tons.* According to both Chinese and Japanese experts, the reserves of Free China are around 300 million. This adds up to a total of approximately 1.5 billion, somewhat larger than the proven reserves of Britain and Sweden, which are, however, much higher in iron content.†

Large coal and iron-ore deposits are close to each other only in southern Manchuria. In independent China, only

* *Japan-Manchukuo Year Book 1940*, pp. 341-3 and 760-2.
† According to the last official estimate the total reserves of China are 1,694,000,000 tons. The Chinese Ministry of Information, *China Handbook 1937-43*, p. 484.

near Chungking has the juxtaposition of coal and iron given rise to a small pig-iron and steel industry. In sum, the Yellow Sea region has the coal and iron necessary for an expanding steel industry.* However, the natural setting precludes its growing to a size even remotely comparable to that of the Soviet Union or of western Europe.

By contrast, India possesses the broad raw-material base for heavy industry which the Far East lacks. Moreover, India is further advanced technologically than any other Asiatic country except Japan, and she is China's equal in manpower.

In the two provinces of eastern India, Bihar and Orissa, vast coal deposits are close to vast iron-ore deposits. The ideal proximity of basic raw materials, nearness of large population centers in Bengal and Madras, and accessibility to transport by rail and sea—these are the elements which have gone into the making of an Indian steel industry capable of unlimited expansion.

Reserves of iron ore are estimated conservatively at 2.7 billion tons in the eastern provinces alone.† Deposits of good grade occur in central India. The Orissa and Bihar ores are of high grade and resemble, in geological formation, those of the Lake Superior district in the United States and Canada. According to a recent study by an American expert, these ores carry an average of more than 50 per cent iron and represent mineral reserves of 1.4 billion tons of the metal, "or enough for at least 500 years at present rate of use.‡ . . . This favorable estimate, it is true, makes no allowance for a marked rise in consumption, but it also discounts the possibility of extending the reserves by further exploration."

In 1939, Indian pig-iron ore production was 1.8 million tons,§ or three-quarters as large as the production of Manchuria. The Tata Iron Works at Jamshedpur is the producer of the lowest-cost pig iron in the world; its plant is the largest

* C. H. Behre, Jr., and Kung-ping Wang, op.cit. See also the excellent analysis of China's raw-material position in D. N. Rowe's *China among the Powers,* New York, 1945, pp. 64-8.

† H. C. Jones, "The Iron Deposits of Bihar and Orissa," *Geological Survey of India Memoirs,* Vol. 63, Part 2, p. 253.

‡ C. H. Behre, Jr., "India's Minerals," *Foreign Affairs,* Vol. 22, No. 1, pp. 78-93.

§ *Statistical Abstract for British India,* Vol. 18, Delhi, 1942, pp. 580-1.

and most modern in the British Empire. Its pig-iron capacity is steadily expanding and, since other India plants have only fairly recently begun to produce, accounts for nearly one-half of that of all India. The pig-iron and steel plants of the Tata concern as well as those of smaller producers, the Indian Iron and Steel Company at Burnpore, Mysore Iron Works at Shimaga, and Bengal Iron Works at Kulti, are designed along modern lines and susceptible to fairly rapid expansion. In addition, steel production enjoys the inestimable advantage of an abundant local supply of manganese. India's output was 1 million tons in 1939, second only to that of Russia.*

India, in contrast to China, will emerge from World War II as a strong creditor country. She has amassed, between 1939 and 1944, a 500-million-pound-sterling credit in London, a sizable backlog against steel-making equipment she may seek to buy from British makers. While the Japanese will hardly let the mines and plants of occupied China fall intact into Chinese hands, Indian plants will have survived the war unscathed. All in all, as regards the rapid expansion of Indian and Chinese heavy industry, the odds are heavily in favor of India.

Summarizing our findings, we may say that only the United States and Russia possess large coal and high-grade iron deposits. India follows as a close third, at least as regards the harmonious side-by-side existence of large and high-grade mineral reserves. Other Great Powers either dispose of large coal resources and inadequate iron supply (Britain and Germany), or have large iron resources and insufficient coal (France), or they are inadequately supplied with both and have gained their Great Power position through the leverage of manpower, strategic location, and historic accident (the case of Japan).

However, it would be fatuous to conceive of the raw-material strength of the Great Powers in terms of their national boundaries, because all of them draw necessary supplies from their zones of influence or control, and because initial conquests may completely alter the situation as it prevails in

* Statistical Abstract for British India, ibid., p. 586.

peace. Close British-French co-operation, for instance, would remedy Britain's deficiency in iron, and cover French requirements of coal. If, however, France's eastern frontier is defended no better in the future than it was in three successive Franco-German wars, then Germany could count with equanimity upon gaining possession of Lorraine iron. In both World Wars, Germany drew high-grade iron from Sweden and Norway, while Britain in the First World War obtained Scandinavian ore only with difficulty and in World War II was barred from it altogether. On the other hand, a French-British bloc enjoys relatively safe access to the iron mines of Spain and, if sea communications are kept open, to supplies from other continents.

Control of Manchuria is the pivot on which swings Japan's military and economic strategy. Upon Manchuria, too, converge the strategic and economic interests of China and Russia in the Far East. For each of these three, Manchuria is the keystone of regional power. The power that controls Manchuria controls Far Eastern heavy industry and enjoys the political and military advantages therein implied.

In terms of coal and iron there are at present only two major powers: the United States with all the resources of the Western Hemisphere at its disposal, and the Soviet Union possessing vast proven deposits in Europe and Asia and having gained strategic ascendancy over additional resources in eastern Europe (Silesia). The mineral resources of the British Empire are immense. Yet as an economic and strategic entity it lacks the integration necessary for the rapid and efficient conversion of potential wealth into industrial produce for war. The power resources of western and central Europe are dispersed among several nations. Were they gathered into one economic unit, its raw-material potential would equal that of the United States or Russia.

9. GEOGRAPHY OF OIL

LACKING abundant supplies of both coal and iron, a state may attain a high degree of military strength—with this proviso: That strength will be as great as powers controlling coal and iron permit it to be. If coal and iron are the materials indispensable for the building of a powerful war machine, unlimited supplies of oil are no less indispensable for running it. Lord Curzon held that the Allies of World War I were swept to victory upon a stream of oil. The question will long be debated how much of United States–British –Russian superiority in World War II was owed to control of about 95 per cent of world oil production. Among the Great Powers—as they lined up for World War II—only the United States and Russia disposed of large reserves of petroleum within their own territory. The British Isles, Germany, metropolitan France, and Japan possessed insignificant deposits or none at all.

Anglo-American sea and air power shielded the supply routes linking the British Isles with American and Caribbean production centers; British strategic control of the Middle East secured the output of the Mosul and Persian Gulf region for Allied forces based along the eastern Mediterranean and in India.

France met defeat with large petroleum stocks on hand; for prolonged resistance she could have counted on the same regional sources which supplied Britain.

Japan within a few months after she had gone to war implemented her (reputedly large) domestic stores by the production of the rich oil fields of the Netherlands Indies.

The case of Germany is not so simple. By 1939, Germany had accumulated large stores of imported oil, and by 1941 she had obtained control of the entire output of the Rumanian oil fields, which accounted for one-fiftieth of world production and had been steadily declining—due to exhaustion, it was generally believed—since 1930. In addition, a large part of the commercial and military oil stocks of conquered Europe fell into German hands. Germany's supply of "natural" oil, i.e., oil in the ground, as compared with the plenitude on the side of the Allies was negligible. Obviously it did not meet the large requirements of the German war machine.

Can German military reverses be ascribed to a shortage in natural oil? Russian and Anglo-American victories from 1942 to 1944 were scored against German forces which, whatever else they may have lacked, were well supplied with petrol. True, German civilian economy had to suffer; but the *Wehrmacht* was not defeated because of chronic oil shortage. Its demands appear to have been met largely by the output of "synthetic" petroleum products. True, it was a shortage of fuel which immobilized German tanks, trucks, and planes in the closing months of the war. But this was the consequence of the Allies' strategic bombing and the German General Staff's misconception of the nature of air power, and not of an initial lack of supplies. The "priority" accorded by American and British air strategists to German synthetic oil plants as target objectives seems to indicate that German chemistry and petroleum engineering had solved the problem of self-sufficiency in oil as it had solved, just before World War I, that of saltpeter.

The processes developed by the Germans are well known abroad, for the patents were sold to foreign manufacturers. Coal is the raw material upon which the most important German processes for the making of oil as well as of rubber are based.* The plants were costly; their construction and operation diverted labor from other sectors of the economy. None the less, military returns appear to have justified the investment.

The case of Germany suggests that large coal-producing powers can divert, should they have to do so for military reasons, enough of their output to open up a new or alternative source of petrol supplies. It is this development which

---

* It is estimated that Germany produced synthetic oil from three raw materials: from coke, 15 per cent; from alcohol, wood, tar, etc., 20 per cent; and from coal, 65 per cent. H. G. Moulton and L. Marlio, *The Control of Germany and Japan*, the Brookings Institution, 1944, p. 32.

has modified the position "natural" oil has held as a raw material of military power second in importance only to coal and iron. It has lessened its importance for a land power like Germany. For genuine naval power and true intercontinental air power, as they have been developed by the United States, oil-in-the-ground retains, and will retain in the foreseeable future, its vital importance. "Uranium 235" may replace it soon as a source of energy; but in the meanwhile, makers of national policy will be loath to gamble military security on experimental physics.

According to figures furnished to the Truman Committee in 1944 by Mr. Harold Ickes, Petroleum Administrator for War, the United States possesses 40 per cent of world oil reserves—20 billion barrels out of a total of 50.7 billion. The combined reserves of Canada, Mexico, and South America were estimated at 7.5 billion; hence more than half of the world's known oil resources are located in the Western Hemisphere and within the American orbit of strategic "accessibility." None the less, the increasing rate of withdrawals for consumption and export has given rise repeatedly to fears that the reserves of the United States, large as they are, will become exhausted and that future discoveries will not keep abreast with demand. The withdrawals from American oil fields in 1944 were approximately 1.6 billion, while discoveries were only 600 million. Were output and discovery to continue at these rates, reserves would be drained by 1965.

The surplus of the United States, huge as it was, did not suffice to meet all the demands of coalition warfare. The oil fields of Mexico, Venezuela, and the Middle East supplied the critical margin which kept the Allied war machine running. Moreover, a large part of American production of crude oil and natural gas was being absorbed by the chemical industry for the manufacture of explosives, rubber, and other war-important materials and hence was not available as fuel. It was undoubtedly considerations such as these which prompted the Petroleum Administrator to declare that the "demands of global war have forced such heavy withdrawals from our petroleum bank account that nothing must be left undone today that might result in the replenishment of those deposits." [*]

It is not the demands of global war alone which have raised the specter of exhaustion. In the period between 1850 and 1940 the United States consistently averaged 60 per cent of world production, i.e., a total of approximately 20 billion barrels, and that figure does not include resources squandered by wasteful exploitation. It is not surprising that pride in record production is giving way to anxiety over the future. The American oil industry is capitalized at several billion dollars; and American military power can strike no further than oil can carry it. Public attention was focused upon "the dwindling oil reserves of the United States," as an official release put it, by the Petroleum Reserves Corporation's announcement of its intention to construct a pipe line from the oil fields of Saudi Arabia and Kuweit on the Persian Gulf to the Mediterranean.[†]

The project contemplated an agreement between the United States government and three American oil companies owning concessions in Saudi Arabia and Kuweit. Its terms provided for the construction of the 1,200-mile pipe line at the expense of the government, which reserved the decision as to its route, operation, and maintenance. The companies were to maintain a reserve of one billion barrels of crude oil at the disposal of the government, especially for military and naval needs. The government was to have a veto right over the sale of oil by the private companies to foreign governments or their nationals.[‡] The project, grandly conceived politically as well as technically, stirred a good deal of controversy in the United States and Great Britain, was debated in Congress and the House of Commons, and was accorded a mixed reception by the oil interests of both countries. It was apparently superseded by an agreement, signed in August, 1944, between the United States and Great Britain providing for a joint commission to study global oil problems and to

[*] Senate Rept. 838, 77th Congress, 2d session, p. 13 as quoted by Herbert Feis in *Petroleum and American Foreign Policy*, Food Research Institute, Stanford University, March 1944, p. 14.
[†] Press release of U.S. Department of the Interior, February 6, 1944.
[‡] Herbert Feis, *op. cit.*, p. 41.

recommend long-range policies for their solution. The agreement, according to official releases, is to be open to those peaceable oil-producing and -consuming nations who may care to join in at a later date. One clause provides that new production shall be brought in "in an orderly manner."

The formal discussions, as reported, did not dwell specifically on American operations in the Middle East. However, the Middle East, the one major producing area where Britain holds a commanding position, is the "heart and center" of the international oil problem. The agreement for an Arabian pipe line as proposed by the United States Petroleum Reserves Corporation carried the endorsement of the Departments of State, War, and Navy. It can be assumed, therefore, that American dealings in the Middle East reflect a considered policy of national security and, implicitly, serious concern by military and naval leaders for the current rate of depletion of American resources.

The thesis of impending "exhaustion" is not universally accepted. Policies proposed in order to replenish domestic reserves from foreign sources have been opposed strenuously from within and without the American oil industry. It has been recalled that oil "panics" have occurred periodically since 1903; that in 1923 a prominent geologist predicted American reserves would be used up in fifteen years' time, unless the United States could secure a larger share in world production; that in 1938 the United States had larger reserves than had been proven fifteen years before; and that throughout the 1930's the problem was not to find new reserves but rather to market at a fair price the all too plentiful output of producing fields.

It is argued, too, that new discoveries will catch up, as they have done in the past, with the rate of depletion; that restoration of pressure has renewed the productivity of fields thought to have been depleted, for example, those of Rumania; that advances in drilling and refining techniques have upset previous estimates and are bound to result in considerable economies in the utilization of proved reserves; that the United States possesses unlimited deposits of oil-bearing shale, particularly in the Rocky Mountain region; that proved American reserves of natural gas are the equivalent of 17 billion barrels, almost as large as present reserves of liquid petroleum, and could be converted into liquid fuel at a unit cost only slightly higher than that incurred in refining liquid petroleum; and that the oil seepages of the Point Barrow region, reserved to the U.S. Navy, and oil wells at Katalla, Alaska, and Fort Norman on the Mackenzie River, Canada, are but samples of the oil riches of the American north which future exploration may confidently be expected to reveal.

The following table appears to sustain the contention that proven reserves of petroleum have kept abreast of consumption. The drop between 1943 and 1944 is slight. Reserves in 1943 were one billion barrels larger than they were in 1941, i.e., at the beginning of the "shooting war." *

TABLE V

UNITED STATES OIL PRODUCTION AND KNOWN RESERVES, 1918-1943
(in 42-gallon barrels)

	Proved Reserves of Crude Petroleum	Accumulated Production
1918	6,200,000,000	4,608,572,000
1928	11,000,000,000	11,243,149,000
1933	12,000,000,000	15,690,379,000
1938	17,348,146,000	21,188,242,000
1940	19,024,515,000	23,806,418,000
1941	19,589,296,000	25,208,646,000
1942	20,082,793,000	26,595,291,000
1943	20,064,152,000	28,098,467,000

Only geologists, petroleum engineers, and chemists are competent to pass on the likelihood of "exhaustion" and the technical problems to which it may give rise. Similarly, commercial and financial problems, higher prices, increased imports, and costs of shifting plant, labor, and the national economy as a whole to the production of substitutes, lie outside the scope of this analysis. What matters here is the relation the oil position of the United States bears to the mis-

* "Trends in the Petroleum Industry, 1918-1944," *Petroleum Industry War Council*, Committee on Petroleum Economics.

143

sions which future exigencies may assign its military forces,
and to the oil resources of other nations.

TABLE VI

(in thousands of 42-gallon barrels)

U.S.A.	1,503,176	U.S.S.R.	240,000
Venezuela	187,000	Rumania	36,000
Mexico	34,500	Germany	7,500
Trinidad	25,000	Poland	3,500
Argentina	24,836	Hungary	8,200
Colombia	14,900	Albania	1,100
Peru	14,600	Austria	6,800 *
Canada	9,958	France	600
Ecuador	2,500	Czechoslovakia	125
Bolivia	250	Italy	60
Western Hemisphere	1,816,720	Europe	303,885

Persia	78,000
Netherlands East Indies	20,000 †
Iraq	26,266
British India	3,000
Burma	750
Egypt	8,994
Sarawak-Brunei	3,000
Bahrein	8,000
Saudi Arabia	5,475
Sakhalin	3,500
Japan-Taiwan	3,500
Middle and Far East	160,485

The following points stand out: (1) Wartime demand for
fuel, lubricants, and sundry derivatives of petroleum is virtually unlimited; wartime demand is instantaneous. Before
military reliance can be placed upon substitutes for liquid
oil in the ground, facilities for their production on a scale
comparable to that of present "natural" capacity would have
to be established. So long as no such facilities exist, national

* 1937:221.
† 1940:62,011.

144

security involves control of the maximum reserves of oil, domestic and foreign. (2) Calculations of future military risks call for consideration not only of reserves upon which the United States can count, but also of those which will be at the disposal of other powers. Its estimated share of world reserves is approximately 40 per cent. However, if all parts of the world were as thoroughly explored as America, the share of the United States might prove to be considerably lower, and the position of other states would have grown proportionately stronger.* (3) Military requirements call not only for control of ample reserves of oil but also for ample supplies, ready at hand, in or near the focal areas of strategy.

Granted that the ramifications of the international oil business are far from crystal clear, the considerations which prompted the United States government to seek a first call on Arabian oil are simple. Their chief significance is strategical, hence power-political, which is not, as a matter of course, the same as imperialistic. Only the fields of the Middle East among the oil-producing areas outside the Western Hemisphere and Russia contain large proven accumulations on which the world in general, and the United States in particular, may rely for supplying their needs for many years ahead. Moreover, control of their output spells control of oil at the crossroads of Europe, Asia, and Africa; i.e., where strategic foresight must plan to meet huge military requirements.

The crux of the strategical problem is this: In three wars for universal domination—the Napoleonic Wars and the two World Wars—the Middle East has proved to be one of the key areas of world strategy; the defense of the British Empire involves control of the Arab lands and Persia. While the Middle East is the classic theater of power conflicts, it lacks the essentials for power of its own. Its manpower potential, 50 million people upon an area two-thirds the size of Europe, is low quantitatively and lacks technological sophistication; its mineral wealth does not include workable deposits of coal

* According to Wallace E. Pratt, geologist and vice-president of the Standard Oil Company of New Jersey, a more thorough exploration of the globe may disclose that only 15 per cent of world reserves lie within the United States. *The Lamp*, vol. 26, no. 6, December, 1943.

and iron. The Middle East excels only in strategic geography —and oil.

Reserves of the Persian Gulf region—southern Persia, northern Iraq, Saudi Arabia, Bahrein, Qatar, and Trucial Oman—are conservatively estimated at 18 billion barrels and probably are much larger; they may ultimately prove the largest in the world. Average annual production in five pre-war years was 100 million barrels, only 4 to 5 per cent of world production.

No figures are available to show how large have been the contributions of Middle Eastern producers to Allied forces operating in Mediterranean and Indian theaters of war; no doubt, considering the slim margin of Allied superiority during "the retreat to victory" of 1940-1942, they were of crucial importance. After the loss of the Netherlands Indies and Burma oil fields, they were critically important for the defense of India. Now and in the foreseeable future, India must look to Persian Gulf oil production for satisfaction of her military requirements. Moreover, the industrialization of India will create an expanding market for petroleum products which may exceed the output of the Burmese and Dutch fields.

It requires little imagination to perceive the leverage Middle Eastern oil will give to those powers who control it, upon the future economic development of India and China, since neither country possesses substantial oil reserves of its own. Thus, states of southeastern and eastern Asia will join that group of countries which, while themselves not of the Middle East, are vitally interested in it. The convergence of power interests in this area is as old as recorded history; modern techniques of transportation and the incidence of oil have added a new chapter without, however, breaking its continuity. Planes instead of camel caravans now travel the ancient crossroads. The effectiveness of a Middle Eastern air force depends, of course, on the number of planes, pilots, and airfields. But no matter how small or how big, it can be fueled locally.

The relations of American and British oil interests form but one aspect, if also an important one, of Middle Eastern politics. These interests have lived, in Herbert Feis's happy phrase, "in uneasy and uncertain friendliness." The main issue dividing American and British oil policies is quantity of production. For Britain, Middle Eastern oil is an important potential source of foreign exchange, doubly important because Britain will enter the postwar era encumbered by foreign debts. The British government, which directly or indirectly controls the British and British-foreign companies operating in Iran and Iraq, must be expected to husband Middle Eastern resources and to adjust output closely to market demand. Not that American companies will quarrel with policies designed to keep prices as high as the traffic will bear and to forestall a recurrence of price wars which in the past have marred international oil harmony! However, the American government is primarily interested in Arabian oil because it could prolong as well as supplement domestic reserves, and hence may foster a more aggressive program of exploitation than would fit in with British policies. There are other, subsidiary issues on which American and British oil interests may divide in the future, as they have done with great éclat in the past, notably in the early 1920's.*

Trade conflicts, however, are of small significance as long as the world oil situation remains what it is now. The United States and Great Britain together control 80 per cent of world output; their joint position in Europe and Asia (Russia excepted) is commanding, and bids fair to remain so as long as their political interests harmonize. These interests now conjoin harmoniously in the Middle East. To that, the pipe-line project bears mute testimony. For its stipulations do not conflict with Britain's system of political controls over the Arab states; rather, Britain's position is reinforced by the presence of the American government as sponsor of the project—an implicit recognition of the abiding strategic importance which the United States as well as Britain attaches to the

* Demands for the open door in 1920 were energetically pressed upon Britain by the U.S. Department of State, acting to secure a share in Middle Eastern oil resources and trade for American business. After a long and hotly fought diplomatic battle the issue was compromised and American concerns ultimately obtained concessions in the Arabian peninsula and on Bahrein. For a vigorous statement of the American position see the U.S. Federal Trade Commission report, *Foreign Ownership in Petroleum Industry*, Washington, 1923.

147

Middle East. Published accounts of subsequent negotiations do not contradict the impression held, in certain quarters at least, that United States foreign policy has come down on the side of the *status quo* in Middle Eastern politics.

The independence of Persia was expressly guaranteed by the joint Anglo-American-Russian declaration of Teheran in 1943. At first glance it is not surprising, therefore, that the Soviet government should have opened negotiations with the Iranian government for oil concessions at Kevir Khurian in the northern parts of the country. For, does not Britain exploit the oil fields of southern Persia, the most productive in the Middle East, and is not Russia free to claim privileges granted by Iran to another foreign power? The question could be answered simply were the Iranian government indeed the master of its fate and hence of its oil. It is neither. The entry of Soviet, British, and American forces into Persia reopens a chapter in Middle Eastern politics which appeared to have been closed when the Soviet Union, shortly after the Revolution, abandoned czarist Russia's diplomatic positions in the Middle East. World War II restored effectually, if not also formally, the delicate balance of Russian and British interests as defined by the Anglo-Russian Agreement of 1907 allocating northern Persia to Russia, and southern Persia to Britain, as respective spheres of influence.

The Anglo-Russian relation in Iran is the "bare bones" of the total Anglo-Russian relationship. For it is the propinquity of British and Russian power in Iran which magnifies the slightest move of either power into an issue involving the world-wide prestige of both. Viewed in that light, a Soviet quest for Iranian oil is fraught with all too familiar historical and power-political implications.

The Iranian government turned down the Soviet proposals. The British Minister "had no objection to the [Persian government's] decision," and the United States Minister addressed on November 1, 1944, a letter to the Iranian government "confirming the latter's decision to postpone talks on foreign oil concessions in Iran until after the war as entirely legal and within the rights of the Government." * Be-

* As reported by the *New York Times*, November 2, 1944.

fore the incident was closed, a sharp campaign was waged by the Soviet press against the Premier of Iran, the presence of American troops in that country, and American oil interests fearful of "losing their European markets because of competition from Near East oil." The campaign subsided under the press of larger issues in Anglo-American-Russian relationships.* It is of interest, however, that a Russian spokesman ventured to surmise that the Soviet Union was running short of oil and needed access to Middle Eastern resources to replenish its dwindling stock.**

By far the largest oil reserves outside the sphere of Anglo-American controls are those located within Russian territory. All available estimates are incomplete. For total reserves a figure of 3.2 billion tons has been mentioned, to which the .5 billion of the Rumanian fields can now be added.† Output for 1940 is given as 240 million barrels. At that rate, Russia appears to face no imminent danger of exhaustion. According to Soviet sources extensive geological surveys have been carried out since 1934 in the far north, east and west of the Urals. Along the Arctic coast, throughout the Lena drainage system, along the Tolba River, and to the west of the Sea of Okhotsk plentiful evidence of vast oil accumulations has been found.‡ Published reports also indicate a steadily rising output from the newly developed fields in Sakhalin, in the Bashkir Republic, and at Emba on the Caspian.§

* The Soviet Union, through diplomatic pressure and support of the pro-Russian Tudeh party, forced subsequently the resignation of Premier Moham-mad Saïd, whom the Soviet press accused of fascist leanings.

** *War and the Working Class*, October 22, 1944. This assertion is at variance with previous statements. Soviet geologists have maintained that the Soviet Union controls half or more than half of world oil reserves. N. Mikai-lov, *Land of the Soviets*, London, 1939, pp. 20-1, and I. M. Gubkin, *Mineral Resources of the USSR*, New York World's Fair Pamphlet, 1939, pp. 15-16.

† Harold G. Moulton and Louis Marlio in *The Control of Germany and Japan* suggest that "because of the substantial dependence of Germany upon Rumanian oil, attention should be given to the possibility of crippling German war power in the future by exhausting the Rumanian oil supplies within a short period of time." It is doubtful that this proposal will find favor with the Soviet Union or with the farm co-operatives of Rumania bent upon establishing tractor farms on the Soviet model.

‡ Wallace E. Pratt, "Petroleum in The North," in *Compass of the World*, New York, 1944, p. 346.

§ B. Plaetschke, *"Die wichtigsten Eisenbahn-Neubauten in der Sowietunion,"* *Petermanns Mitteilungen*, Vol. 86, No. 5, Gotha, 1940, pp. 161-6.

In summary, we may say that both America and Russia, most richly endowed with coal and iron, control also the largest oil reserves. The United States in addition has access to large oil reserves in neighboring countries, while Russia expects to find, according to exhaustive geological and geophysical surveys, additional sources within her territory. The two other main oil areas, the Middle East and the Dutch East Indies, lie outside the zone of direct political control of any Great Power. True, Britain is the dominant power of the Middle East, but her hold remains unchallenged only as long as Great Power conflicts remain suspended. The oil wells of the Dutch East Indies may remain accessible to Britain and the United States only as long as their naval supremacy is maintained over the narrow waters of Singapore and the Java Sea and no other sea power based on Asia challenges the *status quo*. England and France may count on ready access to South American oil, which, together with Holland and the United States, they control financially. Yet in the case of American neutrality, the oil supply of these countries is only as secure as their navies, separately or jointly, can make it. Synthetic oil production in the western European states is hampered by comparative lack of manpower and the strategic vulnerability of their industries. It is probable that all Great Powers will in future be able to provide domestically for their minimum needs in liquid fuels. Yet abundance of oil is an inestimable military asset. Anglo-American co-operation in the Middle East would supply the most essential link in a world-wide chain of supply centers. The Anglo-Saxon countries would then possess virtually limitless oil resources near every focal point of the world's strategic geography.

10. SUBSTITUTES

THE production of substitutes is an integral part of a country's raw-material supply. This topic has given rise to a somewhat stultifying discussion, a "conservative" faction rejecting *Ersatz* in any form, and an "alchemist" faction taking the diametrically opposite point of view. One side maintains that substitutes (a) are too expensive, (b) are of inferior quality, and (c) do not offer a solution of the raw-material problem when really serious shortages occur. The other side advocates a general use of substitutes and insists that military security is not assured unless the country has completely freed itself from the bondage of foreign trade.

Both are extreme views. The whole of technical progress may be conceived as an economy of substitutes. The gasoline motor is a substitute for the steam engine which in turn was a substitute for the mail coach; fuel oil is a substitute for coal, which in turn replaced wood burning. This applies of course also in the military field, where, for instance, the tank may be considered as a substitute for heavy cavalry. In a general sense, the economy of substitutes with its concomitant diffusion of technological skills turned inventive genius toward new ways and techniques. In a more narrow sense, substitution often alleviated tightness in armament production and sometimes eliminated raw-material shortages altogether. Without Haber's invention for producing nitrogen from air, British naval blockade and the subsequent loss of access to Chile's saltpeter would have forced Germany out of the First World War within six months. Without synthetic gasoline production she could not have started the Second World War. Without "synthetic" rubber plants at home, the loss of Malaya would have been almost a fatal blow to American war economy. Some countries, especially the United States, Great Britain, and Germany, successfully replaced scarce minerals with plastics.

These are the success stories of substitute economy. There

were other, less successful attempts at replacing important but scarce materials by more abundant ones. Germany, for example, attempted to produce clothing and food, notably sugar, out of wood—with which, incidentally, she was not overabundantly supplied. Despite this feat of alchemy, the German people appear to have favored wool and cane sugar over wood fiber in any guise.

There are a number of rather inflexible rules governing the workings of any substitute economy. Generally, the substitute is more expensive and more difficult to produce. The price, of course, matters little in war; yet it matters that to produce the substitute, larger industrial and manpower resources must be used than were necessary for the production or importation of the original. The production of many substitutes entails a decrease in other types of production. Certainly the Haber process is the ideal of substitute economy— the new product is made out of air, i.e., of nothing! Yet a closer analysis shows that even this ideal process requires considerable industrial equipment, a good deal of it made of metal, and a large outlay of electricity. The making of other substitutes requires the building of entire new large-scale industries, as for instance, synthetic gasoline production.

Secondly, substitutes do not necessarily improve the over-all raw-material supply. Let us suppose that to meet heavy demands for electric wiring, methods have been developed for replacing copper by aluminum! This would be a great advantage if copper is scarce but aluminum abundant. Yet the substitution creates a heavy demand for aluminum, and to satisfy it, aluminum production may have to be doubled or tripled. Hence a shortage in aluminum may occur, and transportation equipment and electric power, the most expensive "raw materials" in aluminum manufacture,* may have to be diverted from other, no less vital economic tasks.

The making of substitutes may frequently divert valuable reserves of labor, consume inordinately large amounts of domestic raw materials, create new import requirements, and thus open at least as many breaches in the battlements of self-sufficiency as it was supposed to close. On this score Ger-

* Robert Mossé, "Aluminum—A World Industry," *World Economics*, Vol. II, Nos. 5-6.

many furnishes—as always in this problematic field of endeavor—instructive object lessons. The stupendous consumption of crude coal by Germany's synthetic gasoline and rubber plants embarrassed not only shivering householders but also important defense industries at home as well as in satellite and conquered countries—and that in spite of the fact that Germany was the world's second largest producer of coal! In addition, these plants constituted an additional drain on Germany's scarcest resource, manpower.*

Individual substitutes are unlikely to create such dislocations, yet a substitute economy on a large scale cannot fail to do so. There is no way to make a poor country rich by the miracle of substitution. At best it may eliminate single critical shortages.

Thirdly, there are materials for which no substitutes can be found and which, on the contrary, are themselves the foundation of substitute economy. The most important of these materials are, of course, coal and iron. Unless a country has a supply of both, no substitute economy will increase its power by one iota. And unless a country is abundantly endowed at least with coal, it cannot even set up a real working substitute economy.

Oil, too, is not as easily replaced by synthetics as the "alchemists" may wish. It is not yet practical to produce lubricating oil synthetically, or to transform light natural oils into good lubricating oils. It is possible to retrieve a considerable amount of lubricating oil after it has been used. The used oil can be cleaned and used again. However, loss occurs and therefore this process cannot be repeated indefinitely.

Fourthly, countries in need of substitutes are usually not rich enough to afford vast investments in huge industries which cannot produce cheaply enough to compete in peacetime with the natural product, and which thus must be kept idle on government subsidy until an emergency arrives.

Yet on a limited scale, possibly by accepting minor quality in a small number of goods and restricting substitute produc-

* For a terse discussion of the raw-material and substitute problem in war economies see S. T. Possony, *Tomorrow's War*, London, 1938, pp. 151-172, perhaps the most prescient writing on this topic published in the interwar period.

tion to areas where particularly critical shortages exist, countries endowed with large raw-material resources may make up for certain deficiencies in raw materials, replace some minerals by others, and shift manpower resources to employment in industries which, were they not favored by tariffs and government subsidies, could not operate at a profit. The over-all result of the international pursuit of *ersatz* economics has been to render the great military powers less, not more, dependent on raw-material imports. The prospects are dim that they will, in peacetime, abandon their substitute industries, new and old, just because costs compare unfavorably with prices in world markets.

One alternative to substitution proposed by certain military and economic experts is stock piling. This proposal particularly envisages stocks of scarce minerals. It is argued that in the United States stimulation of submarginal production (which was one means for obtaining in wartime such critical items as mercury and tungsten from domestic sources) diverted scarce manpower and equipment from other sectors of the war economy. Moreover, some of the mineral resources of the United States are already beginning to show the effects of the drain upon them.* Although accumulated stocks at the end of the war may be large enough for peacetime purposes, there is no assurance that they will be large enough to meet the demands of another war.†

Stock-piling proposals are fraught with the difficulty of distinguishing between future military necessities and pro-

* For a concise statement of the pessimistic view see Lee Hager's *Too Many People in the World,* Houston, 1943, p. 15-17. "At the present rate of consumption our copper deposits will last, along with the gold, silver, lead, and zinc which they carry as by-products, not longer than twenty-eight years. . . . Our main reserves of high-grade manganese will be used up within twelve years. . . . If worked to capacity our own reserves of tungsten, chromium and vanadium will be exhausted within a few years."

† "The United States is passing from a country of plenty to a country of scarcity in the field of minerals and other essential supplies. We are moving toward an economic position similar to that in which England has found herself, that of having to depend on imports of material from abroad to maintain her very existence. . . . A few of our soundest thinkers propose that the United States take in as much as possible of foreign metals, minerals, oil, and other materials and thenceforth use as little as possible of our own precious remaining supplies."—William L. Batt, in an address to the Bond Club of New York City, February 23, 1944.

ducers' anxiety over market stability in peacetime. It is suggested that military authorities determine minimum goals for certain items presumed to be essential in another war and unavailable in the future within the United States. However, the task of planning such strategic stock piles involves a good deal of guessing, both military and geological. Moreover, there is always the possibility that a stock-piling program will degenerate into a permanent means of subsidizing high-cost producers. Were this to happen, military security would not be served appreciably, and the public in general would have to foot the bill. This is not to say that strategic stock piles will not have to be maintained. But funds required for a large-scale program may yield better returns to the nation if they are applied to research in laboratories, to improving and securing communication with foreign centers of production, and to the development of better techniques for exploiting as well as conserving domestic resources.

In summary, we may say that the United States and Russia are as close to self-sufficiency in all vital materials as any power may approach to that ideal state. The most important item which the economy of both countries lacks, and for which alternatives may have to be adopted permanently, is natural rubber. Both countries will maintain and strengthen facilities for making the synthetic product. Britain, more likely than not, will expand the production of synthetic gasoline. All powers will continue to experiment assiduously in alternative uses of light metals and alloys.

11. HEARTLANDS OF HEAVY INDUSTRY

HOW "accessibility" to raw materials bears upon the world's industrial pattern is clear from even the crudest kind of world map. The workings of this influence on the location of individual industries within the important manufacturing nations is far less obvious. Other major factors—accessibility to labor supply, markets, power and fuel—join in determining the sites of industrial enterprise. These factors act upon each other and are modified in turn by a host of social and political forces. The problem of plant location thus resembles a problem in the resultant of forces. Rarely is the location of an industry or even of a single plant determined by one factor alone. Some of the most important concentrations of population and industry are situated in areas which are physically close to neither agricultural nor mineral resources; they are located where the influences of a variety of factors converge. The steel plants along the Great Lakes are not close to coal nor to iron ore. They were placed at the crossroads of lowest total costs, namely where raw materials could be married most advantageously to ample labor supply and important markets.

Coal is the most bulky and most important raw material, hence many sites of heavy industries are close to large coal mines. Iron being the second raw material in weight and importance, industries tend to seek the vicinity of iron-ore deposits. The ideal location of heavy industry would, theoretically, be there where both raw materials can be united with the least transport costs. There are of course exceptions to this rule. Industry may move to cheap labor, particularly when transport costs have been reduced and wages play an increasingly important role in general costs. Industry may also move close to the consumer and it may move away from strategically dangerous places. No inexorable economic law bars countries poor in coal and iron from equipping themselves with heavy industry. By using water transportation they may in fact be more advantageously located than a country possessing large deposits, accessible, however, only by long overland routes. Yet in time of war they may be cut off from their resources to the detriment of their military security. Such countries cannot afford a truly independent foreign policy since they are always compelled, either by their own military interests or by foreign pressure, to ally themselves to countries which control their maritime communications and are willing to supply in wartime the necessary materials.

The pull of the position factors varies from industry to industry and from plant to plant within each industry. Cheaper and more diversified means of transportation, cheaper and more efficiently transmitted electrical power, tend to decentralize industry. However, this trend is most conspicuous *within* the larger areas of concentration and does not greatly alter the international balance of economic power. Within the national economy, the relation between accessibility to raw materials and other position factors is a highly complex one under any circumstances. Generalizations upon this topic are even less meaningful when "accessibility" becomes an issue of international politics.

The history of the great heavy metal industries is that of the three great steel-making centers of the globe, northeastern United States, northwestern Europe, and England. To these have been added in recent times Russia's Donets basin in Europe and the Magnitogorsk-Kuznetsk combine in Asia, the Japanese-Manchurian combination, and the steel plants of northwestern India.

Throughout the vast regions of Africa, Central and South America, Australia, and the Middle East, production of steel is insignificant. Their total output of coal and iron ore probably does not exceed 2 per cent of world production. It ranges between zero and fractions of one per cent for individual regions. If any one of these regions is to become a prime source of political and military power, this will have to result from material factors other than those associated with the coal-iron complex. In this respect no substantial change need be expected within the period selected by this inquiry, i.e., between 1945 and 1970. Because coal- and iron-using industries require stupendous masses of raw materials, huge transportation facilities, and vast plant, there is little scope for improvisation, no matter how ardently it may be desired in the interest of national self-sufficiency and power. It is in the light of these considerations that divers aspirations to national and political greatness should be tested.

The interdependence of their steel industries upon raw materials has been one of the most powerful and consistent factors affecting the economic and military policies of Britain, France, and Germany. That interdependence must be taken as a concrete fact inherent in geological conditions; it was not the result of entrepreneurial or political conspiracies. It remained comparatively unaffected by changes in the foreign policies and political regimes of the three countries. Britain and Germany imported the iron ore produced in metropolitan France and French North Africa because of its convenient location and properties, in short, because it was the cheapest raw material suited for the kind of plants Britain and Germany had built. For the same reason France purchased British and German coal and Germany and Britain swapped special types of coal.

While in international trade British, French, and German steel firms sought to obtain as much profitable business as they could garner individually, that competition was far from "free." It was hedged by a complicated system of purchasing and selling agreements. Although as a rule these were not intended for the benefit of the consuming public and were motivated by the crude desire for the biggest profits, these arrangements reveal only one aspect, though an important one, of the practices and ethics of the European steel business. Obviously, under ideal conditions of free trade the interdependence of the British-French-German steel economy could have been its virtue. As it was, political and military considerations impinged on its rational organization. Moreover, the area upon which the currents of raw-material exchanges converged, i.e., the triangle formed by the Ruhr valley–Briey basin–Seine estuary, is the historical battle zone of western Europe. It is generally overlooked how fatefully the historical interests of Germany, Great Britain, and France in the strategic geography of Europe were reinforced by the geologically conditioned characteristics of their respective raw-material positions. European frontier arrangements carried forward the politics of the stagecoach-canal age into the era of railroad and motor transportation. National antagonisms kept divided a region which nature seems to have intended as an economic unity.

It is against the anachronism of political frontiers that such proposals as that advanced by Field Marshal Smuts must be assessed. The South African leader, in his celebrated speech of November 25, 1943, called for closer collaboration between Britain and the states of western Europe. His observations were widely interpreted as a sober acknowledgment of the decline of British power vis-à-vis the United States and Russia. He outlined a compact—perhaps to be formalized by a federal constitution—between the European powers of the Atlantic rim which would join not only their European homelands but also their colonial empires into one powerful bloc.

Compelling economic arguments support the Smuts proposal—which, incidentally, comes in the right line of descent from Mr. Churchill's offer to France, on the eve of her surrender in 1940, of political union with Britain. The merging of the political sovereignties of Britain, France, Belgium, the Netherlands, and Luxembourg would be the first step toward a rational integration of the mining and steel industries of western Europe. In 1937 their combined output of coal was 332 million tons, of iron ore 61 million, and of steel ingots and castings 28 million—figures which were surpassed only by those for the United States and which substantially exceeded those for Germany and Russia. The Smuts proposal implies also the integration of African mineral wealth with the industrial capacity of western Europe. The manganese of South Africa and the Gold Coast and the chromium of northern Rhodesia tie in with the alloy requirements of the European sector.

Against this scheme and similar proposals are arrayed not only complex technical problems but also powerful political and economic interests which stand to lose heavily by a metamorphosis of ancient and less ancient sovereignties into a larger statehood, to say nothing of deep-rooted popular senti-

ments. Nevertheless the proposal of the non-European statesman for shoring up the power of western Europe cannot be
written off as a mere trial balloon. A Belgian cabinet minister
endorsed it warmly. Negotiations for a customs union between Belgium, Holland, and Luxembourg, which expressly
left open a door for French participation, recognized implicitly the weight of the Field Marshal's argument.

Because the position factors of heavy industry are imper-
vious to mere arguments, consideration of a consolidation of
western Europe cannot be divorced from the question of
what disposal is to be made of the coal fields and steel plants
along the lower Rhine valley. The Ruhr district is the core
of German heavy industry based on coal. Without it Germany may remain an important manufacturing and trading
nation, but ceases to be a first-class industrial and military
power. The future of the Ruhr district is essentially not a
German but a European problem.

Conceivably Germany can exist without heavy industry;
the heavy industry of the Ruhr valley cannot exist without
Germany unless its trade is given a radically new orientation.
There are the alternatives of razing the plants and gutting
the mines. This measure, however, would not solve the problems of the coal-iron economy of France, Britain, Belgium,
Holland, and Luxembourg, each country having a substantial stake, either as customer or purveyor, in the economic
life of the Ruhr district. It is a foregone conclusion that its
control will not be left to Germany. It is proposed to "inter-
nationalize" it. Whatever measures may be taken to that end
will principally affect ownership, management, nature of
goods produced, and allocation of markets; they cannot substantially alter the pattern of raw-material exchanges. In that
respect the Ruhr has always been "internationalized," for it
is an integral part of the iron-coal complex of western Europe.

The production of Ruhr industry, which, of course, com-
prises many kinds of industries aside from coal mining and
steel making, can be directed toward the rehabilitation of the
countries devastated by German aggression. It is the largest
European workshop suited for industrial reparations in kind.
There are many excellent reasons why it should not be
turned back to German political control for many decades, if

ever. But there is no means, barring total destruction, for rendering it politically and strategically neutral. In the nature of things, its industrial potential accrues to the industrial potential of the region, i.e., western Europe, and the kind of political controls which will govern the relationships of the regional powers, principally those of France and Britain, will determine the political and strategical control of the Ruhr. This contention is borne out, if only negatively, by Anglo-French relations in 1923.*

The task of reconstruction facing all west European peoples to roughly the same degree furnishes a powerful incentive to the rational integration of their heavy industries into one system. Were it to be organized along the lines of functional interdependence, its joint productive capacity would, by all the laws of economic probability, exceed the aggregate of individual national outputs. Suffice it to say that in 1937 the total of steel ingots and castings produced within the narrow quadrangle Sheffield-Birmingham-Briey-Essen, 400 miles in length and 200 miles in width, was approximately 47 million tons—more than one-third of world production and only slightly less than the output of the United States. The foundations of this productive capacity are the unlimited coal reserves of England, Belgium, and Westphalia, and the 8 billion tons of iron-ore reserves of Yorkshire, the Lorraine, and Luxembourg. Were these resources housed under one political roof, they could supply the broadest base for military power in Europe and the most solid guarantee against the resurgence of an aggressive Germany in the short, middle, and long run.

The manpower balance in Europe, it has been argued in a previous chapter, is moving inexorably against Germany.

* British dissatisfaction with French policies stiffened into sharp resistance when French troops, dispatched by Premier Raymond Poincaré, occupied, in 1923, the Ruhr district. France occupied the major German coal and steel center avowedly as a punitive measure in retaliation for German dilatory tactics in fulfilling the obligations of the peace treaty. Had it been extended over a long period of time, French control of the Ruhr would undoubtedly have made German rearmament impossible. It would, too, have resulted in a *de facto* marriage of German coal and French iron under the same political control. It was British pressure which forced what now seems to have been the premature withdrawal of French troops. See Arnold Wolfers, *Britain and France between Two Wars*, New York, 1940, pp. 58 and 77.

A Germany minus the Ruhr cannot retain her status as a Great Power no matter what political regime she chooses or finds chosen for her. Conversely, control of the Ruhr district conveys to whomever wields it a large measure of control over German economy. The plant of residual Germany will be as elaborate as the supply of tools that only heavy industry can make is abundant.

This is not to exaggerate the importance of one among several industrial districts. German industries were well distributed geographically before considerations of air warfare suggested even wider decentralization and dispersion of plants. Moreover, other resources remain open to Germany. For example, several million tons of iron ore can be extracted annually, though at a prohibitive cost, from low-grade deposits located in the Siegerland. Large deposits of iron ore are found in Silesia. The ore, however, contains much silicic acid, and its use for steel making will require the development of a process which gives every indication of being very costly. Germany may increase production from rich seams of bituminous coal in upper Silesia and Saxony—provided these are left in her possession. But these fragmentary resources do not add up to magnitudes upon which a large heavy industry can be built.

No cautious estimate of Germany's future industrial potential will neglect the resourcefulness of her engineers and chemists. They, as all engineers and chemists worth their salt, will seek substitutes for scarce raw materials. However, German techniques of substitution were themselves closely allied with the techniques of heavy industry; coal was the mainstay of German manufacture of "synthetic" gasoline and rubber. Before World War II, out of Germany's 300 major coal mines, 250 were crowded in the Ruhr area.

It was industrial superiority resting upon a unique combination of manpower, skills, and raw materials which enabled Germany to extend her economic and political sway over eastern and southeastern Europe. Her influence was powerfully abetted by the dismemberment of the Austro-Hungarian Empire. The heavy industries of Czechoslovakia and Austria, notable for the quality of their products rather than the quantity of their output, had been complementary.

When the Austrian Empire dissolved, it left the Danubian basin economically divided and unable to compete with German industry, which remained intact. Consequently, the Danubian sector was powerless to cope with the totalitarian trade policy of Nazi Germany, the divide-and-rule technique of bilateralism.

The dissolution of Germany's industrial empire will create, at least for a prolonged period of transition, an economic void which no industrial capacity now existing in eastern Europe this side of the Russian border can fill. Heavy industry and its raw-material base are not subject to facile improvisations. The restoration of east European economy cannot be accomplished without accelerated industrial development and rationalization of agriculture, which itself is an aspect of industrialization. The problem concerns the fate of more than 100 million people, rapidly increasing—one and one-half the number of Germans who will presumably continue to live in the more or less deindustrialized Reich of the future.

To break up German industrial concentration will create a condition favorable for the amalgamation of west European economies based on heavy industry; it settles the German question as it has been put in two World Wars. It does not answer as a matter of course the question of the economic future of eastern Europe. It is this, not the German question, which poses the future problem of Europe.

The heavy industry of Japan is a highly synthetic and none too robust product. Its core is the productive capacity of the home islands; its outer layer consists of a motley system of mining and manufacturing facilities on the Asiatic mainland. Japan proper has neither coal nor iron enough to support her steel-making capacity. Up to 1932, Yawata Steel Works in Kyushu produced three-quarters of Japan's pig iron and half her steel. Their capacity, it is believed, is still twice that of the Showa works in Manchuria. According to a Japanese release, "the great blast furnaces in Manchuria, North China, and Korea, which are operated day and night are a true symbol of Japan's heavy industry," but "the hub of the iron and steel works on the Continent is in Manchuria." * However,

* *Japan-Manchukuo Year Book 1940*, p. 756.

another authority states that by 1942, Manchurian pig-iron production concentrated in the Showa Steel Works at An-shan, and of the Penhsihu Iron Works, had risen "nearly" 200 per cent over 1938 production, which had previously been reported as 762,000 tons.* These figures, if accurate, would indicate a total production in 1942 of well below 2.5 million tons. And again the same Japanese source, which cannot be charged with treasonable lack of enthusiasm, admits that "there are, however, handicaps for these iron and steel industries: the shortage of bituminous coal is very acute and for the better grade of iron ore they are dependent on imports."

When the Japanese have been ejected from the Asiatic mainland, vital questions will have to be answered: Who will control, finance, and manage the economic development of the liberated areas? Will China—Kuomintang, Communist, and treaty China—and Manchuria and Korea form one political unit? If that condition obtains, the development of a large heavy industry, basis of state power, will still be fraught with immense difficulties; if it does not, it is hard to see how heavy industry is to be developed at all.

So far Japan has supplied the managerial and technological personnel of industrial production in north China, Man-churia, and Korea. Japanese industrial management is, by Western standards, mediocre. However, Japanese managers and engineers will have to be replaced by native talent or, if that is not adequately forthcoming, by foreigners. The development of new plant and the ironing out of peculiar technical difficulties such as lack of sufficient coking coal and treatment of low-grade iron ores requires large and continuous capital outlays. The elimination of Japan will create a financial void which, after a long and destructive war, neither China nor, for that matter, any other Asiatic power, can fill.

The future development of Far Eastern industry will be determined largely by the degree of political and economic integration which the peace settlement will have wrought. Only in Manchuria, northern Korea, and, to a lesser extent,

* "Progress of Blast Furnace Operations," *Asahi Shimbun,* January 9, 1944.

in Kiangsu (Shanghai) do conditions permitting the development of heavy industry exist. An independent Manchuria and an independent Korea may constitute the least viable solution of China's economic problem. Political fragmentation may preclude altogether the rational exploitation of the resources with which nature has none too generously endowed the Yellow Sea region.

Not even the most ambitious expansion projects of the Japanese, whose imagination runs to bigness, envisaged for the "Co-Prosperity Zone" a steel-making capacity as large as the German or British, not to speak of the American or Russian. No effort, however prodigious, can within the next twenty or thirty years transform the Far Eastern region into a center of heavy industry rivaling the capacity of these giants. Moreover, other powers will not stand still, and the Far East faces the problem of bettering its position in respect to absolute production and output per head. Locally available resources are totally inadequate for raising per capita production to the levels already attained by the older centers of industrialization.

The Far East, especially China proper, possesses a wealth of exportable nonferrous metals such as tungsten, antimony, and tin. Limestone, salt, clay, magnesite, bauxite, and other nonmetallic minerals provide, together with ample water power, the rudiments for the creation of light industries. Their products will find a broader market as the standard of living of the masses rises. It is, however, the low level of living now prevailing which stands in the way of large-scale industrialization. The vicious circle can be broken only by the intervention of foreign capital and technical assistance. Its corollary is expanding foreign trade. In this respect, an economic quarantine of Japan will not redound to the benefit of the region as a whole.*

If what is left of the managerial and technical resources of a defeated and purged Japan were made to serve the interests

* This conviction is emphatically stated by an Indian statesman: "No scheme which permanently excludes Japan from these areas will have the least chance of success, and it is necessary to emphasize that fact and keep it in mind when discussing any problem connected with Eastern Asia." K. M. Panikkar, *The Future of South East Asia*, issued under the auspices of the Institute of Pacific Relations, New York, 1943, p. 110.

of all the peoples of the Far East, it would lessen their dependence on others. It would still not emancipate them from foreign controls, however remotely and sympathetically applied.

The inequalities of nature slate the Far East for a secondary role in the making of world politics. It will not generate power-political impulses. The forces of world politics will, as they did in the past century, converge upon it. With the eclipse of Japan the Far East is again wide open to the penetration of extraregional influences. These may work a fruitful union of Western techniques with Eastern culture to the lasting benefit of all peoples. Nevertheless, the initiative will be foreign.

While the fact is generally accepted that China does not now fill that role of a Great Power which is formally accorded her by her allies, it is widely assumed or hoped that she will do so in the future, and that she will be stronger in peace than she was in war. Indeed, with the defeat of Japan, China will be the foremost power of the Far East. Yet regional power has a mere token value of world politics.

The rising industrial centers of Soviet Asia are bound to exert a strong pull upon the Far East, politically as well as economically. The strategic interests of Russia in Sinkiang and Outer Mongolia are reinforced by the proximity of the Siberian centers of heavy industry. It is difficult to see how the economic development of these remote borderlands of China can be accomplished without Russian technical and commercial collaboration. The attraction of Russian markets, technical standards, and ways of living is bound to affect Chinese Turkestan far more profoundly than will the future development of the Far Eastern monsoon region thousands of miles away. Similarly, the economic fortunes of Indo-China, Thailand, and Burma, countries which are China's "debated ground" to the southwest, will be more intimately related to those of India as that country unfolds its vast industrial potentialities.

Already at the Bretton Woods World Monetary Conference, Indian representatives pressed for the unfreezing of Indian blocked accounts in Britain and their liquidation through shipments of capital goods, especially heavy industrial machinery. The expansion of Indian heavy industry will proceed as fast or as slowly as special equipment is obtained from foreign makers, native labor is trained, and domestic and export markets are developed. The difficulties a growing Indian heavy industry will have to cope with in the future are large and numerous, but they are not inherent in the "natural" setting. Some of these difficulties were discussed on preceding pages; they are not so much economical and technological as political and cultural. They cannot be separated neatly from each other. They are aspects of one and the same process, as is illustrated by the case history of industrialization in Japan.

Industrialization is perhaps the most potent argument for the political unity of India. It has been pointed out that the division of India into two states, Moslem Pakistan and Hindu Hindustan, would leave the principal coal, iron-ore, and manganese deposits and steel-making centers in the possession of the latter.* Doubtless Moslem-Hindu rivalry is no mere divide-and-rule figment of British imperialist imagination. The conflict is real enough. However, Hindu-Moslem strife cannot change the distribution of India's mineral wealth. Neither side can be entirely blind to the fact that the Pakistan-Hindustan project is a scheme for destroying the economic unity of the country.

Indian industrialization is still in its infancy. Only 3 million Indians, less than 1 per cent of the whole population, are employed in industry.† However, India possesses the raw materials, the core of technological skills, the manpower, and the administrative organization required for large-scale expansion of heavy industry. The war against Japan has forced the growth of armament production in India; Indian manufacturers and workmen are learning rapidly the art of making modern weapons; and Indian troops have learned to use them. The creation of an industrial base of political and military power in southeast Asia is not a matter for future speculation; it is being accomplished under one's eyes. It has quickened the imagination of Indian nationalists, who now

* C. H. Behre, Jr., *op cit.*
† *Statistical Abstract for British India*, Vol. 18, Delhi, 1942, pp. 605 and 617.

contemplate—beyond the attainment of national independence—the global responsibilities of India as a Great Power. "If, as seems clear," K. M. Panikkar writes, "the permanency of the effective defence of [southeast Asia] can only be organized from India, then a free and stable government in that country, willing and capable to undertake these responsibilities, based on the necessary military, naval and air power, and industrial potential, becomes a matter of vital international importance."

In summary, the growth of large-scale heavy industry depends on a great many factors "occurring uniquely together." That unique concurrence is given only in a small number of regions. Their surface area is minute compared to the total land masses of the globe. While there are very few places where natural conditions favor the development of heavy industry, a heavy industry in being exists in even fewer places. At present the United States possesses the greatest and most highly differentiated plant capable of mass production. In addition to the United States, only the countries of western and central Europe can be considered truly industrialized. Due to political division, these countries have developed mass production only on a limited scale. There is in Europe no equivalent for the standard-made American truck, tractor, merchant ship, and many other items which American industry produces cheaply, serviceably, and in huge quantities. On the other hand, political division has fostered in Europe a large number of industrial establishments of a more varied character.

The integration of the west European coal-iron complex under one roof—federation or customs bloc—would be a mighty step forward toward a more rational division of labor and toward consolidation of an industrial system second only to that of the United States in capacity to produce.

The problem of meshing west European industry into one efficient system is inseparable from the problem of the Ruhr district. Ruhr coal mines and steel mills powered Germany's drive for European domination. History is taking care of one half of the German problem. With a minimum of common sense Great Britain, France, Russia, and the United States can take care of the other half. A west European condominium over the Ruhr district will not be a bed of roses for Britain, France, Belgium, and Holland. The syndrome of German nationalism defies quick and easy treatment. The guardians of the Ruhr will not be able to foresee and prepare solutions for all the problems they will encounter. But any peace arrangement which leaves Germany in possession of the Ruhr or of any other major coal- and iron-producing district leaves Germany the power to make war.

The Soviet Union has built a heavy industry solidly based on unlimited mineral resources, notably coal, iron ore, and manganese. Measured by American production records, Russian heavy industry has still a long way to go. However, by virtue of its size and population, compact area and uniform market, the Soviet Union appears headed for the adoption of mass-production methods on a truly New World scale. Despite celebrated pioneering feats in Soviet Asia, the geographical center of gravity appears, for the foreseeable future, fixed in Europe. The development of a powerful heavy industry in Siberia and the Soviet Far East might be retarded by the immediate and pressing needs of European Russia. The bulk of new investment will have to be allocated, for many years to come, to the rehabilitation and improvement of plants west of the Urals. Siberia's transportation problems are far from solved; markets are remote; and the labor force cannot be expanded indefinitely by directed migration. If the cost problem is at all taken into consideration—and Soviet economists aver that it governs socialist economic policies— then the industrial development of European Russia will for a long time overshadow that of Siberia. No one can say now whether by 1970 Russian industry will have reached those goals which Soviet leaders envision as within the grasp of socialist enterprise, to wit, the greatest output in the world. By the nature of international raw-material distribution and population dynamics, if any country can beat American production records, it can only be Russia.

India is Asia's industrial powerhouse of tomorrow. Political and religious strife may retard India's industrial growth; it cannot prevent it for long. The analogies of an industrializing Russia and a westernizing Japan may not fit India in all respects because historical analogies never do. None the less, they suggest caution in accepting rash verdicts on the limitations providence imposes on Indian intelligence and enterprise. The great mineral wealth and manpower reserves of India contain a tremendous "kick" which may, much sooner than now seems likely, precipitate Indian heavy industry into booming expansion.

The Yellow Sea region is the fifth major world region of heavy industry. Because of inadequate raw-material deposits and capital resources its potentialities are limited. In one respect the problem of the Far East resembles that of western Europe on the opposite end of the Eurasian mainland: Political fragmentation inhibits the rational utilization of natural resources. Under the most auspicious circumstances—a united domestic economy and generous foreign assistance—the Far East could develop in twenty to thirty years a heavy industry of a size comparable, let us say, to that of France. It will not be large enough to support political and military power of global scope.

Part Four

ORGANIZATION AND POWER

12. ECONOMICS OF PROGRESS

MANPOWER and raw materials are the crude indices of national strength. Population supplies the animate force; large reserves of raw materials are the elementary prerequisites of heavy industry and hence of genuine military power. Organization, political, economic, and military, transforms these elements of power into world-political realities. Manpower and raw materials are, within limits, measurable. Forecasts based on them are subject to some degree of scientific control. What of organization, the actual use to which these basic factors of power may be put? For organization is just as truly power as is the possession of raw materials.

The predominant tendency of our age is industrialization and world-wide spread of mass-production techniques. How this trend bears upon political and military power is clearly revealed by the rapid expansion of the German, Japanese, Russian, and American war potentials, each accomplished within a few years in the face of different, but equally formidable, restrictions. Each involved enormous concentration of manpower, raw materials, and machines, to be sure. But it was the ability of these countries to organize their whole economies for war that constituted their power. Potential output, not weapons-in-being, was the true measure of their military strength. Manpower organized, technical skills, facility in acquiring new ones, ability to marshal and train large reserves, skill in applying large effectives of men and machines strategically are the characteristic power factors of our age. Thus viewed, quantity and quality are the basic elements of power. Within limits quantity may make up for deficiencies in quality and vice versa. But if either of these basic factors shrinks too far in relation to the other, the net result is absolute loss of power.

As quantity diminishes, quality must increase in order to maintain the balance of power. In terms of technology this means that any economy faced with a relatively diminishing stock of quantitative factors must improve technologically or suffer relative loss of power. And a superior technology, be it remembered, is not merely the result of inventiveness or of the large number of the inventors living in one country, but of the country's entire economic and industrial structure, of which invention is an essential element. Technical superiority reflects a country's scientific institutions, general political conditions, and the absence of restrictions. It is a function of the entire economy.

What then is the relation of technology to an economy in transition? What in particular is the relation of the superior technologies of the Western powers to economies that seem to be changing under our eyes? Judged exclusively from the point of view of power, technology and economy in transition are variable factors whose importance ranks easily with that of manpower or raw materials.

The two World Wars of the twentieth century and the intervening armistice must be regarded as phases in the major revolution which is transforming the pattern of civilized society. This process is widely regarded as the transition from a capitalistic economy to an economy either controlled or directly operated by the collectivity. Now it is not necessary for students of power to ask themselves whether or not they agree with those who regard these economic changes as inevitable. What inevitability there is in human history has been put there by historians. Yet it is altogether undeniable that all trends in the recent past have been toward a greater degree of governmental control, in one form or another, of the actual workings of the major economic systems of the world. That these trends will continue, at least for the near future, seems an equally inescapable conclusion. Therefore, the study of the effects of such trends on power relationships is well within the scope of this inquiry.

It is not necessary to argue here that capitalist economy is a recessive form and will be succeeded by other forms of economic organization, however cogent may be the evidence pointing to that conclusion. Nor, by anything discernible in the present world trends, need we subscribe wholeheartedly to the prediction that the state will reach out its power of direction into every sphere of the community's activity and that "in all countries the process is in its general direction irreversible, because it is the inevitable consequence of modern technical conditions." * But to rule these possibilities out in advance, and to construct a study of power relations on the assumption that they may be blithely disregarded, is to invite disaster. For on the assumption that they are true, or, indeed, even on the generally valid hypothesis that governmental control of economy will increase rather than diminish, we are faced with a power problem of utmost urgency. Technical progress, as we know it, is a function of a free economy. We must, therefore, consider the argument that technological advance has made inevitable the withering away of capitalist economy and the surrender of economic freedom to the state. The question is not whether the state will intervene in this or that sector of the national economy. From its earliest beginnings capitalism has been transformed continuously. It is not now, and it never was, the same thing in every country. At all times and everywhere, governments have intervened in the economic process. The issue today is not intervention but control. Only by central planning, it is said, can the problems of modern industrialization be dealt with efficiently. The validity of this assertion need be examined only in so far as it concerns the external power of the state, which includes the power to wage peace as well as war.

PROGRESS UNDER DECENTRALIZED PLANNING

Modern technology was developed within the framework of capitalist economy. The world's areas of greatest technological advance are also the areas of most highly developed capitalist economy, west-central Europe and North America. If this coincidence is merely accidental, then technological progress need not shorten its strides even though a new economic system takes the place of the old. The assumption, however, that this will happen rests upon a number of hypotheses which experience has not had time to verify. Before these assumptions, plausible as they may be, are made the basis of a prognosis of things to come, it is necessary to recall

* *Planning*, a broadsheet issued by PEP (Political and Economic Planning), London, No. 201, February 9, 1943.

what the dynamics of economic progress in capitalism in fact have been, not what they might have been or should be according to an untested theory of social evolution. The economic conditions under which, in general, capitalist economy was actually brought to its present position are the following:

1) There exist sufficient funds available in the hands of the entrepreneurs; banks are able to furnish credit, and individuals are willing to invest money in stocks or bonds. Not all of the goods produced are consumed. Savings flow into new investments as long as there is an opportunity for making profit.

2) Replacement of human labor by machinery is continuous. Hence funds flow into the capital goods industries. Production methods are being continuously improved or rationalized. Production tends toward increased differentiation and specialization. Mass production, in particular, is based on the subdivision of the product into its elemental parts, and subsequent assembly. The more specialized an industry is, the more easily will it lend itself to the introduction of mass-production methods. Increasing specialization fostered the "round-aboutness" of modern production. Specialization demands a high mobility of capital, as does the growth of new industries. The last factor is important from the military point of view because new industries furnish not only the peacetime market with new goods but also the military establishment with new weapons.

3) Specialization and differentiation foster decentralization even though factories within a certain industry may join in horizontal or vertical combination. Against this centrifugal tendency, implicit in technological progress, the co-ordinating principle is supplied by the market mechanism, i.e., competition. Within the framework of certain restrictions imposed by nature and society, competition plays freely in the internal market, as well as across political frontiers, unrestrained by prohibitive tariffs, trade monopolies, or quota systems. Cartels are not protected against foreign competition. The "goodness" and "badness" of combinations and cartels are known by their behavior under competition: Only those are "bad" which must be protected to keep alive. By the

same token, the test of effective competition is gain of additional customers abroad and lower prices which enable customers at home to buy more goods.

4) Despite these factors of freedom, the obstacles and frictions which impede the effective working of the market mechanism and which in particular cause cycles of depression are many. Economic life has never been free from state interference. Nonlogical motivations and actions impinge on the automatism of the market just as they distort any other rational social or political scheme. Even the most extreme liberalism reckoned with intervention by the state, in, for example, monetary and discount policies. The enactment of laws regulating the conditions of production, distribution, and consumption lies within the province of the state.

Another important cause of economic disequilibrium is the comparative immobility of labor as well as of capital. The importance of this factor was overlooked by most of the classical economists.* *Mobility is the essential prerequisite of working capitalism:* In the first place, labor must be mobile enough to shift from low income spheres to more profitable ones, from depressed areas to those with labor shortages, from unskilled to skilled occupations. A larger proportion of skilled labor reduces unemployment, because employers must introduce machinery into hitherto primitive production. This shift is not only of economic but also of military significance. For the modern soldier is a skilled mechanic, and machine-tool manufacture is militarily one of the most important branches of industry. Secondly, capital must be mobile enough to quit bad investments for investments in new production. It is within the province of the state to loosen capital, especially as regards the rate of depreciation of plant and equipment, and the accumulation of reserves. Reconversion is a permanent problem.

The interplay of these factors shows that in the last resort the market mechanism will function only when and so long as it is triggered by a sufficient number of able and confident entrepreneurs and a sufficient number of workers possessed of the requisite skills and available as labor reserve. While it

* It was not overlooked by Adam Smith, who wrote, "Of all the baggage on the face of the earth, mankind is the hardest to move."

177

is the function of the government in a capitalist economy to intervene against obstructions impeding the orderly functioning of the economic process, it cannot effectively replace entrepreneurs by officials. The decisions to produce how, what, and for whom, and to buy what, where, and for what purpose, remain those of the entrepreneur. The making of a framework within which these decisions are carried out is the task of the government. The regulatory powers of the government extend over currency, banking, interest rates, credit, taxation, modes of competition, and so forth. If the functions of state, entrepreneur, and market are thus divided, then the objective is to mitigate the extreme effects of economic cycles—not to abolish the market mechanism, but to maintain it. Economic crisis weeds out unprofitable, i.e., technologically backward, units of production. Therefore, abolishing the economic cycle would not enhance technological efficiency but embalm obsolescent enterprises. Then entrepreneur and labor are granted economic security in the *status quo,* instead of being helped in adapting themselves to changing conditions.

It becomes clear from the above that a changing and adaptable economy is the main condition of technological progress. Inventiveness cannot be transformed into technological progress as a matter of course. As long as expanding markets and competition impel change, "bottle necks of ideas" will not be formed. For under the rule of competition, the entrepreneur thrives only at lower costs and greater sales, and hence by constant improvement of production techniques. Neither lower costs nor bigger sales can be had without technological progress.

These are the primer facts about the conditions of technological *and* economic progress as we know them from the history of the major industrial countries.

We have noted that all of economic evolution is a process of substitution. Technological progress is among other things the replacement of manpower by machine power *with increasing total employment.* Technological progress involves technological unemployment under a capitalist system as well as under socialism or any other kind of planned economy. Every undergraduate student of economics knows that the making of labor-saving machines afforded more employment for capital and labor than their introduction had displaced, and that the problem of technological unemployment is one of mobility of capital and labor, i.e., the shift of factors of production from contracting to expanding trades. How this mobility is to be paid for is again a question which any economic system faces, be it capitalist or collectivist. The loss suffered by the displaced industry is as real as is the profit accruing to the industry exploiting the new invention. The worker laid off because a machine has taken his place cannot match, as a matter of course, the gain in new jobs which the making of that machine creates, against the very real loss of his old job and status.

We are not concerned, within the frame of reference of this inquiry, with this problem as a matter of social justice. Elementary economic logic dictates that the impact of technological innovations should be cushioned. The burden thus shifted to the community is eased in the long run by increased revenue from the expanding substitute industry, whether in the form of increased production, jobs, or taxes. This is the ideal case. Obviously, in real life, adjustments do not always work smoothly; there are time lags, inequities, and losses sustained by the individual and group which cannot be measured in economic terms only. But no one will argue that for this reason techniques should be used which are less effective economically, and which, while possibly mitigating temporary difficulties, engender permanent maladjustments and a regression of over-all productivity. In brief, the high degree of integration and interdependence technological advance has brought about requires just the kind of pragmatic foresight which the continuous rub of technological advance develops.

The national economy, faced as it is with the prospect of increased governmental control, must discover how to transform the system so as to preserve "play" between the component parts. It must decide how to maintain harmonious growth in the face of increasing technical specialization and differentiation. It must find room, in an economy increasingly given over to planning, for initiative, progressiveness, and, in a word, freedom. This problem is the problem of the relation of technological progress to power efficiency. For students of power, it is the very live and pressing paradox of "planning for freedom."

All conscious life is a continuity of planning. Every rational economic activity is planned. A business concern schedules production on the basis of detailed information. But this is not what in the semantics of economic planning is called planning. It is central planning, the direction of the economic process by government decree, which is deemed the alternative to economic planning by a multiplicity of individual enterprisers. This kind of planning prescribes what the economy shall produce and what the market shall take.

PROGRESS UNDER CENTRALIZED PLANNING COMPARED

War economy is planned economy. Thus it may seem that a planned, a "total" economy is more conducive to technological progress than is the un-co-ordinated "anarchic" market economy. This, indeed, the advocates of permanent economic planning argue, is the conclusion suggested by the apparent proliferation of human ingenuity under conditions of close regimentation. The line of reasoning, incidentally, is not new; it was, for example, systematically propounded as early as World War I by Walter Rathenau, chief of the German War Raw Materials Office and leading literary exponent of technocracy long before that term was coined. Has the history of World War II confirmed this theory? The evidence is, to say the least, inconclusive.

Germany entered World War II with an economy which was held, not only in Germany but also abroad, to be a model of efficient economic planning. British and American economy went to war unplanned. Moreover, neither Britain nor the United States had specialized in military technology. Germany avowedly had funneled her best engineering talent into the development of military techniques, and by virtue of a six- to eight-year head start, should have led the United States and Britain in military inventiveness and should have maintained that lead with comparative ease. Evidence for this is lacking. Indubitably, Germany excelled in devising certain secret weapons which were highly effective—as long as their tactical application was aided by the element of surprise.

Likewise, in what must be regarded as nonmilitary sciences, German inventors designed, and German factories produced, many new and valuable devices. But it remains to be proved that British and American technology was unable to match new German weapons with new counterweapons, that British and American chemical industries were unable to produce drugs as potent in the treatment of injuries and cure of disease as those developed by the Germans. In short, it would have to be proved that British and American brains and enterprise, so sadly lacking in centralized direction until the outbreak of war, could not have drawn level with, and surpassed, German *"gleichgeschaltete"* science and production. The only conclusive proof of this would be for Britain and the United States to have lost the war.

Another aspect of the question requires emphasis. Germany, Great Britain, and the United States entered, in that chronological order, the race of war technology. These three powers have produced the bulk of the new devices which have revolutionized modern warfare. Other nations have exercised their ingenuity with distinction, but the majority of new inventions in land, naval, and air warfare were either made or adapted to mass production by these three leading industrial powers. Their contributions to the technology of war are distinguished by certain features shaped by geographical and economic environment.

Distribution problems inherent in United States geography and a huge internal market have channeled American inventiveness into fields other than those upon which British and continental European technology has concentrated. American techniques of mass manufacture, road building, railway engineering, transportation, packaging, etc., have set the standard for the world and have been adopted eagerly by other nations. On the other hand, German chemical industry is, in part at least, a product of weakness inherent in the German raw-material and trading position. It is this weakness which has focused German attention upon the procurement of raw-material substitutes. Some of the best processes for the manufacture of new materials now used in this country and abroad are of German origin. The growing competition of industrial nations in world markets has shifted many sections of Britain's old-established engineering industry from mass articles to high-quality goods. The outstanding performance of British aviation engines and electrical devices is largely the result of a functional determinism based on geographic as well as economic factors.

Few of the radically new devices introduced in World War II appear to have originated in the United States. In ordnance, the Germans lead in the development of the dual-purpose gun of high muzzle velocity and the rocket. The Germans, and the British too, scored in designing jet-propelled planes. German and British laboratories appear to have developed new uses for plastics in military equipment. Gyroscopic controls and the pilotless plane are products chiefly of European research. The heavy, highly mobile, thickly armored tank has originated in German and British arsenals. By contrast, American war technology excelled in the mass output of a great variety of weapons and in solving logistic problems. While it is much too early to assess certain controversial issues, it can be said that on the whole the quantitative superiority of American matériel, supplied by a unique system of mass manufacture, and mastery of the science of logistics have proven decisive factors in American strategy. Conversely, the pinch of quantitative shortages has directed British and German inventiveness toward radically new solutions. Significantly, the *furor technicus* generated by the Soviet Union strives toward size and mass, while the Continental types and certain common features of physical geography make American machinery more suitable than British and German for Russian use.*

American power is based on the direct adaptation of mass-production and mass-construction devices to war uses. It is nourished by an unparalleled plenitude of resources and a high average of skills. By contrast, the drive behind British and, to an even greater extent, German inventiveness is triggered by the necessity for stretching inadequately supplied natural resources, and the pressure of international competition. This national distinctiveness should not be stressed unduly. American, British, and German inventiveness overlap in countless fields.†

* *Economic Bulletin on the Soviet Union*, Russian Economic Institute, New York, Vol. I, No. 1., December, 1944.
† See page 283, Note 1 to Chapter 12.

Nationalist propaganda extols the contributions of a nation's great men of science and industry and readily claims this or that discovery as a "first." Wartime secrecy, too, beclouds the pedigree of certain important inventions. Some of the most important discoveries in aerodynamics, electronics, and medical drugs were made simultaneously in several countries and represent the co-operative effort of scores of workers claimed by scores of nations. None the less, the position of the United States, Great Britain, and Germany is thus-far a commanding one. The superior technology and industrial strength of each have been developed within the framework of the capitalist system. That system, despite substantial modifications, has remained in force in the United States and Britain until now. That system too, though mutilated and distorted, was far from completely abolished in Nazi Germany. It is a matter of dispute how far in these three countries the forms of capitalist society have yielded to diverse etatist pressures. It cannot be a matter of controversy that the scientific and managerial personnel of each country is by education and social status rooted in the capitalist "way of life."

Do not Russia's achievements in technological progress challenge the claims of liberal economists? Do not her collectivized science and economy vie with the best the capitalist system has to give? The answer to both questions is no, so far as we can see.

Undoubtedly there are Russian scientists of international stature. Their contributions in physics, chemistry, biology, plant physiology, psychology, medicine, and mathematics are recorded in learned journals the world over. In military technology many new devices, such as the Stormovik plane and rocket-firing mortars, attest to the skill of Russian engineering. However, the vast majority of the great names of Russian science are borne by men of middle age and over. Virtually all the celebrities of Russian applied science were compelled, by force of circumstance, to obtain their early schooling in a prerevolutionary society; many are distinguished by plainly bourgeois antecedents. According to Harvey C. Lehman's exhaustive study, *Man's Most Creative Years*, the medium age of practical inventiveness lies in the neighborhood of forty. It is at that age that the 499 outstanding inventors of the last hundred years entered upon their most prolific periods.* Most Russian inventors do not appear to deviate from this pattern of age and creativeness and therefore can hardly be claimed as typical products of pure collectivism.

The intellectual and social conditions making for inventiveness are not easily measured statistically. Patents are not granted under uniform conditions everywhere, and the available statistics are incomplete. The United States, Great Britain, and Germany have published the number of patents granted annually; the Soviet Union has not. The table below shows the number of patents per million of inhabitants granted in the former three countries: †

	1938	1939	1940
Great Britain	429	396	444
United States	277	332	317
Germany	190	209	247

The patent law of the Soviet Union is unlike that of other countries. The inventor may ask for an author's certificate or a patent. Soviet statistics do not reveal the number either of certificates or of patents granted during the period of the Five Year Plans, presumably an era of high technological activity.‡ However, patents are high on the list of invisible exports, and the United States, Great Britain, and Germany derived in peacetime a sizable income through patents sold abroad. It must be assumed that the Soviet Union, too, would have sought to market abroad the products of its inventors, the more so since its policies called for increased holdings in foreign currency. However, the U.S. Patent Bureau lists in 1938 only one patent as having been issued to residents of the Soviet Union. In 1940 that number had risen to eight. The totals for Great Britain for those two years were 1,288 and 1,308 respectively; for Germany 2,480 and 2,595, which figures, incidentally, are far higher than those of any other country. France is fourth with 634 patents granted by the United States. Even Japan, with 57 U.S. patents in 1939 and

* *Scientific Monthly*, Vol. LIX, No. 5, November, 1944.

† This computation is based on figures furnished by the Secretariat of the Convention for the Protection of Industrial Property, Berne, Switzerland. The Soviet Union is not a member of the convention.

‡ A. Meyer, *The Patent and Trade Mark Laws in the U.S.S.R.*, Russian Economic Institute, New York, 1944, pp. 8-9.

44 in 1940, topped the Soviet Union. By contrast, the Soviet Union has been an eager buyer of foreign patents, having paid during the period of the first two Five Year Plans several millions of dollars to American patent holders.

It will not be claimed here that this is a conclusive test of technological creativeness. By far the most reliable yardstick for a nation's technological potential is economic progress as a whole—not progress in any one branch of engineering or industrial activity, but the advance along the entire front of national productivity.

PROGRESS AND NATIONAL INCOME

For any country, the only valid and complete measure of progressiveness is the national income—the annual value of goods and services available for consumption or investment. Tons of steel, car loadings, and kilowatt hours of electricity can give some sort of an indication even when expressed in percentage increases over a base period, although a wrong impression can easily be given by selection. By far the most significant yardstick of progress is national income. For improved productive processes will be reflected by a higher national income, i.e., a greater value of goods and services produced and available for consumption and investment.

The best data for national income are those compiled by Colin Clark in his *Conditions of Economic Progress*. They are expressed in International Units: one International Unit is the equivalent of the goods and services one dollar would have purchased in the United States over the average period 1925 to 1934. Because of World War II, data later than 1937 are not available for many countries. The data thus obtained show the general order of magnitude, but are subject to a rather large possibility of error. According to Clark's computations, the annual income per capita in the period 1925-34 was 541 for the United States, 477 for Great Britain, 274 for Germany, 101 for the Soviet Union, and 91 for Japan.*

* Real income produced per head of working population 1925-1934: U.S.A., 1,381; Great Britain, 1,069; Germany, 646; Japan, 353; U.S.S.R., 320. "In different parts of the world ratio of dependents to workers varies considerably

Clark distinguishes between primary, secondary, and tertiary production. Primary industry includes agriculture, fisheries, and forests. Secondary industry includes all types of industrial productivity, mining, building, and power plants. Tertiary production includes the value of all sorts of services which raise the standard of living without the actual production of new goods. Transportation, recreation, education, government services, hotels, garages, doctors, clergymen, and scientists are factors in tertiary production. The more prosperous a country is, the more it can afford to pay for such work. Many of these services increase the productivity of primary and secondary production, and improve diet and health. The percentage of population engaged in tertiary industries is, next to national income, perhaps the most important index of a country's standard of living and, because of the diversity of skills contained in this item, of a country's progressiveness. More important still, it is from the part of the population engaged in tertiary trades that are drawn many of the skills essential in the prosecution of modern war. In 1937 in the United States 45.8 per cent of the population was engaged in tertiary industries, in Britain 43 per cent, in Germany 37 per cent, in the Soviet Union 9 per cent, in Japan 27 per cent, in India 12 per cent.

Clark estimates income per capita of gainfully employed population as follows: 1,485 IU's for the United States; 1,275 for Great Britain; 406 for Japan; 379 for the Soviet Union; 200 for India; 100 to 120 for China. These are 1937 figures, and thus do not allow for increased income due to the normal rate of progress which up to World War II may have boosted workers' real incomes, nor for whatever rise in workers' real wages may have been produced by armament booms in the United States and Britain, nor for the expansion of Russian industry scheduled under the third Five Year Plan 1937-1942, nor, of course, for the destruction of plant by military action. None the less, as an order of magnitude, these figures are probably as revealing as any kind of compu-

and figures of average income produced per head give a misleading impression."—Colin Clark, *The Conditions of Economic Progress*, London, 1941, p. 32.

tation of such highly volatile relationships as national income differentials.*

More significant than a comparison based on an arbitrarily selected year is a comparison of rates of growth. Colin Clark calculates variations of Russian income per head of working population as follows: 264 IU's in 1870; 288 in 1900; 306 in 1913; 117 in 1921; 185 in 1923; 280 in 1925; 290 in 1928; 267 in 1934; 379 in 1937. It is obvious that the period from 1914 to 1928, years of war, revolution, and economic convalescence, cannot be taken as a criterion of Russia's capacity for economic progress, nor as a basis for estimating what Russia's progress would have been had she not engaged in war and revolution.

H. R. Knickerbocker writes that by projecting the graph of Russian industrial productivity in 1900-1913 over the next twenty-six years it can be shown that czarist Russia would have produced more in 1940 at the same rate of increase than Soviet industry under the Five Year Plans. This statement infers that Imperial Russia would have maintained an uninterrupted rate of progress, a somewhat unlikely supposition no matter what political system had presided over the economic development of the country.† Moreover, Clark's computations show for the period 1900-1913 an increase only from 288 IU's to 306 IU's, whereas for the period 1925-1937 much larger improvement is shown, namely, from 280 to 376. However, the growth of Soviet economy is not impressive when compared with capitalistic countries who are latecomers to industrialization. Income per head of working population has grown in Japan from 172 in 1914 to 406 in 1936, in Italy from 262 in 1901 to 343 in 1914, and even the "mature" economies of the United States and Britain show a rate of growth not substantially below that of the Soviet Union.

"There would seem to be a good reason to believe that,

* Ellsworth Huntington, expanding Clark's data for productivity and income, calculates real income per worker in secondary industry during the period 1924-1936 as follows: 1,728 for the United States; 1,151 for Great Britain; 810 for Germany; 450 for Japan; he omits any figure for the Soviet Union.—"The Geography of Human Productivity," *Annals* of the Association of American Geographers, Vol. XXXIII, No. 1, March, 1943, p. 4.

† H. R. Knickerbocker, *Is Tomorrow Hitler's?*, New York, 1941, p. 123.

other things being equal, the later a country embarks on an intensive process of 'catching up' to modern industry the more quickly it would run through the process once the main political and social obstacles have begun to crumble." *
The development of industries and communication systems should proceed more rapidly since a "young" industrial country can benefit from the experience of the "older" countries, and draw upon the international reservoir of technical knowledge. The essence of Russian industrial planning was to follow, or try to follow, foreign models. It drew its inspiration for steel-making techniques from Germany; in automotive engineering it sought to copy American methods. Thus the homeland of socialism could choose among the paraphernalia of the great capitalist economies, learn by their achievements and mistakes, and select in a competitive market the most efficient productive techniques, just as Japan, in an earlier period, was able to select the latest inventions and manufacturing methods displayed on the bargain counter of the West. Regarded in this light, the rise in the industrial output of the Soviet Union constitutes a respectable achievement, particularly when viewed against the background of devastation, heritage of ten years' revolution. But measured by the pace of capitalist rates of growth, it is not extraordinary. It could have been extraordinary only had Soviet industry indeed begun from scratch. This was not the case. The transformation of a feudal into an industrial society, which is so readily claimed as the accomplishment of Soviet management, was in full swing long before the First World War began.

Compared with the highly industrialized countries of the West, the Russia of 1913 was a backward country, and so is, in many respects, the Russia of today. Yet the Soviet Union has not stamped out of the ground the industries and skills which now make it powerful. While czarist Russia was only semi-industrialized, the industry which existed in the Petersburg, Moscow, and Tula districts was of a very modern kind, equipped with up-to-date German, English, and Belgian plants, and staffed by efficient Russian and foreign managers

* Eugene Staley, *World Economic Development*, International Labour Office, Montreal, 1944, pp. 73-4.

and engineers. Large factories employing more than a thousand workers accounted for nearly half of all factory labor, or nearly as large a number as in the United States before the outbreak of World War I. Despite the ravages of defeat and civil war, disuse and obsolescence, a part of that plant was salvaged by the Soviet.

More important still was the nucleus of skills which, depleted as it was by war losses, political purges, and famine, the old regime was able to hand down to the new. In certain branches of the metallurgical industry and particularly in ordnance, czarist Russia need not have shirked comparison with the rest of European industry. Graduates from Russian engineering colleges attained renown not only at home but also abroad; in World War I, for example, the first and best long-range planes were of Russian make. While before World War I most peasant farms were worked with primitive tools, many large estates were operated as efficiently as the best-equipped farms in the United States and Canada.

The Soviet government fell heir to an invaluable legacy of bourgeois know-how and a bourgeois trained working force. It inherited from the czarist era the impetus of eastward expansion. The vision of Russia behind the Urals had stirred many Russian minds before it came to dominate Soviet strategic planning. Scientists, industrialists, and soldiers urged the rapid development and settlement of Siberia and the Far East long before World War I. Indeed, Dimitri I. Mendeleiev, the great chemist, predicted in 1897 that the center of gravity of the Russian population would shift, by the middle of the twentieth century, to Omsk in Siberia.

If the achievements of twenty-five years of socialist economy are measured by the yardstick of industrialization everywhere, then the absolute rate of the socialist "development of productive forces" constitutes no challenge to progress under capitalism and does not reflect a superior grasp of technological problems. It was accomplished by the prodigious use of Russia's vast labor reserves, and a low wage rate and standard of living per head of population.

How has socialist economy met the test of World War II? The contribution of the Soviet Union to the triumphs of the military coalition fighting Nazi Germany was so immense that the sacrifices it entailed may easily escape the attention of the Western world. It was made despite the serious shortcomings of Russia's economic war potential. Russian manpower was exchanged for Western matériel.

The list of items lend-leased to the Soviet Union by the United States illustrates some of the quantitative and qualitative gaps in the Soviet economic system. By March 31, 1945, 8.4 billion dollars' worth of American lend-lease goods had been shipped to Russia. On June 30, 1944, British "mutual aid" to the Soviet Union totaled 1.17 billion dollars.* The United States shipped to Soviet arsenals not only tanks and planes but also aluminum, copper and copper alloys, chemicals, and a hundred thousand tons of toluol and TNT. In addition to hundreds of million dollars' worth of tools and industrial equipment, the bulk consisting of precision machinery of all kinds, refinery equipment, and electric generating units, a whole tire plant was crated and shipped to the Soviet Union.†

Expressed in dollars, American and British subsidies to Russia represent only a small share in Soviet armament— probably less than 10 per cent. However, in many Soviet plants the key equipment was of foreign make, a fact confirmed by Soviet managers as well as foreign visitors. The importance of certain highly complicated tools cannot be measured by their price. A plant equipped with only a few of these strategic tools may accomplish miracles of production; without them it may not be able to produce at all.

It would be absurd to deduce from these facts that Russians are less capable of acquiring technical knowledge. We may surmise, however, that Russian industry lacks as yet the degree of specialization and versatility which are the mainsprings of American, British, and German industrial strength.

BIGNESS, COMPLEXITY, AND PLANNING

It is a Marxist thesis that the very logic of modern technology requires that production be concentrated in fewer

* "Second Report on Mutual Aid," a White Paper prepared by the Chancellor of the Exchequer, November 23, 1944, p. 11.
† See page 283, Note 2 to Chapter 12.

and increasingly larger plants. Looked at more closely, all arguments in favor of government planning and collective controls of the national economy are found to be rooted ultimately in this conviction. Is modern technology really increasing the optimum size of the productive unit? The evidence is inconclusive. Modern developments lead at the same time to more concentration here and to less concentration there—a circumstance which does not simplify the task of central planning. It is obvious that electrical power, the internal combustion engine, and elaborate machines of the smallest size have gone a long way toward diminishing the superiority of the bigger plant. The modern development of motor highway transportation surely signifies, to a large extent, the triumph of the smaller over the larger unit, though against this fact there must be set the triumph of mass production in the automobile industry. Some steel plants recently constructed in the United States are smaller in size than the famous giants in Pennsylvania and Indiana, yet have proven efficient producers, economically as well as technologically. The rise of many new service industries reflects a tendency toward diffusion rather than concentration.

Trends toward decentralization in certain branches of production, while belying the popular notions about "bigness," meet with modern strategic requirements. For modern war, notably air warfare, suggests decentralization of physical plants as well as managerial functions, not extreme dependence on one mammoth production unit or one central planning agency which can be incapacitated by one blow. It remains to be seen, however, whether even the highly concentrated industries are not capable of being broken up quite profitably into those parts which must remain centralized for technological and organizational reasons and those which lend themselves to decentralization.*

British industry, that pure-bred creature of capitalist econ-

* It is widely held that motor-car manufacturing and concentration are synonyms. A leading manufacturer appears to hold the contrary opinion. "Industry should be decentralized. Plants in more places should be the objective. The result is a better balanced local economy, hence a better balanced national economy."—Alfred P. Sloan, Jr., in the *Proceedings* of the Academy of Political Science, January, 1945. Henry Kaiser's steel plant at Fontana, California, completed in 1943 and capable of producing 700,000 tons

omy, has worked miracles of adaptability. The story is told in the British White Paper of November 28, 1944, from which it is evident that the expansion of British armament manufacture from 1940 to 1944 was prodigious. British industry, as the emergency proved, was highly flexible and adaptable. Thousands of British shops are small and are capable of making almost anything out of metal. From these workshops have come countless types of parts, gears, precision tools, complicated devices, and innumerable revolutionary inventions.

In the light of British experience, the argument for mere bigness, for a centrally controlled economy, and for uniform standards is not as convincing as it looks in textbooks for planning. Also in the United States countless small and owner-operated plants have made vitally important contributions to the war effort. In 1943, 30 per cent of all American [*] and 40 per cent of all British war production was handled by "small business," i.e., plants employing under 500 wage earners. True, in Britain, as well as in the United States, industry worked to the specifications, priorities, and allocations determined by government agencies, and a large part of the output of small firms was for the account of large concerns holding prime contracts. However, the role of small business in the war effort cannot be assessed by its direct contributions to the armed forces alone. For the task of keeping the country's basic economy running came to rest more heavily than in peacetime upon the shoulders of small business.

PLANNED ECONOMY AND THE PROFIT MOTIVE

It is necessary here to separate as sharply and as clearly as the subject will permit the essential dualism in the question of the profit motive in its relation to national power. One is

---

of steal ingots a year, is hailed as an important step toward a better regional distribution of the industry and a milestone in the reversal of past trends toward concentration in steel making. See "Steel in the West," *Fortune*, Vol. 31, No. 2, February, 1945, p. 261.

[*] *Program and Progress Report*, Smaller War Plants Corporation, November 2, 1944, pp. 27-31.

the ethical aspect of profit as the drive to production of wealth and the advancement of human welfare. It goes without saying that whereas students of power cannot ignore the necessity of taking a stand on this matter as members of the human family, they must, as specialists, rule out *ab initio* this side of the question from a survey of power factors in modern economy. There remains the question, delicate and complex, of what role profit can have assigned to it in the actual development of the national economy as an instrument of power. The profit system rewards with profits and punishes with losses. To the extent that profit supplies the main incentive to increasing production and improving techniques, profit is a factor in national power. Indubitably, this is a real and present aspect of capitalist economy as historically developed. Profit is roughly the margin of saved costs in production. An economy that dispenses with this incentive does not, of course, abolish the effect of costs on production. For costs operate just as inexorably in a socialist as in a capitalist economy. The problem remaining after profit is abolished is precisely how to guarantee the constant incentive to reduced costs or, to put it the other way around, "increased production in a socialist economy."

If the capitalist entrepreneur is spurred by profit, he is curbed by costs, and costs are the gauge of the efficiency of his undertakings. It is precisely to this problem of costs that Soviet economists have lately given their concentrated attention.* The Soviet economic system, as Calvin Hoover remarks, lays claim to the same distributive principle as does capitalism. Soviet economists as well as practical managers appear to be groping for a market mechanism of a kind. That market mechanism is to function, as the Soviet economists see it, for social purposes in which capitalist countries allegedly fail of satisfaction. But it is the same market mechanism which, this past hundred and fifty years, has been described

* "Some Questions in the Teaching of Political Economy," *Pod Znamenem Marxizma (Under the Banner of Marxism)*, No. 7-8, July, 1943, pp. 56-78. For a critique of this manifesto of Soviet economy see Calvin B. Hoover, "Capitalism and Socialism, a New Soviet Appraisal," *Foreign Affairs*, Vol. XXII, IV, July, 1944, pp. 335-356; P. A. Baran, "New Trends in Russian Economic Thinking," *American Economic Review*, Vol. XXXIV, No. 4, December, 1944.

by the classical economists. In the Soviet Union, costs, prices, and wages are to be fixed by state-owned factories, and thus by the state. In capitalist economies this same task is performed by private entrepreneurs exposed to the pressure of the market and the bargaining power of organized labor.

A free economy allows, like every efficient mechanism, for "play," while the tightly fitted parts of a command economy make for friction. Yet it is precisely the "play" of a free economy which its critics condemn as wasteful. The "effecting of new combinations," experiments with new techniques and ventures upon untrodden paths of production, involve willingness to assume risks. Scrapping a serviceable tool because a better one has been devised, and experimenting with radical departures from the norm, entail "waste." But to the extent that this calculated waste nourishes new productive forces, it is a source of national power, produced at a cost, to be sure, but power, none the less. It is theoretically conceivable that a different economic system can operate more rationally. But it remains to be seen whether any system other than capitalism is capable of developing the same or a higher degree of national power. A planned economy purports to achieve better distribution; a free economy purports to achieve higher production.

Under capitalism many technologically sound inventions prove a bad risk and are eliminated by the market. A technologically sound patent may not be of any use to the community. This, too, is waste of a kind. A planned system, however, stands in danger of not developing enough new devices to insure technical progress because there is no profit incentive and bureaucratic management is, as a rule, unsympathetic to change, and of foisting technological innovations upon the community, simply because they are technologically sound, in spite of the fact that they will not benefit the public.

The "wastefulness" of private business, it is alleged by some, is illustrated by the fact that it fails to use fully its productive facilities. In the United States, for example, throughout the most prosperous years a part of the productive equipment remained idle. This is statistically true. Changeovers to new techniques will halt this or that assembly belt. Moreover, a reserve capacity must exist lest breakdowns, obsolescence, and sudden demands find the producer incapable of making the necessary adjustments. More important still, it is this reserve capacity which cushions the impact upon the national economy of such an emergency as, for example, war. Potential production, not production-in-being, is the true measure of an economy able to sustain the incalculable and unpredictable demands of large-scale warfare.

By far the most serious charge brought against the capitalist system is that it is wasteful of men, and that it demands a pool of employable unemployed workers as a requirement for its efficient operation.

"Full employment" is an absolute which, like other ideological slogans, is meaningless when analyzed in the light of historic facts. In 1929, 47 million Americans were engaged in gainful work, i.e., only 36 per cent of the total population. In the same year more than 60 per cent of the total population of Germany were gainfully employed. None the less, national income per head in the United States was twice that of Germany, while total U.S. income was four and one-half times larger than the German. Full employment is thus no convincing test of a nation's capacity to produce and consume.

The problem of unemployment in the United States has changed signs since war expanded the demand for labor. Although this demand is huge, not all men and women capable of work and for whom jobs are available are working—patently a case of voluntary unemployment. By contrast, Germany had solved the problem of unemployment long before it went to war. There was, during the years of world economic crisis, no unemployment in Nazi Germany; hence war found Germany fully mobilized on the labor front. How was this triumph achieved; has it made Germany a more productive, stronger country? So much ideological nonsense has been uttered on this question that it has become difficult to grasp the elementary facts.

German economy was run avowedly as a war economy, for the German people were assured by the Nazi leaders that the pluto-democratic powers were bent upon crushing the one and only national socialist state on earth which had solved the problem of full employment. Incidentally, it was this achievement of the Nazis which impressed even some of their severest critics in this country and abroad. German leaders declared that not only had all employable Germans been put to work but that the problem was to overcome manpower shortages in industry and agriculture. The question, it appears, must be put differently: Does "full employment" in Germany reflect the virtue of the system or, to the contrary, failure to produce efficiently?

Soviet employment statistics cast a revealing light on the problem of full employment. The 1937 census of the Soviet Union disclosed that the intelligentsia, i.e., government employees and intellectual workers of all kinds, had reached a total of 9,591,000.* To these must be added a larger number of minor employees and an indeterminate group of officials of the Commissariats of the Interior and Defense, of the trade unions, and of the Communist Party. The total number of white-collar workers was larger than, for example, that of all workers employed in Russian heavy industry, and amounted to 8 per cent of the total population of the Soviet Union.

On November 30, 1944, the number of federal employees of the white-collar class in the United States was 2,535,000.† The number of state and municipal employees was 3,168,000, making a total of 5,703,000, or approximately half that of government employees of the Soviet Union. It can be argued that the Russian figure includes a large number of white-collar workers, the equivalent of whom would be classified in the United States as business employees and professional personnel in private practice. None the less, if allowance is made for the much lower national product and income of the Soviet Union, the size of Soviet bureaucracy in peacetime dwarfs even the inflated wartime bureaucracy, public and private, of the United States.

The bottom layer of the social pyramid in all totalitarian countries is made up of millions of workers who are being

* The 1937 census was declared invalid by the Soviet government. The tabulation of the intelligentsia contained in the 1939 census is incomplete. Engineers, technical personnel, scientific workers, professional workers, and medical personnel total 5,839,000. The figure for bookkeepers and accountants is 1,769,000. *Bolshevik,* Vol. 10, 1940, p. 22, as quoted by the *American Quarterly on the Soviet Union,* Vol. III, No. 2-3.

† This figure does not include civilian workers in shipyards and ordnance plants operated by the War Department and Navy Department, respectively.

paid wages which, by American standards, may be described as infinitesimally low. These workers for whom there is no equivalent in the American system have completed, or broken the ground for, some of the most celebrated public works of totalitarian regimes.*

Employment statistics in the Soviet Union are organized differently from those compiled in the United States. Moreover, Soviet statistics are published with different ends in view than those emanating from the United States Department of Commerce. None the less, certain distinct features of labor in the Soviet Union can be discerned quite clearly. They do not suggest that the Soviet solution of the employment problem is susceptible of adaptation by the United States or any other Western country. There is no unemployment in the Soviet Union, but it is obvious that "full employment" in the Soviet Union does not mean what this term implies in American public discussion. Clearly, what is meant in that discussion is a job for everyone willing to work *at not less than the average wage rate.*

"Full employment" is not a measure of economic and technological progress; it may be incompatible with it. Full employment of a nation's labor force can be achieved only provided there is willingness to change trades. If the right of everyone to work is recognized as a fundamental right of citizenship, this agreement does not of necessity imply the right to a particular job in a particular place at a particular wage. To extend it that far is precisely to guarantee permanent unemployment, a policy which could be defended on various grounds, but which should be formulated deliberately and without ambiguity.† As many explanations of chronic unemployment have been advanced as there are schools in political

* David Dallin, in *The Real Soviet Russia*, New Haven, Yale University Press, 1944, draws a somber picture of forced labor in the Soviet Union. Some of the information on this category of Soviet labor is being disseminated abroad by quarters openly hostile to the Soviet regime; some accounts are patently inexact. It is, however, no secret that the Soviet government disposed of such politically undesirable elements as Kulaks, counterrevolutionaries, and Volga Germans by mass deportation, and that the contingents of forced labor are large. Mass deportation and forced labor are traditional Russian institutions. Russia, incidentally, is not the only country to exploit convict labor without compensation except bare subsistence.

† See page 284, Note 3 to Chapter 12.

197

economy. Among the causes cited are lack of capital, restrictions on production and foreign trade, faulty adaptation between production and consumption, and technological change. In the last resort, all causes of mass unemployment in the interwar period can be traced back to the disintegration of the world economic system.

Widespread dissatisfaction with the characteristic features of capitalism, and political animosities converging upon it, still derive their virulence from the world economic crisis a decade ago. It is by the failure of capitalist society to meet that test that its *raison d'être* is being judged. We may suspect that the staggering costs in lives and wealth of World War I, the ensuing tariff wars, quotas imposed on immigration, and the geographical contraction of the free market system due to the self-immolation of Russia, were not unrelated to the Great Depression. None the less, the bulk of economic thought generated by that period sought the cause of economic crisis in structural faults of the system. This is about as consistent as attributing the collapse under shellfire of an apartment house to a faulty design of the architect.

A free economy has proved itself adaptable enough to wage war successfully. It developed an entire system of controls, political, social, and (in a narrow sense) economic, required for the attainment of military power. For example, in the sphere of political economy, wage, price, and manpower controls were devised to carry out this policy. But the system is irreconcilable with an economy on a permanent emergency footing. War economy is planned economy; it is planning heedless of costs and consideration of human welfare as a good in itself. War calls forth inventiveness and draws upon untapped forces of production. These, however, are the legacies of peace, latent accumulations which are gathered up and discharged in the war effort.* The process cannot be continued indefinitely. It is for this reason that comparing the purposefulness of war economy with the

* Professor Robert Millikan recently expressed the opinion that war is not, as it is widely believed by laymen, a pressure house of progress in science and technology. While certain developments are accelerated by the special demands war creates, science would have advanced just as purposefully without the stimulant of war. Peace, not war, is "the father of all things."

(seeming) anarchy of peacetime economy is not as meaningful as the advocates of basic change allege. Conversely, constant doctoring of a country's economic structure is the
surest way to make it less fit even for military purposes, just
as wholesale militarization of society is apt to dull the qualities most needed for successful warfare. Adaptability to
change is inherently an individual characteristic. It cannot
be regulated by law.

The orderly functioning of a free economy depends on the
observance of certain rules and voluntary restraints. This is
so despite the immense amount of effort expended by liberal
as well as Marxist economists upon showing that it functions
by virtue of some motivating force generated from within itself. There is in economics, just as in mechanics, no perpetual
motion. Let us put the question again: Must the economic
system under which the United States has grown rich and
strong beyond the imagination of past generations yield inevitably to another form of economic life? Will the survival
or demise of historical institutions be decided in a clash of
ideologies or, if one prefers the terminology of Mosca and
Pareto, by the struggle for power between the in-and-out
elites? The victory of this or that contending faction will confirm this or that doctrine of inevitability—depending on
which side will be able to arrange for the writing of history.
That victory will not decide the question whether a free or a
planned economy is more conducive to human welfare, just
as the Religious Wars did not deliver a verdict on the dilemma of faith and reason, and the French Revolution did
not reconcile the Rights of Man with the rights of the state.
Be that as it may, socialism is not inevitable; neither is the
decline of creative imagination under freedom. Our problem
is to examine the industrial potentials of the systems as they
now exist and to project a picture of what they will be like
in the discernible future.

13. THE BURDEN OF THE PAST

THE power of the United States in the decades to come will be fatefully conditioned by the rate of technological progress it is able to maintain. Technological progress in the United States has developed within the framework of a free economy. So far, the United States and Britain have proven the adaptability of a capitalist society, despite its many real and alleged shortcomings, to the demands of war. The state of the arts and the condition of the economic system are not chance companions on the road of progress.

The right kind of military economy is the one which develops the greatest war potentials. There is no gainsaying the fact that a country which has planned its economy fully in peacetime may have a considerable temporary advantage; but the longer the war lasts, the more this advantage will turn into a clear disadvantage, as the decision will more and more pass from arms-in-being to potential output of weapons. This is precisely the test which the economy of the United States has met.

The next war—if it comes, and come it may—will be even more a contest of skills and productive potentials than this one. But there is no guarantee that American matériel will ever again exert such an overwhelming weight upon the enemy and that the United States will again have such powerful industrial allies as it had in this war.

The decade preceding the entrance of the United States into World War II was marred by curtailed industrial growth and deepening economic pessimism. Restrictive trade policies and resistance to adaptation hobbled enterprise. Labor unions penalized production by limiting working hours and pegging industrial efficiency, hence industrial output per head of population. A virtual ban on immigration coincided with a slackening of population increase, thus walling in one source of economic progress, to wit, population growth, while patent pools and reluctance to incur risks attending the introduction of innovations threatened technological progress.

The experiments of the 1930's with methods for promoting economic recovery were tried with much greater determination and vigor than the public realized. Public expenditure for purposes of social reform and economic recovery were nearly as large as the outlay for running World War I.* The record of production and employment from 1930 to 1940 was taken by some economists as evidence that the economic system had run down, and that a "mature" economy could not generate enough activity to absorb the available labor force into employment. This conviction nourished a body of theories purporting to explain the paralysis of the economic system and to devise means for its reorganization. These means were public spending, the extension of public regulation, and unrestricted taxation of the rich. While these measures were enacted with intensity and speed, they failed to attain their avowed purpose, full employment. The new theories met with the demands of the majority of the people. Progressive taxation and public bounties promised to replace toil and insecurity with the pleasures of spending and prospects of a carefree age. Yet as the influence of these doctrines grew, so diminished the dynamism which competition had supplied to the economic process. High taxation enfeebled the stimulus to new economic ventures, to wit, the profit motive. The overconcentration of industry, and bureaucratic routine, braked technological progress and discouraged the use of the most modern instruments of production.

The entrepreneur, venturing forth upon new ways of doing things and risking his resources upon untried ideas, is of necessity a nonconformist. He is troublesome to his competitors and not always a stickler for adhering to the rules, some of which safeguard true public interest, others of which protect none but the entrenched few, and still others no one at all.

The inventor often upsets settled investment. Most outstanding inventions, great additions to knowledge, or radical

* Leo Wolman, "Readjusting the Working Population," *Proceedings* of the Academy of Political Science, Vol. XXI, No. 2., January, 1945.

innovations come from outside the laboratories of the mammoth industrial organizations and government bureaus. Elaborate research organizations controlled by large concerns dispose of luxurious facilities far beyond the means of individual scientists and most institutions of learning. Yet bigness may foster complacency and a false sense of superiority. Eccentricity is understandably not encouraged by the chiefs of huge research organizations. However, some of the greatest inventions are the result of inspired borrowings from techniques developed in seemingly unrelated fields. The true inventor is an individual still too often found hidden among failures. Frequently, he is a troublesome and imperfect individualist.*

There is in this conflict between centralized organization and individual initiative the same clash of group against individual which cleaves through the social and economic problems of our time. From this clash arise dangers not only to the traditional forms of American society but also to the political and military power of the United States. Before World War II a process of arteriosclerosis had overtaken not only sectors of the peacetime economy but also institutions of research and learning. Some vital techniques had nearly been lost or had become atrophied. The pressure of war has swept away much of the dead matter which has clogged the stream of American production and inventiveness. American ingenuity and the far from negligible technological inspiration of its British allies have reanimated the venturesome and productive genius of a nation which by heritage, natural endowment, and character possesses the wherewithal necessary for leadership in industry and science.

However, the burden of the past, with its experiences and preconceptions, weighs upon the thinking and planning for the future. It is likely that the doctrines of the 1930's will determine American policies in the postwar period and that the Malthusian features of American economy will be hardened by the strain imposed by a gigantic national debt, veterans'

* For an excellent discussion of this problem, see "The Bottleneck in Ideas," editors of *Fortune*, Vol. 27, No. 5, pp. 82-85, 184-8. According to the *National Inventors Council* 80 per cent of all inventions accepted by the armed forces came from individuals, 15 per cent from small companies and 5 per cent from large corporations.

pensions, outlay for vast public works, subsidized foreign trade, more massive governmental intervention, and a variety of fiscal charges which, despite technical modifications, will conform to the principle of progressive taxation. The very momentums of wartime technological progress and dammed-up consumer demands are guarantees against a sudden lapse into economic stagnation. However, if sole reliance is placed on energies accumulated in the past, the growth of American industry will slacken, and so will the growth of the United States war potential. Such a purely mechanical increase, as, for example, a closer integration of Canadian industry with that of the United States, may add to the bulk, not to the vitality, of American economy.

The situation in Britain appears somewhat similar in character, though less favorable as regards the immediate outlook. Britain's course appears set toward a planned economy. Unlike the United States, Britain has not been able to wage war chiefly by drawing on excess plant and labor capacity. On the contrary, she has had rigorously to reduce her own home consumption, abandon her trade, surrender her foreign investments, and borrow abroad.

Also in Britain technological advances will have increased output per man hour from 1938 to 1945, inclusive, by approximately 10 per cent, i.e., somewhat above the normal rate of progress for western Europe.* However, in the United States almost the whole of the war effort of 1941-1944 represented increased production; in Britain one-half of it was defrayed by cutting back peacetime trades. Colin Clark predicts that the outflow of capital from Great Britain will continue in the middle run chiefly because her working population will tend to decline, a contingency not faced by the United States in this generation.†

The British Empire is still a vast storehouse of wealth. But

* This estimate is based on the calculations published by Nicholas Kaldor in his "Quantitative Aspects of the Full Employment Problem in Great Britain" in Sir William H. Beveridge's *Full Employment in a Free Society*, New York, 1945, p. 370.

† Colin Clark forecasts for Great Britain a decline of capital required per head of working population from 4,860 IU's in 1935 to 4,610 in 1960. See *The Economics of 1960*, London, 1943, pp. 80, 85.

its economic center, England, has lost in this war the comfortable economic margin which played so large a part in the control it exercised over the economic development of the Commonwealth, its dependencies, and colonial possessions. Britain is still rich; but she has become poorer. She is the prey of the psychological disturbances that a relative impoverishment is apt to produce in minds unaccustomed to this harrowing experience. This fact dominates British thinking on trade, and conditions the determination of the level at which Britain's power can be made to balance her world-political commitments.

Britain's crucial problem is now, as it always was, trade. But the accumulated reserves consisting of foreign credits and investments are gone. It was these reserves on which Britain drew to pay for imports in excess of the purchasing power of her export trade. How to replenish these reserves and restore foreign trade, on which every fifth Englishman depends for his job, is the question which conditions Britain's outlook on the future.

The large majority of Englishmen appear agreed that government controls of foreign trade must be retained for years after the cessation of hostilities, and that, because Britain's domestic economy is largely governed by foreign trade, domestic production, too, must long remain controlled. The slogan is "controlled de-control." Significantly, because it is hard realities, not theories, which compel the continuation of planning after hostilities will have ceased, the idea of planning stands in danger of losing its ideological flavoring. "The British business man . . . has reached the stage of demanding that the government should intervene sufficiently to set the stage on which he can pursue his craft. . . . On the other side of the fence, virtually every one of Britain's socialist intellectuals has spent four years serving his country in the Ministries and Departments of Whitehall, and many have come to realize the limitations of bureaucracy and the virtues of leaving a very large sector of the national life to individual decision." * Britain may reach, more quickly than the United States, the middle ground where, unhampered by doctrinal

* Geoffrey Crowther, "British Twentieth-Century Economics," *The Yale Review*, Vol. XXXIV, No. 2, pp. 210-224.

bickering, state and business join as well as separate their functions. However, this likelihood is no better than Britain's chance to recapture her old markets and open up new outlets for her manufacture.

At the end of the war Great Britain will owe $15 billion to other nations. India alone will be a creditor to the tune of not less than and probably more than 500 million pounds sterling. As these sterling credits are being converted into British goods after the war, there will be a tendency for British machine tools, automobiles, and electrical equipment to flow abroad, while imports will be reduced to a trickle. All this will be good for British employment, but it means that Britain will be paying off debt rather than increasing real income.

Britain's merchant marine will have lost nearly half of its prewar tonnage, namely, 10 million tons out of 21 million. That tonnage may be speedily replenished by the shipyards on the Clyde, by purchase, and by charter. Yet the merchant fleet of the United States will have grown more than fivefold, namely, from 11.6 million tons to an estimated 57.5 million tons.* Even under circumstances most favorable from Britain's point of view, only part of this gigantic fleet will be withdrawn from operation or sold or lent to Britain. In this sector of world trade alone, American policies can shape the economic destiny of Britain.

When Prime Minister Churchill, speaking on British problems in Europe, stated, "Other powerful States are with us on every side, *some more powerful, perhaps, than the British Empire and Commonwealth of Nations*," † he was not engaging in somber rhetoric, but stating a bald fact which speaks to the British people through the deterioration not only of their "power position," a somewhat abstract notion, but of their place in world trade. For Britain, more than for any other nation, political power depends on trade. Yet the productive capacity of British industry has not grown in proportion to expanding strategic commitments and the increas-

* "Merchant Marine II: The World View," editors of *Fortune*, Vol. XXX, No. 6, December, 1944, p. 169.

† The Prime Minister's address on Poland in the House of Commons, December 15, 1944. (Italics are mine.)

ing population of the empire. The empire's annual steel capacity is probably in excess of 18 million. These 18 million tons must be spread over the economies of the United Kingdom, the Dominions, and India. Out of the British Empire's 18 million tons must come the tonnage of the merchant marine, the rails and the rolling stock, and the machine tools of the British Commonwealth of Nations containing more than 550 million people. In addition, the Royal Navy has first call on a part of British steel-making capacity.

The emergence of great and compact continental empires, the vulnerability of widely dispersed holdings, inferiority in manpower, and exhaustion of economic reserves—these are the bleak realities before Britain. It is not surprising that a neurosis has taken the place of serene assurance nourished by centuries of British might. Because the British Empire is world-wide, its adjustments necessitated by political, strategic, and economic change are a world problem. The making of these adjustments is the foremost problem in world politics before the United States.

The successful accommodation between American and British economic policies will largely determine how well and how smoothly these adjustments can be made. The premise of constructive collaboration is that "both countries must act in the belief that in any future great crisis they will prove reliable allies and come to each other's defense." * The interests of the two countries are complementary and interlocking. The conception that Britain, by seeking the shelter of state-managed trade abroad and a state-managed economy at home, can perpetuate a socialized, closed monetary system rivaling the United States does not jibe with her political and military self-interest. War has, in a fashion, mixed up the economies of both countries, and forced free trade upon both sides against their will. Both countries now profess an abiding interest in the revival of a truly international system of exchanges. It cannot be recreated without their co-operation.

Enlightened economic policies alone cannot restore Brit-

* Herbert Feis, former adviser on international economic affairs in the State Department, in his *Sinews of Peace*, New York, 1944, pp. 183-189, argues cogently the imperative need for Anglo-American collaboration and the formulation of common policies in foreign trade.

ain to the position of power she held formerly. A renascence of British foreign trade does not spell substantial increase of Britain's industrial potential, unless there is a far-reaching economic integration with the countries of western Europe as proposed bluntly by Field Marshal Jan Smuts and more cautiously suggested by Prime Minister Winston Churchill and Mr. Anthony Eden.

Among the countries of the west European coal-iron complex only France appears in a position to venture upon a program of increased industrialization, if for no other reason than that she is now by British or American standards an underindustrialized country. Even this postponed industrialization of France may require a larger population; it may be inhibited altogether should France not pursue a liberal policy of immigration.

Finally, whatever industrial growth there may be in western Europe, it will be balanced by the growth of east European countries which under a bipolar system would accrue to the industrial potential of Russia.

In the foregoing pages it has been assumed that industrial advance and technological progress are aspects of economic growth and that they are indivisible. If this assumption holds, then a slowing up of industrial advance implies a slackening of technological progress. Thus the absolute and relative weakening of the industrial potential of the traditional European allies of the United States tends to offset whatever future gains American industry may make, and whatever technological advances American inventors and engineers may score.

14. TRADE AND TECHNOLOGY: THE EXPORT OF KNOWLEDGE

THE power-driven tool began to encroach upon the techniques of water, wind, and wood only a little more than a hundred years ago. The use in commerce and war of the steam engine, steamboat, and steam railway dates back to the era between the Napoleonic and Crimean Wars. European science devised machines which were to transform European civilization; peoples of European stock used these machines to pry open the gates of "backward countries" to commercial exploitation, and Western traders pressed upon these countries the keys which had gained them entrance, i.e., the tools designed by Western science.

A later, more skeptical philosophy of empire questioned whether the long-range benefits of this exchange would accrue to Western wealth and power; but the West had been far too confident of the abundance of its creative energies and its lead in inventiveness and skills. It had been far too successful in scattering its tools among the other peoples to restrict that flow of exchanges which it had set in motion so impetuously and profitably. In this latter stage, motherlands attempted to inhibit the industrialization of their overseas possessions; European industrial nations sought to prevent overseas producers of raw materials from setting up factories of their own.

On the whole, restrictive practices recoiled upon those who practiced them. For competition between the great trading nations assured backward countries of the continued supply of goods as well as technical instruction—if not from one Western exporter, then from another. But for that circumstance, modern Japan would not exist. True, already before World War I some European manufacturers attempted to join in common defense of their trade secrets; preoccupation with keeping the most essential of the formulas and techniques out of consumers' reach played no small role in the formation of many cartels. Europe did become anxious about its technical secrets. The fact is, Europe had kept them badly. By the beginning of this century European technology and science had spread to the whole world. Europe's fund of knowledge had become the possession of all mankind; her peoples no longer hold the monopoly of the technical instruments of power. In the war that has been waged since 1914, the age of Europe's economic and political preponderance passes into history.

The first break in the international system established as a result of the Allies' victory in World War I occurred in Asia, not in Europe. Indeed, since the war of 1905 between Japan and Russia, the latter herself a power based on contiguous Eurasian land masses, the balance of power in the Pacific has lain with non-European powers, namely, the United States and Japan. The eclipse of European power modified the balance of power in the Pacific and set in motion the events which were to converge upon Pearl Harbor. It is widely held that future dangers of world political disequilibrium will arise again in central Europe. This is writing history backward. "Germany," an American demographer writes, "like her Western neighbors, has passed a period in which she could become a dominant world power *owing to the diffusion of technological civilization to peoples that are growing more rapidly.*" *

The techniques of mass production are being universalized. Competition is no longer confined to the exclusive circle of the old industrial nations; industrial progress is no longer tied to the apron strings of Western culture. In the power conflicts of Asia the comfortable margin of Western technical superiority is wearing thin. Competition has shifted to qualitative refinements, just as it did in the West a century ago. In peacetime industry it is no longer the power-driven loom against the hand loom. In war it is no longer the automatic rifle against flintlocks. The issue has come to rest with the superiority of the latest, more perfect type of weapon over that which only yesterday was hailed as a triumph of engineering. Backwardness has become a matter of degree.

* Frank W. Notestein, "Population and Power in Postwar Europe," *Foreign Affairs*, Vol. XXII, No. 3, April, 1944, p. 403. (The italics are mine.)

That Asiatic peoples will indefinitely limp behind those of European stock in fields of applied science and industrial skills is no longer a "safe" assumption. The transcendent result of World War II may, in retrospect, prove to have been that it consummated this process of universalizing Western technology.

If this is indeed one meaning of the struggles through which the world now passes, then the problems of the redistribution of world power resolve themselves into a question of crucial importance to the United States: Will the "younger" industrializing countries be able to catch up in the foreseeable future with the "older" countries, namely the United States and the powers of western Europe now leading in industrial output and inventiveness? The answer will depend upon such imponderables as the zest and intelligence that the industrializing countries may demonstrate and the future conditions of world trade.

The process of industrializing involves certain restrictions: a young industrial country cannot concentrate its energies upon technological innovations to the same extent as a mature one. This need not imply that it lacks inventiveness. In the early stages of industrialization the bulk of a country's capital is devoted to textile factories, railways, and steel mills. There is no room for important technological changes, since not enough capital to invest in laboratories and pure research is available. Skilled technicians are being used for more elementary, if also more pressing tasks.

We cannot assume that the older industrial countries like the United States and Britain will stand still. Their future development, however, will be less rapid in the primary and secondary than in the tertiary industries, while the younger countries like Russia, India, and China will above all expand their coal and iron output and metallurgical industries, i.e., their crude war potential. Hence crude war potentials will tend to equalize. Yet the growth of tertiary industries, itself an important element of technological progress, will necessitate the further expansion of primary and secondary industries. Thus, for example, the development of civilian flying in the United States could impart stimuli to many secondary industries, besides contributing valuable matérial and skills to military air power. Housing construction and the renewal and modernization of railway equipment may also call for further growth of such secondary industries as the metallurgical trades and electrical engineering. The huge investments and savings of the highly industrialized countries allow for large expenditures upon experimentation and the increasing refinement of industrial techniques.

Estimates of the future growth of Asiatic industries vary considerably. Virtually all of them are based on the assumption that termination of World War II will be followed by an era of comparatively free movement of capital. The modernization of Japan supplies a rough measuring stick for estimating the future developments of other Asiatic countries. Eugene Staley believes * that if China and India were to develop their economies at the same rate as Japan after 1900, they might add in the first decade about 13.6 and 7.2 billion dollars' worth of new capital equipment, in the second decade 23.1 and 14.6 billion, in the third decade 44.9 and 27.7 billion, and in the fourth 51.6 and 31.4 billion dollars, respectively. These figures are based on 1936 prices and would have to be increased if allowance is made for the higher prices that prevail now and may prevail after the war.

The assumption underlying this calculation is that China and India will develop in the same proportion to population and area as Japan developed one generation earlier. It is doubtful, however, that the modernization of Japan can be taken as the perfect model for the future progress of other Asiatic countries. In the first place, the rise of modern Japan was favored by international conditions which may prove to have been unique in history. Japan was able to take advantage not only of the broad markets for capital and goods afforded by the nineteenth century, but also of the Great Power rivalries in the Far East. Moreover, the Japanese were a homogeneous people, their country was relatively small, and their rising industrial centers were easily accessible by sea. It is by no means certain that any other Asiatic nation would have borne so docilely the tremendous strains imposed upon it by its rulers, determined upon the rapid transformation of a me-

* Staley, op cit., p. 71.

211

dieval agricultural society into a modern industrial state. None the less, the industrial development of Japan is typical, at least in so far as the process of industrialization was undertaken "from scratch" and without more than a polite pretence of acquiring Western culture. Japan became industrialized; she did not become Westernized. The lessons which can be gleaned from the example of Japan are significant if for no other reason than that other Asiatic peoples are seeking to read into these lessons analogies pertinent to their own future development.

Against the likelihood that China and India will develop as rapidly as Japan stand weighty arguments. Their industrialization might be greatly slowed by population pressure, internal political and ideological conflicts, and foreign political influence. Particularly the latter factor, which played a comparatively small role in the case of Japan, may affect decisively the direction the industrialization of China and India may take. For the infiltration of Western welfare ideologies into Chinese and Indian thought may steer the industrial development of these countries toward the expansion of consumers' goods industries rather than heavy industry, i.e., that kind of industry which increases a country's war potential.

However, it is possible to marshal other arguments which suggest that China and India will develop even more rapidly than Japan. India and China, like the Soviet Union at the start of the Five Year Plans, will be able to draw upon techniques which have made gigantic strides since 1900. New processes for blasting low-grade ore may enable China to expand her steel-making capacity far beyond present estimates based on proven iron-ore deposits. American industry expanded so rapidly under the impact of war that it was able not only to meet vastly increased national demands but also to furnish Allied powers with gigantic quantities of lend-lease goods. This enormously expanded capacity for exporting the most modern kind of machine tools, planes, trucks, and locomotives might be put at the disposal of China and India, who may thus obtain the wherewithal of industrialization more rapidly than did Japan in 1900. If the great industrial nations of Europe and America were to collaborate after World War II in promoting the development of India and China, to train Indians and Chinese in the requisite skills and furnish large numbers of specialists, then "the results could well exceed past experience, for the world has never tried systematic cooperation to this end." *

Perhaps one of the most important facts brought home by wartime experience in the East is that Western technology is quite readily transmissible to peoples of other races and cultures who only yesterday were possessed of none but primitive techniques. Information is as yet incomplete. It is possible, however, to fit from the scraps and bits which have come to hand a preliminary picture of the adaptability of Indian and Chinese labor. In it some features can be recognized which are easily gleaned from the experience of Western industrialization. Others are specifically relevant to the East.

In India, for example, American-owned automotive plants located in Bombay province met wartime demands by rapid mobilization of native labor. Native workers have shown themselves as capable as American and European workers in learning how to operate multiple- as well as single-purpose machine tools. Indian men and women were trained to operate these tools by the same job-training methods which yielded such spectacular results in the United States. One difference was noted in respect of delicate operations requiring particular manual dexterity: Indians proved more "machineable" than Americans. Output per head was in general no lower than in the United States—provided Indian workers were being supplied with, and persuaded to avail themselves of, adequate bulk and protective foods. This not-so-strange discovery confirms the conviction long held by American production experts: The relation between sustained output per head and diet is about the same everywhere.

A large percentage of the Bombay labor force recruited by American concerns had previously been employed by the city's large textile mills. It may therefore be argued that it was not representative of Indian labor in general. However, the agents of the companies scoured the countryside and hired ever larger contingents of Indian peasants. The prob-

* Staley, *op. cit.*, pp. 21-32.

lem of training these villagers was found to be substantially the same as that of introducing recruits from the farming areas to industrial work in the United States. Obviously, the "personality problems" were not the same; in India management was faced with the problems of religion and caste. But parallels for these can be found, without particularly straining one's imagination, in the race problems complicating American personnel relationships.

As regards the "machineability" of Indian village labor, one production expert suggests the parallel of European immigrant labor to the United States in the 1880's and 1890's, which was probably as raw a human material as Indians who had left their ancestral acres for the assembly line of the Ford Motor Company of Bombay. It is against this evidence, slender yet highly suggestive, that we must examine such schemes as the so-called Bombay Plan, proposed by a group of up-and-coming Indian businessmen.

This plan provides for the postwar industrialization of India to dimensions that are colossal measured even by American standards. It calls for an expenditure of 30 billion dollars and proposes "to bring about a doubling of the present per capita income within a period of fifteen years from the time that the plan comes in operation." * In fifteen years industry would contribute 35 per cent of the total national income instead of its present 17 per cent, agriculture 40 per cent instead of 53 per cent, and service industries 20 per cent. It is calculated that at the present rate of population increase this would involve a trebling of the national income. The plan envisages the speedy development of the basic industries, namely electric power plants, mining and metallurgy, machinery (particularly machine tools), chemicals, communication, and armaments. A gigantic educational program is to be financed by a contribution of one-half of 1 per cent out of the total national income, about as large a proportion as is spent in the United States for this purpose, i.e., the largest proportion the world over. The problems of agriculture are touched only lightly by the planners, among whom the most prominent is the greatest industrialist of In-

* Howard Daniel and Minnie Bell, "The Bombay Plan," *Asia and the Americas*, Vol. XL, pp. 341-4.

dia, J. R. D. Tata, chairman of the largest steel combine of India, which also includes the biggest steel plant in the British Empire.

The plan has been called "the programme of Indian Fascism." The London *Economist* concluded that it explains "in the naïvest way [how] India can be made into a Great Power by 1960 by large-scale industrialization." This is indeed what the plan would accomplish were it to be put into effect—no matter whether it is proposed to bring about precisely that or, as the followers of Nehru will have it, to minister to "that forgotten creature, the Indian peasant, who has borne so many grievous burdens for centuries, [and] must find relief and . . . advancement in any plan."

It is one of the contradictions of Indian politics that the native industrialists behind the Bombay Plan are also the most influential backers of Mahatma Gandhi, foe of machine civilization and champion of village handicraft. The plan prescribes for India a concentrated dose of industrialization as remedy against want. That remedy may "take"—ultimately; there is surely nothing "gradual" about the proposed treatment. What it would do to India's growing mass of humans is easily foreseeable. After fifteen years there would be available a real force of skilled manpower, but also vastly more people. It does not matter whether or not the Mahatma takes seriously the archaic views he expresses; they do envision a future development which is to be less grandiose, but also less cataclysmic, than that advocated by the go-getting nationalists of the Bombay Plan.

It is to be noted that the Bombay Plan is not the only plan for Indian industrialization. A second plan, called the People's Plan, was put forward by the Indian Federation of Labor. Finally, there is the plan propounded by the government of India. The People's Plan is forthrightly anticapitalist. A spokesman of the Committee of the Indian Federation of Labor, sponsors of the People's Plan, stated the problem as follows: "The fundamental problem of Indian economic life is the problem of poverty. It cannot be solved on the basis of the capitalist system of production. . . . Production is to be planned not with the object of increasing the purchasing power of the people but with that of supplying their requirements. The plan aims at increasing agricultural production by 400 per cent and industrial production by 600 per cent in ten years." *

The authors of the Peoples' Plan propose, therefore, to nationalize all land in India, and to restrict the profit of private capital to 3 per cent. Should this figure not be reached by any privately operated business, the state would help to make it up. As their fundamental political assumption the authors have taken an India which would be a federal democratic state. Unlike the Bombay Plan, the People's Plan favors the consumers' goods industries rather than basic industries.

The plan of the government of India is far more modest. Its emphasis rests on the postwar development of agriculture, civilian aviation, education, and hydroelectric power, and the expansion of railroads. It is at this moment impossible to say which of these plans, if any, will be adopted. There can be no doubt, however, that India contains vast potentials of industrial skills and the entrepreneurial initiative necessary to release them.†

China, too, is slated for a five-year reconstruction program after the war. According to Mr. Wong Wen-hao, Minister of Economic Affairs for the Chungking government, this program provides for the investment of 10 billion United States dollars. Within ten years the annual steel output is to be raised to 5 million tons, and 3 million tons of ships are to be built. This program, which Dr. Wong Wen-hao deems "modest enough to be within the means of the people," ‡ is to be implemented by American co-operation.

The United States Foreign Economic Administration released details of a plan for building 600 industrial plants equipped to manufacture 104 varieties of goods to be distributed over northern, southern, and central China. The objective of these first five years of industrialization is to provide China with telephone and telegraph, a transportation system, and factories producing buses, bicycles, electric bulbs, glass, plumbing fixtures, canneries, cotton, wool, rubber goods, and refrigerator equipment. Selected groups of Chinese are to

* See p. 285, Note 1 to Chapter 14.
† Sirdar Ikbal Ali Shah, "Three Post-War Plans for India," *Fortnightly*, No. 933, New Series, September, 1944, p. 175.
‡ Rowe, *op. cit.*, p. 88.

be trained in the United States as technicians, administrators, supervisors, and training experts. These specialists would receive instruction over periods ranging from six to eighteen months.

The pace of industrialization of the backward countries of Asia (as well as industrial rehabilitation and expansion of Soviet industry) will depend in part on the willingness and ability of the industrially advanced countries to trade and to invest. There is no need to review in these pages the stultifying arguments which are being advanced in favor of tariff protection and against foreign lending. Foreign investments, in raising living standards elsewhere, do not necessarily lower the standards of the capital-exporting country. Low-paid workers in the industrializing countries cannot as a matter of course compete successfully with the highly paid workers of the capital exporting country. The case of Britain and Germany is apposite. In the middle of the nineteenth century British trade with Germany increased rapidly when Germany began to use modern tools. The high standard of American wages is not the result of tariff protection, but of American technological efficiency.

Eugene Staley in one of the most cogent books recently published on world economic problems forecasts the rapid industrialization of backward countries the world over, particularly those of Asia.* He proposes that it be accomplished by international co-operation, and that the leading industrial countries furnish the necessary capital and technological advice. He holds that "economic development of new areas brings both opportunities and dangers to existing industrial areas, but . . . it is definitely possible, by policies of mutual co-operation and intelligent adaptation, to make the advantages far outweigh the disadvantages."

We may agree that the freeing of world trade from its shackles, a goal pursued with such vast patience by Mr. Cordell Hull that it has become synonymous with American foreign policy, will accrue to the mutual benefit of all trading

* Eugene Staley, *op. cit.*, p. 21.

nations. It is therefore of more than casual interest that Eugene Staley writes:

Industrial development is not only a means of attaining higher standards of living, but is also the basis of modern military power. This incentive will certainly play a major role in China, for example, after the present war. The adoption of modern industrial methods in Asia, Africa, South-eastern Europe and Latin America will ultimately have the effect of enhancing the influence of the peoples of these areas in determining the political destinies of their own regions and of the world. Economic development of new areas will no doubt lead to a more even distribution of world political power.

Will the rise of all these newly developing countries in the world power scale mean a lengthy series of wars for power and position, until some new "balance" is established, or until some super-dictator subjugates most of the world and establishes a Roman peace? . . . Or will the newly developing countries throw their influence on the side of a world system of security and orderly change under law, thus assuming in a more peaceful manner the new responsibilities that will come with rising power? *

This, precisely, is the question, and those who are charged with planning the political and military policies of the United States will have to speculate on the answers.

For it is not true that industrialization of a country must *invariably* engender an increase of purchasing power and thereby a widening of the market for new industrial productions to be imported. It would surely be dogmatic to take this for granted. The method by which industrialization is carried through is of decisive importance for judging its effects. The collectivist industrialization of Soviet Russia, after the initial phase characterized by an enormous increase of capital goods, finally resulted in a decreasing importance of foreign trade. The particular economic structure of a country like Russia makes such a development exceptionally easy. It is, moreover, questionable whether, even under the most optimistic assumptions, this industrialization of the earth can be continued indefinitely so that all countries would become richer and richer, and so that world trade would consist

* Staley, *op. cit.*, pp. 216-7.

more and more in the interchange between industrial countries.

It is high time that a note of caution should be sounded when an economist opines that "capital exports, of a dimension that exceeds all past experience, may become a basic condition for the establishment of full employment at home, at least if the framework of free enterprise is to be maintained." * The same economist finds the 7-billion-dollar estimate for American foreign trade after World War II issued by the Department of Commerce much too low, and considers that the United States needs outlets abroad for from 12 to 13 billion dollars' worth of goods. Gratifying as this prospect may be for the advocates of full employment at any price, it contains some terrifying implications, particularly if we consider the position of other trading countries.

Rapid industrialization of backward countries may call for capital goods exports far surpassing the value of that item in American foreign trade before World War I. Obviously, this will be good for business and employment. Wartime demands have not increased consumers' goods industries in the highly advanced countries. On the contrary, they have imposed considerable restrictions upon the civilian market. Capital and workers have poured into factories making machinery, aircraft, ships, and electrical devices. In 1943, American machine-tool output, for example, was fifteen times as large as the annual average for 1929-1939. The tool and metallurgical industries of other industrial countries have been greatly expanded, while such countries as, for example, Brazil, the Argentine, and Australia have learned to make out of metal all kinds of complicated devices which they formerly obtained by imports.

It appears, therefore, that war has expanded the capital goods industries of the older industrial countries while increasing competition in some of their export markets. The greatest excess capacity will therefore exist in the typical war industries, notably those making heavy goods and manufacturing equipment. This circumstance greatly favors the industrializing countries, seeking just these kinds of products.

* Fritz Sternberg, "The United States in the Future World Economy," *Social Research*, Vol. II, No. 3, Sept., 1945, p. 293.

It also limits the choice of alternatives before the prospective exporters whose trading policies stand in danger of reflecting disquieting bulges of their own economy rather than long-term considerations of economic and political equilibrium.

America's capacity to produce and to invest abroad will be much greater after World War II than it was after World War I. However, it is worth recalling that up to World War II new international investment has never exceeded 2 billion dollars per year, and that by no means all of it turned out from the investors' point of view to have been invested soundly and profitably.

Opening the floodgates of American productivity may smother the trade of the traditional friends of the United States. Some may be inclined to brush this argument aside. For is not lusty competition the life blood of world trade? The answer is that "competition" of this kind cannot be had without generous government subsidies, and subsidized foreign trade has the annoying tendency of exceeding the quantity of business which can be done with a reasonable expectancy of profit and repayment of credits. Dumping by any other name is still dumping.

Were we to accept the thesis that after World War II everything will be different, that new investment will increase by leaps and bounds, and that foreign debtors will square their accounts punctually, there remains still the question of the benefit backward peoples derive from industrialization.

In India, for example, the process of industrialization has thus far been accompanied by disorganization of communal life. At the end of the last century, machine-made textile goods were underselling the hand-woven khaddar, chief produce of Indian village skills. The Indian village had been a self-sufficient economic unit. Importation of cheap manufactured goods and the pull of new industrial-urban centers have tended to break up the Indian village community. A similar development can be discerned in China, where it remains to be seen whether the village co-operatives (which have meant so much to the war effort of China and were so vividly described by Western observers) will be able to meet the competition of large-scale enterprise.

How a Chinese sociologist views the human factor in the industrialization of his country can be gleaned from a study recently published in this country. It presents the results of a survey conducted in a government-controlled and -operated plant located in Kunming. It casts an interesting light on working conditions and training methods in Chinese state industry. This plant "with about 500 workers . . . is fairly typical of the publicly owned factories in interior China . . . and does not regard profit making as its sole concern. . . ." How this public-spirited enterprise recruits a skilled labor force and harmonizes regional differences in skill of local (Yünnan) workers and immigrants from eastern China is told best in the words of the Chinese scholar:

The apprentices lived in a special dormitory and were controlled entirely by the authority. They were prevented from close contact with the "bad habits and ideas" of the mature skilled workers. They were not allowed even to go home, because previous experience had shown that frequent family visits were followed by reduction of efficiency. A strict training camp is thus instituted in the factory. . . . The young boys had no definite role in their own community, no previously fixed occupational habits, and no prejudice against the rigid organization of modern industry, i.e., to being tied to machines. They form a group in the factory and work together, live together, and play with their young fellow workers. Management is happy in the belief that they have discovered the fundamental solution of the labor problem in modern industry. . . . But, what will be the outcome for these young men of years of rigid training in isolation? What kind of personality will be formed in a collective life unrelated to a normal environment? What will be the social consequence for China if her industry is filled by workers trained under this new system? *

This vignette of Chinese industrialism is drawn from life, whereas Aldous Huxley's Brave New World is mere fiction. None the less the resemblance is uncanny.

If, actually, the process of industrialization in India and China were to transform the lives of the people gradually,

* Kuo-heng Shih, *China Enters the Machine Age,* Harvard University Press, Cambridge, 1944. pp. 212-3. See also H. F. MacNair's pungent review in the *Annals,* Vol. 237, January, 1945, pp. 22-3.

while dislocations were smoothed over by expert planners, then its benefits would outweigh whatever temporary suffering it involves. Thus far there has been nothing gradual about the impact of the machine upon agricultural and handicraft civilizations anywhere, neither under the capitalist system nor under the planned economy of Russia. No one can now say whether or not a cultural catastrophe far greater than that engendered by the impact of industrial revolution upon Western countries will follow in the wake of the industrialization of India and China. If such a catastrophe occurs, it will be exacerbated by unrelieved population pressure. In the West, increase of population was one of the consequences of industrialization. By contrast, in India and China industrialization is being grafted on populations already perilously close to the limits of subsistence.

The masses of Asia who are losing their old communal cohesion and have not yet conformed to the stringent pattern of modern industrial living may prove the most inflammable material for nationalist propaganda. Is it not probable that spiritual values far more primitive than those discarded in the process of economic transformation will fill the void of the Indian and Chinese soul? In the West, nationalism took the place of the old allegiances, political and religious, which Western society renounced in exchange for the promises of economic progress and of the natural sciences which had made that progress possible. Nationalism, just because of its all-inclusiveness, is the most ready substitute for all the values men have cast aside in the pursuit of the material goals implicit in modern civilization. In view of the latent tensions already now existing in the East, it requires no second sight to predict the rise of intense nationalisms as aggressive and as aspiring as those fostered by the formation of masses in the West.

The Indian industrialists behind the Bombay Plan are, above all, nationalists. Indian imperialism is not a figment of the imagination of a few intellectuals. Indian capitalists exercise virtual economic control of Burma; Indian settlers outnumber British in Kenya and Fiji; and many Indians are prepared to claim for India the leading role in a southeast Asiatic federation which would include Burma, the Malay

222

States, the Netherlands Indies, and possibly Siam. Only the exigencies of coalition warfare have muted the voices calling for re-creation of China's imperial realm and the annexation of Burma, Thailand, and Indo-China. That these aspirations have thus far not elicited the enthusiasm of the average Indian or Chinese is no proof that they will not do so in the future. Rapid industrialization will increase existing internal tensions and create new ones. If past experience is a guide to the future, the rulers of an independent India and China will seek to externalize these tensions by the familiar devices of nationalist propaganda. The existence of powerful Indian and Chinese communities throughout eastern Africa and Malaysia may furnish those irredentist issues which lend themselves so readily to exploitation by would-be imperialists.*

At present rates of output American industry could furnish but a fraction of the goods required for raising appreciably the standards of living of the Chinese and Indian peoples. But assuming that the American economy can be expanded indefinitely, that resources depleted by the insatiable demand of mass manufacture will always be replaced by suitable substitutes, and that for industrializing backward countries only certain key equipment is needed anyway, it does not follow as a matter of course that American export trade must always be a blessing for other peoples and for the American people themselves. When Indian and Chinese markets have become saturated with canned food, water closets, and motorcycles, the ensuing gain may not be as substantial as may appear from purely economic calculations.

It is proposed that India and China, in order to raise the living standards of the common people, expand consumers' goods industries rather than heavy industry. It is by no means certain that they will abide by this injunction and will not want first to install the plants suitable for making heavy machinery and weapons. Thus the issue of international cooperation in industrializing India and China cannot be dealt with in purely economic or humanitarian terms.

* K. M. Panikkar, *The Future of South-East Asia*, issued under the auspices of the Institute of Pacific Relations, New York, 1943, pp. 59, 104-5.

Only a strong central government can create a strong and united China. The destruction of the Japanese Empire does not alone secure the unity and independence of China. To draw the parts which now compose the geographical expression "China" into one state, the central government will have to base its authority upon military power. By the same token, the fulcrum of the Far Eastern balance of power is the national independence of China. The dilemma of any Chinese government, no matter what its political complexion, is how to build up its war potential while raising the standard of living of the Chinese masses. The rulers of China, like those of Russia in the 1920's and 1930's, may choose to impose staggering sacrifices on their people in order to strengthen the power of the state. In China's case, such a policy involves the freezing, for decades to come, of living standards which are desperately low even compared to those of the Russian masses throughout the era of forced industrialization. Only the future can reveal whether the results will warrant the costs of the experiment.*

Industrialization is an educational process. The industrialization of Japan and Russia was speeded by imports of foreign capital. But it was accomplished chiefly by imports of Western science and industrial techniques. Under a reign of international law and free trade, "borrowed knowledge" does not impoverish the countries which supply it, for the export of ideas and skills adds to the knowledge of all of mankind. The larger the common fund of knowledge, the greater is the share of "exporting" and receiving country alike, for knowledge "increases by being applied under new circumstances and by cross-fertilization of ideas passing back and forth among many minds." Under a reign of Great Power rivalries and bilateral trade, the export of knowledge may prove the most expensive kind of foreign trade. The costs of engineering advice exported by the United States and Britain to Japan are still being paid for by the blood and sweat of both nations. Similar exports of technological know-how to India and China, we are told, will be crowned by very

* For an excellent impartial discussion of the problem see Rowe, *op. cit.*, pp. 30, 84-9.

different rewards. For industrialization will come to India and China as a series of graduated steps carefully supervised and guided by their foreign friends, purveyors, and preceptors, and "improved living standards help to stabilize peace." *

On economic grounds the case for economic collaboration is strong. Every undergraduate student of economics can argue it convincingly against the minions of economic Malthusianism. However, the efficacy and beneficence of free trade depends on the observance of principles which, like those underlying the peaceful adjustment of power-political interests, are essentially moral.

A large share in international exchanges—be it ever so satisfactory on a commercial basis—does not necessarily enhance the power of a nation. Trade with Japan yielded the United States solid commercial profits; however, on balance, Japan waxed stronger by drawing upon America's store of wealth. Japan purchased machines, oil, scrap iron, and knowledge, while no proportionate gain accrued to the United States from the importation of far more easily replaceable materials, for example, silk. Japan gained easy access to American oil and iron by purchase. Subsequently she obtained access to Britain's principal source of rubber by conquest. The possibility may be excluded that the arrangement will be repeated. Yet these painful experiences do not strengthen the argument that foreign trade invariably serves national interest and that each nation should concentrate upon the output of those goods it is able to produce cheapest.

The United States and Great Britain enjoyed free access to the low-priced rubber supplies of the East Indies; so, for that matter, did any other trading nation. All the canons of the international division of labor and cost accounting ruled out the large-scale development of rubber plantations in Latin America or the manufacture of substitute products in Britain and the United States. Yet no one will argue that the United States and Britain were unwise to weigh the price of military security against the economic advantages they en-

* Alexander Taub, Chief Engineer of the Foreign Economic Administration, as quoted in an interview by Margaret Davis, Washington *Post*, December 7, 1944.

joyed from the international division of labor, to wit, the specialization of Malaya in raising low-cost rubber.

It is by no means self-evident that industrializing, and thus enriching, backward regions is *under all circumstances* in the interest of those nations who promote it by exporting their tools and skills. Improved living standards do not necessarily help to stabilize peace. The great war-making nations are rich nations. Poor nations cannot afford making war. Germany and Japan were "have not" nations only by the definition of their own propagandists. Compared to the great mass of mankind, the German and Japanese peoples were fabulously rich.

A share in the world's trade stands in no direct relationship to a nation's political interests, and its best customers, whether in bilateral or multilateral trade, may be its most powerful political enemies. Today, this proposition is self-evident; to labor it borders on naïveté. Yet the termination of World War II will unleash tremendous productive forces upon the world market. The creation of new jobs through foreign trade stands high on the postwar agenda of all the principal trading nations. The prospects are for intense competition and vigorous assertion of sectional interests. Pressure for jobs and outlets will determine commercial policies. It is not so difficult to test their soundness by rules every good merchant applies to his business dealings. The formulas, to be sure, will be new. The emphasis upon grandiose humanitarian goals to be obtained through foreign trade may make it more difficult to distinguish between group and national interests, profits and losses. The danger of over-trading and over-lending does not become smaller because foreign trade and lending will proceed to the tune of sonorous declarations, ambitious planning, and governmental subsidies. Over-trading and undertrading are both negations of the principles of free trade, the former being perhaps the more dangerous form of economic maladjustment. For exports without proportionate imports impoverish the exporting country, and hence result in a net loss of national resources and military power.

Under a system of free trade the peoples of backward countries will be able to improve their agriculture, expand their textile industries, and gradually develop their basic industries, provided the latter dispose of the requisite supply of raw materials and labor. They may not always be able to buy and to borrow what they want from the richer countries. While this retards their development, it lessens the dangers of sudden dislocations and assures a more gradual transformation of the social structure. A noble impatience with the squalor and poverty of backward peoples should be tempered by the prosaic patience which the work of transformation, fraught with so many imponderable risks, calls for in mutual interest. Inflated lending and dumping camouflaged as "development loans" may foster the very social and political tensions they are supposed to alleviate. It is conceivable that tools and skills so exported are returned in the form not of goods and profits, but of bullets. It is conceivable because it happened.

15. THE INDUSTRIAL POWERS OF 1970

"TECHNOLOGICAL PROGRESS" cannot be defined as easily as we may wish for the sake of neat tabulation. We agreed that it is a function not only of inventiveness but also of general economic progress which is measured most conveniently in terms of national income and capital per head of working population. The problem of projecting future technological progress is like a problem in the resultant of forces. Its direction is determined by many factors—such as resiliency of social structure, vitality of the race, and many others—while in turn it determines the force of all of them. Like national power, technological progress cannot be measured accurately. Hence, projecting this highly composite development will furnish but a crude diagram—a picture of conditions which might prevail were certain observed changes to continue at observed rates. In addition there is the problem of evaluating statistics which no nation compiles in just the same fashion or with just the same ends in view as any other nation.

In the preceding pages the attempt has been made to determine the relationship of a nation's economic strength and technological progressiveness to its military and political power. This relationship is plausible, although it may not be as direct as purely material factors may indicate. The following table is a sample of how a comparison between various "power potentials" can be set up on the basis of a few important indices of productivity. The "power potentials" of Great Britain, the Soviet Union, Germany, and Japan are expressed in percentages of that of the United States, allowance being made for differences in population and relative dependence on imports of essential raw materials and foodstuffs:

TABLE VII

"POWER POTENTIALS" OF WORLD POWERS, 1940

	Great Britain and Empire	U.S.S.R.	Germany	Japan and Empire	U.S.A.
Coal (B) * (thousands of metric tons) 1940	296,804	130,000	220,000	50,000	453,245
Iron ore * (thousands of metric tons) 1940	22,432	30,000	15,000	4,500	74,879
Steel (thousands of long tons) 1940	16,400	19,465	25,130	7,000	59,806
Electric power † (millions of kw. hrs.) 1937	30,700	30,000	55,238	26,714	120,997
Horsepower-hr.‡ (daily output per capita) 1939	7.96	2.21	5.72	1.75	12.27
% of U.S.	32	30	35	11	100

This table appears to agree fairly well with the facts of World War II, particularly if allowance is made for the comparatively large portion of the resources of the United States and Great Britain tied down by the maintenance of their basic economies or diverted, for political and other reasons, to areas lying outside the war zones.

What will be the future growth of the United States and Great Britain, the old industrial countries par excellence, the Soviet Union, an industrializing country well ahead in the adaptation of modern techniques, and India and China, the industrializing countries of tomorrow?

Colin Clark estimates that capital required per head of working population will increase in the United States between 1940 and 1960 from approximately 5,150 to 6,310 IU's. The Soviet Union, according to Clark, will increase its work-

* T. S. Lovering, *Minerals and World Affairs*, New York, 1943, pp. 357-366.
† League of Nations *Statistical Year-Book*, 1937-38, Geneva, 1938, pp. 130-1.
‡ T. T. Read, "The World's Output of Work," *The American Economic Review*, Vol. 35, No. 1, p. 145. British output is calculated for the United Kingdom only. The U.S. produced about 40 per cent of the world's energy.

ing capital from 1,130 to 2,450, while in India capital per head of working population will increase from 580 to 1,040, and in China from 180 to 420 IU's.* For Britain he predicts a slight decrease as a result of an over-all decline of population.† This assumption appears too pessimistic, for a positive population policy, such as that suggested by Prime Minister Churchill, may achieve at least one modest goal, namely, maintaining Britain's population stable for the next twenty-five years.

It should go without saying that these estimates are based on numerous and highly audacious assumptions. They do not purport to forecast actual developments. Their value lies rather in the orders of magnitude they postulate. None of these estimates, however assumes a rate of capital growth in India and China as well as in the Soviet Union which will be sufficiently rapid to overtake the lead of the United States. The national wealth of the United States as well as capital equipment per head of working population will, by, let us say, 1970, be larger than that of India and China, as well as that of the Soviet Union—provided the past rate of economic growth of the United States is not curtailed.

Clark's estimates are substantially in accord with the calculations of other leading economists,‡ who agree that the annual rate of growth of output up to World War II was roughly 3 per cent in western Europe, and 4 per cent in the United States. Slightly less than half of the annual increase in western Europe and somewhat more than half the annual increase in the United States can be assigned to the increase of labor supply. Thus it appears that in western Europe and the United States 1.5 to 2 per cent of the annual rate of growth can be attributed mainly to changes in technique and to the exploitation of new material resources. As the Soviet Union is slated for substantial population increases by 1970, growth of physical output may be expected to increase roughly at a rate of 4 per cent per annum, the rate maintained by the United States up to World War II.

India and China must now be classified as overpopulated

* Colin Clark, *The Economics of 1960*, London, 1943, pp. 80-1.
† *Ibid.*, p. 83.
‡ Computations of growth of real capital formation in England, 1875.

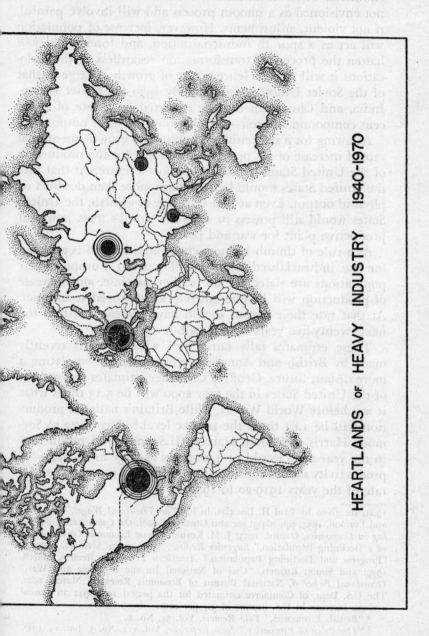

HEARTLANDS OF HEAVY INDUSTRY 1940-1970

countries. Their industrialization, it has been pointed out, is not envisioned as a smooth process and will involve painful, if not violent, adjustments. However, increase of population will act as a spur to industrialization, and foreign aid will hasten the process of transformation regardless of the dislocations it will cause. Hence a rate of growth as large as that of the Soviet Union is assumed. By 1970 the Soviet Union, India, and China can thus be expected—at a rate of 4 per cent compound interest—to treble their physical output.

Allowing for a slackening of population growth, an annual rate of increase of 2.5 per cent is assumed for the production of the United States—probably too low a figure. At that rate the United States should by 1970 have more than doubled its physical output. Even at that slow rate of growth, the United States would still possess in 1970 the world's most powerful productive plant for war and peace.

As a rule of thumb 1.5 per cent annual growth is assumed for the industrialized countries of western Europe. Their populations are slated for no further increase, and increase of production will be due entirely to improved techniques. At that rate their output should have increased within the next twenty-five years by one-half.

These estimates tally fairly well with forecasts recently made by British and American economists contemplating a more distant future. Geoffrey Crowther estimates that output of the United States in the year 2000 will be 5.13 times what it was before World War II, while Britain's national production will be 1.64 times the prewar level.* According to Seymour Harris and Alvin Hansen, U.S. industrial production in the year 2000 would be 4.58 times as large as in 1940—"if productivity should continue to rise from 1940 to 2000 at the rate of the years 1919-20 to 1940." †

1909, are given by Paul H. Douglas, in his *The Theory of Wages*, New York and London, 1934, pp. 464-5; see also Gustave Cassel, *On Quantitative Thinking in Economics*, Oxford, 1935; J. M. Keynes, "Some Economic Consequences of a Declining Population," *Eugenics Review*, April, 1937; Alvin H. Hansen, "Progress and Declining Population," *American Economic Review*, March, 1939; and Simon Kuznets, "Uses of National Income in Peace and War," *Occasional Paper 6*, National Bureau of Economic Research, March, 1942. The U.S. Dept. of Commerce estimated for the period 1919-1942 an annual average increase in U.S. income of 3.4 per cent.

* "British Economics," *Yale Review*, Vol. 34, No. 2.

† "The Price of Prosperity," *New Republic*, Vol. 112, No. 3, Jan. 15, 1945.

In terms of heavy industry the United States would by 1970 have raised its production of steel from a peacetime level of 59 million tons (1940) to between 125 and 130 million tons, while Russia would have increased her production to 60 million tons, a figure somewhat higher than the 50-million-ton goal set by Marshal Stalin in his conversation with Eric Johnston, and in line with a 50- to 60-million-ton goal mentioned by V. Molotov as being "a gigantic task, a task which is far beyond the bounds of the third Five-Year Plan." * By the same method we arrive at a figure of approximately 18 to 20 million tons for India, which would approximately equal the production of the Soviet Union in 1940, and a figure of 25 million for China, provided she controls the combined resources of the North China–Manchuria–Korea coal and iron-ore complex and be able to finance iron ore imports from overseas—India, the Philippines, the East Indies, and the United States, i.e., the producers who formerly supplied the steel mills of Japan.

Offhand, there is nothing in these figures resembling a serious challenge within this generation to the lead of the United States, nor to the per capita productivity and standard of living of the American worker. There is little likelihood that levels of productivity and consumption in the Soviet Union can be raised within the next twenty-five years to those of the United States. Any theory that these levels in India and China can be brought even within shooting distance of American standards is fantastic nonsense. These probabilities, pleasing as they may be from the point of view of America's lead in economic progress, require important qualifications, particularly as regards the military security of the United States:

1) The potentialities of growth in Great Britain and France, the European allies of the United States, may be greater than mere prospects of population growth indicate. However, absolute gain relative to that of the non-European powers will be insignificant.

2) It is a reasonable, not a safe, assumption that Germany

* V. Molotov, *The Soviet Union in 1942*. Report made to the Eighteenth Congress of the Communist Party of the Soviet Union, March 14 and 17, 1937, Workers Library Publishers, New York, 1939, p. 25.

and Japan will be kept disarmed not only militarily but also technologically, and that their power potential, no matter how reduced, will not again become a makeweight in the international balance of power.

3) The consolidation of Russian hegemony over the European "shatter zone" would add the manpower of predominantly Slavic, demographically young countries to Russia's own growing population. It would merge the considerable raw-material resources, metallurgical and ordnance plants, and highly skilled labor forces of Silesia, Czechoslovakia, Austria, and Hungary with Russia's own expanding industry.

4) The political unification of the European continent under a single power would profoundly alter the distribution of technological and economic potentials as charted in our diagram. The total population of continental Europe, excluding Russia, is 325 million. Productive age groups total 240 million—a figure exceeded only by China and India. As regards skills, inventiveness, and technological equipment a unified Europe would rank first among the world's great powers. In 1939, 50 million workers engaged in mining and industry, operated engines developing 75 million horsepower, and produced 50 billion dollars' worth of industrial goods. The secondary industries of the United States and Canada, combined, employed, in the same year, 20 million workers and turned out industrial products valued, too, at 50 billion dollars. The fact that the output of two and one-half times as many workers in Europe was no larger than that of the United States and Canadian workers is due not only to the less abundant resources but also to the political and economic divisions of Europe. The potentialities of a unified Europe would, in all likelihood, be much greater than a mere aggregation of its many parts would indicate. The United States fought two wars to prevent the concentration of all the resources of Europe under one master, namely, Germany. Under any other master a unified Europe would be the strongest unit of world power.

5) It does not follow as a matter of course that per capita figures of industrial productivity will portray the military potentials of nations more faithfully in the future than they have done in the past. Notwithstanding a comparatively low

industrial productivity and small amount of real capital per head of population, the Soviet Union has managed by a prodigious use of manpower to build up a formidable war machine. By throttling and confining industrial progress to comparatively small areas of the national economy and population, the younger industrial countries of Europe and Asia can substantially increase their war potential. The United States and the states of western Europe may not pursue this aim as single-mindedly. They may seek to spread the benefits of technological progress evenly over their populations. In World War II the output of the civilian (basic) economy of the United States had by 1945 not been substantially diminished, at least not in comparison with that of other belligerent nations. Dependence on an elaborate transportation system and high living standards, and political resistance to their curtailment, barred the diversion of *all* available resources to the business of war. Both the Soviet Union and Germany have shown that rigid consumers' controls, preferential treatment of certain sectors of the population, and enforced labor will boost military potentials far beyond what seems likely on the basis of per capita figures of national income and capital equipment.

A higher standard of living is, all else being equal, a positive factor in a country's military strength vis-à-vis another country. However, this holds true only within limits. It does not hold true when a country enjoying a high standard of living is faced by an aggressor superior in manpower and possessed of an industrial establishment devoted principally to the satisfaction of certain strata of society, as for example, bureaucracy, skilled labor, and the army, at the expense of the living standards of the population as a whole. It does not follow as a matter of course that such a state will be militarily "inefficient." Such a maldistribution of national income can be perpetuated indefinitely without causing much distress to the ruling groups, and may be accepted stoically, perhaps even enthusiastically, by the masses, offensive as this fact may be from the point of view of welfare economics.

Part Five

WORLD POLITICS AND POWER

We cannot deny that power is a factor in world politics any more than we can deny its existence as a factor in national politics. But in a democratic world as in a democratic nation power must be linked with responsibility and obliged to defend and justify itself within the framework of the general good.

—President Franklin D. Roosevelt

16. AMERICAN POWER IN TRANSITION

THE fabulous story of United States military might in World War II is told best by the following figures: The production of American war industries rose from 2.8 billion dollars in 1940, one-third the British total, to 86 billion dollars in 1944, six times the figure for Britain. Naval tonnage increased from 1,230,000 to 3,900,000 on November 1, 1944,* or twice the total tonnage of the British navy and as large as all the prewar navies of all the Great Powers combined.† Military aircraft production in total weight of air frames increased from 6.6 million pounds in 1939 to 667 million pounds in 1943, exactly a hundredfold increase.‡ In 1944 military aircraft production averaged approximately 9,000 per month, despite the fact that weights of individual aircraft consistently increased. Thus the output of the United States averaged three times that of Britain, and one and one-half times the combined Anglo-Russian production. Combined effectives of the army and the navy were 12 million. In 1944, 18 million workers were engaged in war industries and the civilian labor force of the United States exceeded 55 millions.§

As this pageant of military and industrial power unfolds there seems to be scant reason for pondering a future in which the conditions now making for the industrial and military pre-eminence of the United States will not hold. Yet we can clearly perceive forces at work which tend to reduce the commanding lead the United States now possesses. Because of the increase in the rate of change, contemporary international power relationships may prove to be of a far more

* *Our Navy at War,* official report by Admiral Ernest J. King, U.S.N., covering combat operations up to March 1, 1944; Washington, 1944.
† See page 286, Note 1 to Chapter 16.
‡ *The Official Guide to the Army Air Forces,* New York, 1944.
§ *Labor Force Bulletin,* U.S. Department of Commerce, Bureau of the Census, November, 1944, p. 11.

transitory nature than the present distribution of strength indicates.

In the preceding pages some of the trends and estimates affecting our population and raw-material resources have been passed in fragmentary review. As regards military man-power, the United States may have in 1970 less than two-thirds of that forecast for Russia, no more than that projected for Japan, less than one-fourth of that predicted for India, and only one-third of that estimated for the Soviet Union and eastern Europe combined. As for mineral resources, some appear in no danger of exhaustion, others are already begin-ning to show the effects of the drain upon them. As regards the industrial lead of the United States, it will, in 1970, still be a formidable one. However, other nations are gradually whittling away the lead which the United States now pos-sesses. Despite glaring deficiencies, inherent in the political system rather than in natural conditions, the industrializa-tion of the Soviet Union will proceed vigorously. Similarly, centers of heavy industry in India and the Yellow Sea region are slated for substantial expansion. By 1970, Soviet Asia, India, and perhaps the Yellow Sea region may have become broad, economically independent bases of military power.

The United States is superior to any other country on the sea and in the air. Yet the total military strength of the United States is not so great that it could fight alone against a coalition of other Great Powers. Hence the over-all security of the United States would not be assured were it to rely en-tirely on its own forces. What under present conditions seems a comparatively safe position will be considerably weakened two or three decades hence. For the relative strength of the United States will also be determined by the position of its traditional allies. Great Britain and France are slated not only for relative but also for absolute declines in manpower, a condition heretofore not faced by the Atlantic community. Their industrial productivity is scheduled for slow expan-sion; their share in total world output will decline.

In 1870, Britain produced half of the world's pig iron and coal; today Britain has only one-tenth the industrial war potential of the world. Britain's power declined while her commitments outside Europe grew. Nationalist movements and expanding military power in Asia are bound to tie down a larger part of Britain's decreased strength; only a smaller part of British manpower and productive plant will be available to meet strategic requirements in Europe.

France will come out of this war less strong than in 1918. Her obsolescent plant will be the worse for wear after four years of occupation. The incalculable loss of prestige France suffered through defeat will, for many years to come, sap her political initiative. She may, because she escaped widespread devastation and her new rulers will not shirk the utmost effort, resume the position of a secondary power. The decline of her influence in world politics appears, within this generation, irreversible.

The decline of Britain and France in Europe is compounded by mounting pressures which will impinge upon their empires from within and without. The increase of the power of the United States will thus be balanced by the decrease in the power of Britain and France.

It is, then, only a seeming paradox that the United States, notwithstanding a smaller war potential, exerted a more powerful diplomatic influence upon the settlement of 1919 than she is likely to exercise in the settlement after World War II. Japan was Britain's ally. The United States fought only on one front. The disintegration of the Russian armies and the defeat of Germany resulted in a concentration of overwhelming power in the hands of the western Allies. And among these western Allies the United States, by virtue of its uncommitted reserves, was the strongest. So vast has been the increase of its war potential since then that the relative deterioration of its diplomatic position is hardly ever recognized.

A fashionable analogy likens the position the United States will hold on the morrow of victory to the dominance Britain exerted in the nineteenth century. There is indeed a suggestive likeness. Britain's economy emerged from the Napoleonic Wars intact. Insular position and sea power had kept the enemy from the shores of the British Isles while large areas of the European continent had suffered the depredations of mass warfare. After World War II the United States, like Britain in 1815, will be able to outproduce any and all economic rivals. But the parallel can be stretched no further.

The United States does not enjoy the strategic leverage vis-à-vis the land masses of Eurasia which Britain throughout the nineteenth century enjoyed vis-à-vis the European continent. The concentration of all military power on the European continent was a unique condition which, while it lasted, insured Britain's hegemony at a minimum of military effort.

Geography had endowed England with the advantage of a central position. The British Isles lay athwart the approaches of northwestern Europe to the Atlantic Ocean. Against any fleet based on the Continent the British fleet could operate along interior lines and without exposing its line of retreat to its bases. British forces in the English Channel and North Sea could intercept and prevent the junction of the fleets of northern and western Europe. Similarly, British naval forces based on Gibraltar could intercept hostile fleet movements between the Mediterranean and the Atlantic. No single European power could build a fleet powerful enough to challenge Britain's command of the seas, and Europe's political divisions happily guarded Britain against the one eventuality which could have threatened her dominant position, namely, a coalition against her of all the Continental powers.

In the nineteenth century no major power saw fit to challenge the *status quo,* and Europe appeared to accept Britain's sublimated version of the balance of power as the norm of international relationships. Neither the dissemination of Western techniques nor nationalist doctrines had yet aroused the backward peoples of the East to the consciousness of their own potential strength. Japan had not yet tested her naval and military power against that of a European state. The United States was still absorbed in the task of consolidating and exploiting its vast continental domain. Europe was the unchallenged power center of the globe, and Britain controlled European power at its source.

The rise of extra-European powers, the world-wide diffusion of Western techniques, and the disintegration of the international economic system closed that era which might be labeled the "European Age." World power is based no longer exclusively on Europe.

In a strictly military sense, the United States will lack one advantage, perhaps the most essential one, which Britain enjoyed in the past: safety from direct attack. New developments in ordnance bid fair to bring the entire territories of the United States within the range of enemy fire, whereas it was imperviousness to direct attack that, up to the age of flight, was the core of Britain's political and military policies. Uncle Sam is thus faced with problems which did not crease the brow of Britannia.

It is now being asserted glibly that American power, preferably in the form of air power, can be made effective in the remotest corner of the globe. The weapon of Pax Americana is to be the plane, just as the ship of the line was the instrument of force which kept the Peace of Britain. It has been pointed out that the keeping of that peace depended on a host of nonmilitary factors. But let us examine the question of whether the purely military facts suggest that the United States can repeat through air power the feat achieved by Britain in the era of sea power.

Britain's naval supremacy was gained in the age of sail. By a singular coincidence the fleet of sailing ships that fought the battle of Trafalgar was based on a coal- and iron-bearing island. Britain was the first country to industrialize. The Industrial Revolution revolutionized naval technology, and British steel makers compounded the supremacy the British navy had gained under sail. Britain's historical opponents did not or could not avail themselves of the new industrial techniques which rendered obsolete the wooden hull.* Thus British experience runs counter to some of the most cherished axioms of history, such as "The technical superiority of the victor passes to the defeated," and "The conservative military mind prepares to fight tomorrow's war with yesterday's weapons." Britain's is the rare case of a nation which was able to revolutionize in peace the military techniques which

* Bernard Brodie, *Seapower in the Machine Age*, Princeton, 1940, p. 41.

243

had given it victory in war. It is possible that another nation, for example, the United States, will be so singularly favored by fortune as was Britain, but it would be the height of folly to take this possibility for a certainty.

The present distribution of air power favors the United States. The United States not only possesses the biggest air fleet but also the biggest potential for building aircraft. The United States by virtue of its human and industrial resources possesses genuine air power. Air power is based on air force, air commerce, and air industry—just as in Mahan's analysis British sea power is conceived as resting upon fighting ships, merchant marine, and the great yards of the Clyde and Tyne —an integrated whole symbolized by the three-pronged trident of Neptune. An international air force such as that contemplated by the Dumbarton Oaks proposals * would be powerless without the support of the United States; or—to put it differently—for the time being, only the United States is capable of "keeping the peace through air power."

The history of World War II has thus far failed to confirm the claims of the extreme proponents of "victory through air power." So spectacular have been the exploits of air power, so eloquent the voices of its exponents, from Douhet to Seversky, that supremacy in the air is now being widely accepted as axiomatic in planning for security in peace and victory in war.

The conception of the most extreme and most popular exponents of air-power-and-nothing-but-air-power can be fairly and simply stated as follows: an air fleet powerful enough to seek out the enemy's air fleet, to defeat it in battle or destroy it on the ground, then to pound the enemy's territory into submission by massive bombing.

Thus far no victory of this kind has been won. Russia, for example, refused to comply in just that way with the claims of the air-power enthusiasts. Well-defined trends in industrial and communal planning are modifying the geography of the world's aviation targets—if they have not profoundly modified that geography already. Air power will, in wars to come,

* Proposals for the Establishment of a General International Organization, Section B. 5, *Dumbarton Oaks Documents on International Organization*, U.S. Department of State, Publication 2192, Conference Series, 56.

remain the sharp edge of a nation's total fighting power. Preponderance in the air has been tactically decisive on many a battlefield and will be so on many more. But the case histories of Warsaw, Rotterdam, London, and Cologne can no more be taken as the final and conclusive evidence of what planes can do to civilian targets than the triumph of the Stuka over massed Polish cavalry can be accepted as the final verdict in the case of plane versus mobile ground forces.

Important factories, especially ammunition plants, will be equipped increasingly with underground facilities for both work and recreation, and fortified by heavy concrete construction. No plausible arguments can be advanced why underground factories, equipped with modern devices of air conditioning and lighting, should not operate as efficiently as surface plants.

Military reality is much too complex to permit any kind of weapon to become all-important. Air power made war more complicated. It has also made war more costly, but it has not done away with traditional weapons. Modern war is an undertaking in which all weapons must be harmoniously employed according to their special limitations. Air power is not a substitute for the older branches of the armed forces. On the contrary, due to the emergence of air power, the army and navy tend to increase rather than to decrease their size and their commitments. The kind of warfare the United States has waged in Europe and Asia is triphibian, i.e., a highly intricate combination of all the weapons of the air, the sea, and the land.

Moreover, every technique, every new invention, is subject to the law of diminishing returns. The introduction of artillery into the art of war gave the power which enjoyed superiority in this novel weapon supremacy on the battlefield. Later, when artillery became one of the chief weapons in all the armies, superiority in artillery, though still of high importance, did no longer of itself insure victory. There are indications that air power is now entering a zone of diminishing returns. Like automobiles, new planes, essentially, are improved and streamlined older models. Some experts assert that new aerodynamic designs and new kinds of propulsion by jet and rocket herald the beginning of a new phase in aviation. Major B. H. Liddell Hart hails the flying bomb as the harbinger of "automatic warfare" which cancels out, "except in a passive form," human qualities in warfare.[*] However great the technical progress of aviation may be, improved technology has only an indirect and perhaps even a remote bearing on the future of air power. It is fallacious to assume that a technically improved weapon is of necessity also a more effective weapon. Technically more perfect weapons have their rudimentary prototypes, which profit less from performance than from surprise. The submarine and the tank of the Second World War were infinitely better weapons than their prototypes of the First World War, and yet during the first war the individual submarine and tank scored greater tactical successes. Although operating under less favorable conditions, they were not checkmated by the effective counter weapons which now oppose technically more perfect models.

Today the United States is industrially equipped for building and maintaining the largest air fleet in existence. After twenty or thirty years, American air preponderance will no longer be relatively as great as it is today. By that time, another power may have become as strong in the air as the United States, and it might even become stronger. All other things being equal, a nation can far more rapidly compete in a race for air power than for naval strength. There was for about a hundred years only one first-class navy; today there are several first-class air fleets. Whatever the case may be, air power does not endow the United States with a special dispensation in world politics.

Would America's interest not be served best if she emulated Britain's nineteenth-century policy of "splendid isolation" made possible by naval supremacy? If America, trusting in her superiority of air strength, withdrew into isolation, a new major war could hardly be averted. Granted that air power in that next war would yield the huge returns its proponents now predict, it would nevertheless have failed in one of the principal purposes for which a political instrument of

[*] "Some Lessons of the European Warfare," *Yale Review*, Vol. 34, No. 3, Spring, 1945, p. 425.

force, as for example the British navy, is designed, namely, preventing war by its mere existence. The purpose of militant isolation, we must presume, is to prevent America from being dragged into war; yet this goal can be attained only by timely prevention, not by inactivity in world politics.

History passes, geography remains, and narrows and island chains retain their strategical importance despite changes in military technology. Gibraltar, Malta, Singapore, and Corregidor are strategic focal points in the age of power-driven craft just as they were in the age of sail. In a contest between powers who are equals in techniques and manpower, possession of geographical advantage spells decisive military advantage. In war the greatest asset is position. It would seem, therefore, a strategic imperative that the United States should maintain a system of outposts in the Atlantic and Pacific—relay stations along supply routes, listening points whence home bases can be alerted to impending danger, and screens designed to hold, in case of surprise attack, until counteroffensives can be mounted.

The bases of the traditional allies of the United States are bases of American power, and the United States should seek to lend assistance in making these bases stronger. The strongest strategic outpost of the United States is Britain. A strong Dakkar in the hands of a friendly France is a powerful element in the joint defense of the South Atlantic; a strong France is the vital bridgehead of Anglo-American power in Europe.

But should the United States not seek, in the image of globe-girdling Britain, to anchor its world-wide commitment in a truly world-wide system of strong points? Shall the United States acquire bases on the African, European, and Asiatic continents? This proposal has met with wide acclaim.

It has been suggested that the United States should shake off its diverse complexes which thus far have inhibited its acquisitive instincts in world politics, and retain all the important bases the world over which are now controlled or serviced by American forces. It requires but elementary knowledge of the world's strategic geography to see that by far the greatest number of the sites proposed as strong points at sea and on land and as ports on the sky are now the property of one or another of the allies of the United States.

According to some it is an anthropological law that victorious tribes acquire the culture pattern of the defeated; the proponents of American hegemony resting upon a generous assortment of bases to be established wherever strategic logic suggests it, appear to be bent upon having the American people verify this "law." The search for new American Gibraltars may recommend itself to the adepts of geostrategy, or rather, global intuition. Any nation that conducts its quest for military security heedless of the antagonisms created may ultimately prove to have increased the dangers that quest sought to diminish. Moreover, the best way to insure weakness at the decisive point is to attempt to be strong everywhere. Every decision in strategy and world politics is a choice between alternatives. It is impossible to provide for every emergency in every respect. The problem is how best to integrate political and military policies with available resources and to apply these to a concrete case at hand. A far-flung net of American bases obtained by pressure may become the most effective means for dispersing resources, and freezing mobility altogether.

Although it is impossible to determine now what value each of these bases would have in a future war, the shape of which we can hardly yet perceive, it is certain that this policy would make doubly sure that in a future war the United States would have no allies and that the allies of today would be at best the stony-faced neutrals of tomorrow.

The character of the diverse doctrines of American neo-imperialism—or extroverted isolationism—is becoming increasingly apparent; the road from isolationist illusion to blustering realism is paved mainly by the half-understood precepts of *Realpolitik*. The phrase "American Century" has the same brassy ring as the term "Manifest Destiny" had two generations ago. Will this century be American? The answer is, hardly. A gratuitous flexing of muscles is not necessarily the mark of world leadership.

Behind the swaggering is the craving for a mechanistic, and therefore more satisfactory, explanation of changes in the world political pattern. This dynamic and popular "cycle" theory—borrowed in the main from German historicism—reduces the political development of nations to youth, adolescence, maturity, and old age. The European Age has passed. Europe, yesterday's theater of world power, will serve tomorrow as the arena in which forces generated from without will operate. Her aging, exhausted peoples must yield leadership to the young giants of East and West. The emergence of regional power blocs heralds the new balance of power. These blocs are symmetric, and power will be so nicely balanced that no individual Super Power will care to seek aggrandizement through war. For each will be equally strong, equally content to exploit its abundant riches, and equally peace-loving.

To be sure, in order to obtain this symmetry some changes are required: A few nations must dispense with their independence, surrender their colonial possessions, and furnish the missing bases which are needed to make the regional Super Power all-powerful. It should be obvious to what catastrophic consequences the adoption of this grossly oversimplified theory of geopolitical evolution must lead. If the United States were to follow a policy of this kind, it could do so only by weakening its traditional allies.

No matter how far civilized nations may have departed from the precept that it is nobler to "war down the proud" than to coerce the weak, history does not confirm the wisdom of turning that precept ·upside down. Moreover, history abundantly demonstrates that its cycles can be reversed, that even in "decline" nations may still demonstrate remarkable vitality, and that the decrepit powers of today may be the strong ones of tomorrow.

The dictates of common sense are thought by Spenglerian fatalists and Malthusian pessimists not to apply to the government of states. If populations cease to grow in countries which are far from overpopulated, this is, we are advised, because they conform to biological "laws." That they obey such "laws" is not only inevitable, but also socially desirable. If nations tend to slacken on the road of economic and technological progress, the reaction of the "cyclic" philosophers is not that something should be done about it, but that it is impossible to do anything. Rise and decline of political power are considered to be outside the reach of human decision, like the movements of planets or the laws of gravity.

Is this indeed a satisfactory explanation? Are nations not masters of their fate? Obviously, no amount of initiative can alter certain facts. The population of the United States will not increase in the future as rapidly as it did in the nineteenth century. The mineral treasures taken out of the earth cannot be put back. There is no longer a whole continent to be opened up for exploitation. No vast personal fortunes will be made by the entrepreneurs of this generation. The United States can no longer afford the luxury of a "no-foreign-policy" foreign policy. The rise in Asia of great nations cannot be halted. The world has become smaller and, for Americans, more dangerous. These are the things which cannot be changed. But there is left a broad area within which political decisions can determine, one way or another, the strength of the United States.

The populous nations of Eurasia will sooner or later, as a result of industrialization and urbanization, pass the maximum point of their demographical development. The United States must seek to maintain its relative position until the rate of increase of the other powers, too, diminishes. If this delaying action is successful, the equilibrium has been maintained. It will have to be fought principally on three fronts: population; natural resources; industrial productivity.

In the past, attempts to influence population trends by government policies were largely unsuccessful, although a good case may be made for the view that intervention was either too late, as in ancient Rome, or too timid and inept, as more recently in European countries. By contrast, there is the tremendous improvement effected within the last hundred years in mortality rates and expectancy of life, which obviously has been influenced by political decisions, i.e., by sanitary and educational measures of all kinds. Recent experience in population policy has shown that limited successes can be achieved. In three countries, Germany, Italy, and, to a lesser degree, France, a low in the birth rate was overcome. Great Britain and Russia have recently adopted population policies. If financial assistance to large families and generous maternity benefits are enacted into law, and if provisions similar to those proposed for Britain by Sir William Beveridge should be adopted by the United States, the population trend may be altered. It has been said that babies cannot be bought. This is true in a sense. Pro-natalist policies will fail if they rely on purely materialist incentives. A population policy must operate in several sectors at once. Ideologies, habits, and customs are not fixed for all eternity and are subject to human control.

Demographical rearmament as a patriotic duty cannot easily be sold by governments to highly sophisticated and individualistic peoples. When Western man seeks to limit births and thus pursues a demographical policy harmful to the power of the nation, there is nothing illogical in his conduct. For he observes quite correctly that his urban-industrial environment is not conducive to the rearing of large families. In a nationalistic race for babies the Western powers would be handicapped from the start. Moreover, in a straight competition with eastern Europe, not to speak of Asia, the ground lost by the Western powers cannot be regained—no matter how greatly the fertility of the present populations may be increased. The problem is, therefore, to adopt population policies which harmonize with the ideas governing the moral and economic conduct of Western man. This means in effect a population policy of limited objectives—the maintenance of the rate of growth at least at the present level. Even these limited objectives can be attained only in a free society. A society is truly free where the greatest number of men own property, possess real independence, and regard economic liberty as a matter of course.

The United States has no population policy worthy of the name. On the contrary, the policy of the United States, as made into law, *aims* at restricting population growth. Throughout history, population growth has followed increase of wealth and productivity, partly because more children could be reared, partly because it stimulated immigration. The United States still exerts a powerful pull on the surplus populations and uprooted peoples of Europe. A huge capital of manpower, brains, and skills is America's for the asking. An intelligent policy of *laissez passer* is today as much in the true interest of the United States as it ever was in its history.

The industrial empire of the United States is built in the main on coal, iron ore, and oil. For generations to come, known coal deposits will be sufficient to meet the demands of an expanding economy. The iron ore reserves of the Mesabi range may be used up within another ten to fifteen years—if the rate of mining continues at the current level. As regards oil, the United States does not face the threat of imminent exhaustion. Yet military fuel requirements virtually know no limit, and in peacetime, civilian demands may increase substantially if anticipated increases in private cars, farm tractors, and civilian planes are realized.

A number of strategic raw materials, notably manganese, tungsten, chrome, industrial diamonds, mica, and tin, are either unavailable within areas controlled by the United States or supplied only in inadequate quantities. Stock piles of the less bulky of these scarce raw materials, sufficient to last for several years at present rates of consumption, can be built up at a small cost, measured by the scales of wartime expenditure. Imports of high-grade iron ore from Canada and Brazil may supplement domestic output and help to conserve the remnants of the Mesabi range. Oil from the Middle East may have to take the place in foreign markets of part or all of American oil exports. However, the threat of exhaustion should not become a stick for beating steel makers and oil producers into radical realignments of their raw-material policies. Stock piles should not become devices for stabilizing markets, camouflaged as military necessities. Improved methods for exploiting available resources and the development of substitutes have proven thus far the best answer to domestic shortages in raw materials.

Mass production, as an institution, has but a short history. No one can chart its future requirements for many years ahead. Machine warfare is an even more recent phenomenon. It is impossible to predict what all the machines of another war will be like and what special, perhaps as yet undeveloped, raw materials will go into their construction. A vigorous sub-

252

stitute economy (in the sense in which this term has been used in a previous chapter) is the backbone of military technology, not any one raw material, be it scarce or abundant. Better methods for using low-grade mineral deposits, research for new materials, and a program for fighting waste of natural resources of all kinds are the best means for assuring both military security and national prosperity. The crux of the raw-material problem, just as of the national economy as a whole, is adaptability.

An expanding, adaptable economy is the essential prerequisite of American world leadership in technology. As long as the collective mind does not succumb to Malthusian doctrines, production will continue to increase. Production—this should be plain—cannot be increased by cutting down profits for capital and incentives for management and labor instead of alleviating the frictions which cause hardships in, and opposition to, the operation of a free economy. The task is to restore competition, because under the competitive system profit rates tend toward disappearance, hence an incentive is created to maximize production in order to raise profits by a larger output, or to enter production branches with higher rates of profits, i.e., new branches. Without such a powerful driving force it is unlikely that entrepreneurs will "effect new combinations," at least not as readily as if compelled to do so by economic compulsion.

It is much too early to say where, precisely, the line between government intervention and private enterprise will be drawn. The precondition of a fruitful partnership is that the government abides by the rules of competition, that government-financed bodies do not take the place of the very monopolies which are now being castigated as the foes of fair play, economic adaptation, and technological progress, and that taxation does not devour profit—"the most important adaptive force of all in a private enterprise system." Similarly, technological progress entails a high degree of individual freedom which appears to conflict with the rigidities of massive planning. The oddities of educational institutions and research laboratories do not fit in with grand schemes of

253

co-ordination, nor does the creative mind.* Neither the adaptiveness of workers and entrepreneurs to the play of economic forces nor scientific progress, both being fundamental conditions to the well-being and military security of the nation, can be planned by an absolutist technocracy.

That military procedure if applied to industrial society is inefficient has not yet dawned on many observers. Transformations in the character of war necessitate subsequent adaptations of social and political institutions. Nothing would be more apt to thwart such adaptations than to cast postwar society into the rigid mold of wartime organization.

American power will be dependent upon the military force available at any given moment. The dangers of the future can no longer be met by the improvisation of a large fighting establishment. A minimum of strength will have to be available at any time, not only on paper, but so equipped that it can intervene on distant battlefields at short notice. Never again will the United States have three or four years to arm in wartime while the enemy is being kept at a safe distance from the centers of America's power. However, security of this kind cannot be had by limitless armaments. It would be dangerous to maintain a military force of such a size that it chokes, as it did in the case of Poland and France, the country's economic development by devouring half of the national budget. Nor should the organization for war be so large that its mere maintenance exhausts the military budget, thus preventing modernization.

The next war will have been won or lost in the laboratory long before it has broken out. A few hundred able scientists may tip the scales far more effectively than a few hundred thousand draftees. The word of these scientists will determine precisely what part of the nation's manpower shall be used in the armed forces and what part in the factory.

The policies the United States pursues in its domestic affairs will largely determine the internal policies of its allies.

* A highly flexible scheme for military research in peacetime has been proposed by James V. Forrestal, Secretary of the Navy. It would team private and institutional scientific research with the research organization of the Army and the Navy. See the *Annual Report*, fiscal year 1944, of the Secretary of the Navy to the President of the United States, released February 21, 1945, p. 13.

Rigidities in the American economy may spell the rigor of death to international trade no matter how energetically American exports of capital and goods are being pushed. The externalization, by indiscriminate dumping, of economic problems the United States fails to solve at home will clash with other nations' all-important interests in foreign trade, press upon them the Nessus' shirt of self-sufficiency, and poison international relations at their roots.

In World War II the military power of the United States has been deployed against the enemy from territories controlled by Britain and France. The logic of geography suggests that, whatever the shape of future warfare, American might will again have to be transmitted to theaters of operations through the territorial possessions of the old allies of the United States. It borders on the trite to repeat what should be obvious from every waking hour, yet it needs restating: The strength of America's allies is America's strength; only by pooling the sum total of their experiences in government, trade, technology, and culture can the Western world, the world of which the United States is an integral part, survive the trials of the present and those which lie ahead.

17. ALLIANCES AND THE BALANCE OF POWER

*Negotiate from strength, not from weakness,
else you will find yourself negotiating first at
some one else's expense—which is dirty—and
then at your own—which is disastrous.*

—Lord Vansittart

THIS book has been written on the assumption that a third World War within this generation, though neither foreordained nor probable, is none the less possible. While it is being argued whether the United States should enter military alliances to safeguard its security or should rely on the workings of an international security organization, or should spurn both, the alternatives of American foreign policy are being narrowed by a shift in the power-political equilibrium so massive that it can be ignored only by means of deliberate self-deception.

It is true that military alliances will not suffice for guarding the security of the United States. They are the minimum requirement of its defense. The foreign policy of the United States, unlike the cabinet diplomacy of the eighteenth century, cannot pick its allies among the most powerful countries. The United States must join with those countries whose interests are parallel to or identical with its own. Alliances with countries too feeble to defend themselves effectively may only put additional burdens upon the shoulders of the American people. However, all those countries with whom the United States, on the common ground of political ideology and general interest, can most readily conclude long-term arrangements of military collaboration have entered the phase of relative and perhaps absolute power decline.

All strategic planning must include not only every likely but also this or that improbable hypothesis. If, for example, the United States should become involved in a future war in which Great Britain, France, Holland, and Belgium are presumed to resist in Europe, Africa, and Asia until the military power of the United States can be transmitted to overseas battlefields, then the defense of Great Britain, France, Belgium, and the Netherlands is the first line of defense of the United States. Conversely, to weaken the power-political position of these countries in Europe and their strategic hold upon their empires in Africa and Asia is to breach the outer walls of American defense.

The size of population and manpower potential of the west European peoples are of vital concern to the United States. The United States may have to seek by material aid and ideological influence to implement the population policies of these countries.

Each country must tailor its demographic policies to its own needs and the characteristics of its people. The United States cannot play fairy godmother to the cradles of Europe. But the political and economic policies of the United States will largely determine with what degree of confidence such countries as Britain and France will undertake long-range demographic measures designed to underwrite their national future.

During the immediate postwar period the competitive position of the United States, its physical plant intact and its excess capacity ready to burst forth in a vast tide of exports, will be far stronger in international markets than it ever was throughout its history. However, future international economic arrangements must be satisfactory to the potential allies of the United States, which are also the world's great trading nations. These arrangements will be acceptable to these nations only if the United States recognizes their vital need for expanding their exports, rebuilding foreign investments, and developing aviation and shipping activities. On the other hand, they must be made to recognize the American desire to share in the economic development of their European homelands and overseas connections.

Foreign economic policies of the United States must be harmonized with its strategic interests. If it is the task of the

United States to strengthen the economies of its friends, it must step warily where trade by inflated credits would tend to strengthen the economies of those nations which might be aligned against the United States in a future struggle. It is being argued that to curb certain kinds of exports to politically unreliable countries constitutes a breach of faith with the principle of free trade. This is a specious argument; for uneconomic loans, stock piles of strategic raw materials, and tools for manufacturing weapons do not increase the well-being of the masses. Foreign investments, if these involve the export of American machine tools and patents, to wit, capital goods in all forms, are instruments of foreign policy. Although an international agency may preside over world economic development, capital goods exported by the United States cannot be neutralized power-politically.

There is no reason why the United States should not derive general advantages, including strategic ones, from its investments. In the nineteenth century, private investments and direct subsidies were closely teamed in support of Britain's foreign policy. French investors between 1890 and 1914 not only aided the economic development of Russia but also strengthened Russia's war potential. French investments in Russia proved financially a total loss. They were probably the decisive element in prolonging Russian resistance in World War I, and thus saving France from the very fate which befell her in 1940.

In terms of the future balance of power this war is being fought over two objectives: (1) control over the heavy industry of western Europe and the Yellow Sea region; (2) the preservation of the colonial empires of Europe as major power units.

If peacemaking is viewed in the light of these facts, it becomes immediately obvious what are the true and long-range interests of the United States and the Western powers. There are many schemes advocated by the partisans of various races, colors, and creeds. Some of these have no importance in relation to the problem of American security. Others, however, are plainly inimical to the security of the United States. Well-meaning and well-intentioned though they may be, they would diminish the strength of the United States, reduce the number of its friends, and create power-political disequilibriums that foster future conflicts—the very conflicts they were designed to avoid.

It is often said that refusal to grant India complete independence will ultimately force Britain to take up arms for the maintenance of the *status quo* and that the United States may find itself involved in the ensuing struggle. A successful domestic revolution in India now seems improbable. It could be brought about only by the active support of another Great Power. Barring such hostile intervention, Britain should be able to hold in peace what she was able to hold in war.

The transcendent result of World War II may well be not the defeat of Germany and Japan, and the rise of Soviet power, but the industrialization and urbanization of India, just as the transcendent result of World War I was not the fall of Hohenzollern Germany but the economic transformation of Russia. None the less, this eventuality does not relieve the present generation of American and British statesmen from insuring the strategic security of their nations, a task which might, but need not, be synonymous with fostering Indian independence. The alternative would be to emancipate India now.

The ineluctable result of immediate emancipation would be either that India herself would venture upon imperialist expansion or that other Asiatic powers would assume the tutelary role abandoned by Britain. The balance of power would then be upset not only in Asia but everywhere else. Such an alternative would more likely than not involve Britain and the United States again in a major war in which, precisely because of the loss of the Indian bases, both would find themselves deprived of strategic advantages they now enjoy. Hence little practical gain could be derived from the change.

It may be noted in passing that voluntary liberation will assure neither the American nor the British people of India's friendship. For as long as Britain rules India she will have friends among at least some groups of India's population. When she leaves, an entire propaganda machine will be set up, not only against Britain, but against all Western powers. The new government will seek to shift responsibility and blame for its inevitable difficulties and failures. The West will remain in Indian eyes forever tainted with its past sins, to wit, colonial exploitation and racial discrimination. In a major crisis it is unlikely that India would side with the United States and Britain.

Being a human creation, the British Empire is imperfect. Yet the progress it achieved must be assessed against the difficulties of introducing modern government into countries with basically undemocratic traditions and customs. It is not enough to initiate progressive political procedures. These must be adapted to existing conditions, and, in particular, precautions must be taken that they are not abused in the interests either of a minority or a majority. The maintenance of the colonial *status quo* does not imply stagnation. The cohesion of the British Empire has not been purchased by dogmatic resistance to change, but by a pragmatic gradualism which has always moved too slowly to satisfy the advocates of basic change, too fast to please nostalgic Tories. Gradual change is the leaven of the colonial *status quo*.

Devolution of central controls, a colonial charter, and international supervision are proposals to which representatives of widely differing views and interests such as Lord Hailey, Julian Huxley, K. M. Panikkar, Bertrand Russell, and Jan Smuts have subscribed. International supervision is to be limited to inspection, advice in technical matters, and inquiry into complaints. Without abdicating her sovereign rights, Britain would invite the participation in regional councils of other interested powers and accord increasing representation to the colonial peoples themselves.*

On the economic side of the ledger, dependence is not without solid benefits to the dependent peoples. Within the framework of the empire it is easier to provide "freedom from want," and for that matter also "freedom from fear." The British Empire is the most perfect form of international co-operation yet devised. Its structure has proven a flexible

* See page 286, Note 1 to Chapter 17.

one; the devolution of central controls has been continuous. The task is to improve, not to dissolve, the only working model of international organization.

Yet dwarfing all these arguments is the fact that the dissolution of the empire would by necessity lead to a series of major wars and would benefit other would-be imperial powers which do not possess the heritage of English common law, political representation, and trusteeship.

Many critics in this country have argued that though Britain may be the bulwark of Western liberties, the British Empire should be dissolved because colonial rule is archaic or immoral or simply impractical, and that the dependent peoples should be given greater political freedoms than they ever enjoyed in their long history. In the first place, there is in the record of the human race no precedent for the voluntary renunciation of empire.* Secondly, it should be obvious that dissolution would be accompanied by new power struggles over the fragments of that empire. World War I was fought over the liquidation of the Turkish Empire—which confirmed Metternich's prediction that the dismemberment of the Turkish Empire would signalize general war in Europe. World War II can appropriately be called the Second War of the Austrian Succession, for Germany's annexation of the succession states of the Austro-Hungarian Empire, namely Austria, Czechoslovakia, and Poland, presented the concrete issues on which the Great Powers lined up for war. The dissolution of an empire creates a power-political vacuum, and a power-political vacuum breeds war.

The integrity of the British Empire depends on the military power of Great Britain and on her ability to resist aggression in Europe. Only by pooling her resources with those of the old democracies of western Europe, i.e., by merging the war potentials of the west-European coal and iron-ore complex, can Britain, as well as France, Belgium, and Holland,

* "No nation ever voluntarily gave up the dominion of any province, how troublesome so ever it might be to govern it, and how small so ever the revenue it afforded might be in proportion to the expense it occasioned. Such sacrifices, though they may frequently be agreeable to the interest, are always mortifying to the pride of every nation. . . ."—Adam Smith, *The Wealth of Nations* quoted by E. M. Earle in *Makers of Modern Strategy*, Princeton, 1943, p. 127.

develop the real power which will correspond to their widely dispersed strategic commitments. Divided and isolated, their colonial holdings are hostages to fortune.

Sir Halford Mackinder's concept of the "heartland" is today, no less than when it was first presented in 1904, the fundamental axiom of world politics. If domination of the landlocked plains-lands of European Russia is joined to the domination of east-central Europe between the Baltic, Adriatic, and Aegean, then the condition obtains which Sir Halford conceived as the final step to the mastery of Europe. If the control of Siberia and central Asia is joined to the control of north China, Manchuria, and Korea, then the monsoon countries will be bracketed by the power which, in Sir Halford's metaphor, controls the "pivot of world history," and the "world island" will be dominated by a single master, the final step to mastery of the globe.

The demarcation of British and Russian spheres of influence in the Balkans and the Mediterranean, too, is not a grand design, but an accomplished fact. No amount of inspired skullduggery can eradicate from the pages of history the expressed views of European statesmen, Continental as well as British, which support Mackinder's thesis on the consequences which must flow from the consolidation of the "heartland" with the populous countries of east and east-central Europe. Palmerston deemed the independence of Poland the essential prerequisite of European freedom from single-power domination. Bismarck said that he who controls Bohemia controls Europe. The balance of power in Europe has changed, and with it the position of Great Britain and all the countries of western Europe. It can serve no rational purpose to pretend that precisely the condition which four centuries of British statesmanship attempted to forestall is now *not* present. With the demise of the old balance disappears that geographic remoteness which buffered the arc of British power resting on the British Isles and the promontories of Eurasia against the greatest land empire of the globe.*

Miliukov, the exiled Russian historian and liberal, proph-

* See page 287, Note 2 to Chapter 17.

esied at the beginning of World War II that Russia's aim would be "to recover the heritage of the old Russian Empire." If the historical pattern of Russian diplomacy has re-emerged in Europe, the question presents itself whether it will not reappear in other areas in which Russia is traditionally interested. "The Eastern question," a question which turned upon Russia's influence in the Black Sea, the Danube basin, and the Straits, and extended to Persia, Afghanistan, Chinese Turkestan, and Manchuria, has been reopened. The center of Russian industrial gravity has moved eastward. In Soviet central Asia a great new industrial empire has been opened up, "for whose safety Russia must be at least as much concerned as it has been in the past for the Ukraine."

The ideological principles which dictated Russia's withdrawal from the Middle East in the twenties no longer determine policy. The change is not only ideological; it is a departure from the early policy of economic isolation. The direction is set, and there can be little doubt that in the next twenty-five years Russian influence in the Middle East will have an economic basis. The industrial areas of Transcaucasia, Kazakhstan, and the other border republics will be the nearest, if not the most efficient, workshops available to the Middle East.

In the postwar world, Russia may intend to do no more in the Middle East than exercise the influence that her power and proximity make inevitable. Europe may remain her principal strategic interest. In a sense, Russian policy in the Middle East is derivative. Russia exercises pressure on the dominant power in the Middle East, Britain, in order to influence British policy in the vital European arena. As the Russian statesman and general, Skobelev, bluntly put it: "The stronger Russia is in central Asia, the weaker is England in India and the more will she be conciliatory in Europe."

Britain is the dominant power of the Middle East. The United States, by virtue of its many economic and political commitments and strategic interests, has a vital stake in that region. The better the relationships of Britain and the United States with Russia in Europe, the less likely is it that

Russia will intervene actively in Middle Eastern politics. However, the ascendancy of Soviet influence in the Balkans, the Mediterranean, and central Asia now places Russia in a position far more favorable than in the nineteenth century for exercising pressure on Britain's vital interests in that region.

Russia, it appears, does not seek territorial aggrandizement. But federation with neighboring peoples has been her policy in Europe. Technically, there is no reason why any people, having purged itself of its anti-Soviet ruling classes, cannot vote itself into the Soviet Union, an additive racial mosaic. Russia has not annexed Lithuania, Estonia, Latvia, and Karelia, but these same Soviet republics applied for, and gained admission to, the Soviet Union. The Mongolian People's Republic acknowledges the suzerainity of China. Its political constitution and military organization were created in intimate association with the Soviet Union. The pull of Russian policies of racial assimilation, economic development, and traditional foreign policy, backed by military might, is disintegrating the coherence of China's borderlands in inner Asia. The attraction of the Soviet Union upon an independent India would be the greater, the larger the number of different units into which India would split.

To many Indians this vista is not displeasing. For the inclusion of India in the Russian orbit would release revolutionary forces which would sweep away the caste system and feudal tenure as well as the capitalistic forms borrowed from the West. Lenin's formula for Russia—"Soviets, electricity, and accounting"—many Indian intellectuals believe, is just as applicable to India as it was to Russia twenty-five years ago. After a heroic period of revolution and experimentation patterned on Russia's example, India would take her place as a modern nation. Despite the barrier of the Hindukush, Russia is thus a party to the balance of power in India. The increasing prestige of the Soviet Union is a powerful lever on British policies in India, and technological as well as psychological changes in modern warfare have immeasurably complicated Britain's strategic problems.

Whoever controls Manchuria determines what kind of industry China can develop. Manchuria is the keystone of a Far Eastern system of heavy industry. Possession of Manchuria is hence the essential condition of Chinese military power and political independence. Were China's sovereignty not to extend anew over this, her ancient domain, her economic development would mainly center in the expansion of light industries, while China would remain dependent on foreign imports of steel and weapons made of steel. Soviet domination of Manchuria—through federation or a controlled government—would restore to Russia that access to the Pacific she lost in 1905, and secure her most exposed outpost in Asia, the Primorski Krai. Strategic logic urges Russia to restore her former position. Yet the inclusion of Manchuria in the Russian orbit would exclude China from the circle of Great Powers with finality. In this sense it can be said that whoever controls Manchuria controls Far Eastern Asia. It is a historic doctrine of U.S. foreign policy that no foreign power shall control the land and people of China. The Cairo Declaration, which pledges China the return of Manchuria, Formosa, and the Pescadores, reaffirms John Hay's thesis of the Open Door and Charles Evans Hughes's insistence upon the territorial and administrative integrity of China. The United States, by virtue of its traditional stake in the China trade and maintenance of the balance of power in the Pacific, has a vital interest in the fortunes of a strong and independent China. A Chinese state which does not control Manchuria might conceivably be independent; it certainly will not be strong. The extension of Russian influence over Manchuria and Korea would thus call for a readjustment of American foreign political and economic policies which hardly jibes with a fundamental concept to which the United States has adhered consistently for nearly half a century, and prevailing sentiments and expectations. Basically, the situation, as regards both its strategic and ideological implications, is closely similar to that confronting Britain and the United States in the Middle East. If India and the Far East were to enter the Soviet power sphere, the greatest and most populous land empire of history would have become a reality surpassing the creation of Genghis Khan and the vision of Lenin. "The Eastern question" cannot be separated from the problems of Great Power relationships as neatly as we may wish for the sake of symmetry in spheres of influence. Great

Power unanimity in Europe cannot freeze into immobility the population dynamics and ideological ferment of the East, nor can it modify the strategic interests converging upon the crossroads of the Old World. If it is in the overriding self-interest of the United States to underwrite the security of the British Commonwealth, United States commitments must extend to the *status quo* in the Near and Middle East. The United States *is* committed to restore the territorial and administrative integrity of China. It will be in these areas that the Great Powers' capacity for compromise will undergo the crucial test.

In sum, the closing in of spheres of influence upon the areas which heretofore isolated the Great Powers from one another tends to render the Great Powers far more sensitive to one another's moves. It shows, therefore, a severe case of geographical astigmatism to argue that the neat demarcation of Super Power orbits is the most promising augury of an era of stability.

It is possible to conceive of all of Europe as a vast buffer zone interposed between the peripheral powers, the United States and Britain to the west, the Soviet Union to the east. But will the pacification of Europe remain for the next twenty years task number one on the agenda of American foreign policy? To establish the primacy of this task on the agenda of American foreign policy, one would have to assume that every major power aligned against Germany in World War II will repeat faithfully every mistake it has made before, and that general power relationships will have remained unchanged.

Preconceptions of the past have frequently encumbered the diplomacy of other times; prestige of power, as a rule, long survives decline in power. The prestige values of Venice in the seventeenth century, of Spain in the eighteenth century, and of France after the Franco-Prussian War, stood in no relation to their real power. The fear value of Germany will be greater for many years than her real power. This will by no means be an unhealthy symptom; it will make for prudence on the part of the victors. But it tends to foster an exaggerated image of a declining power, and to detract attention from very real power changes in other parts of the globe.

Russia has been victorious by a narrow margin. Could she have vanquished Germany in a straight duel, nation against nation? Could she have won without that tenth share in her equipment which represents the direct contribution of American and British war production to the Soviet arsenal? Could she have driven the enemy from Stalingrad to the Spree had Allied forces not tied down German strength in Africa, Italy, and western Europe? Narrow as was the margin of Russian superiority over Germany, it is not the measure of Russian strength today and tomorrow. Victory has created a new condition. The New Frenchman who planted Napoleon's eagles on the capitals of Europe was not the ragged citizen who repulsed at Valmy the army of Europe. The New American who defeated Britain's picked troops at New Orleans was not the starving militiaman who shivered at Valley Forge. The struggle against Germany bequeathed to Russia the tradition of victory.

Nice dialectical distinctions—Leninism, Socialism-in-one-country, Stalinism, and all the other way stations of ambulatory Marxism—pale into insignificance before the national achievement. That national achievement hallows the social and economic system, whatever its definitions. It is therefore pointless to argue as to whether the New Russian is going Left or Right, is more or less inclined to do business with the capitalist democracies, is more nationalist or is still pledged to world revolution. He has been victorious; his prestige is immense; and he would be a strangely introverted being did he not know that for decades to come the eyes of the world will be fixed upon his every gesture. Has victory kindled his imagination to the visions of greater conquests? He would be less than human had it not. If defeat breeds revenge, victory stimulates ambition. Will Russia venture upon imperialist expansion which in the nature of things must lead to conflict with the other world powers? There was and is no major conflict between the United States and Russia. There are many issues dividing Russia and Britain, but they are substantially the ones which have troubled their relations for nearly a hundred years. They were handled without recourse to war.

The boundaries of the new Russia will be the frontiers

which any strategist looking from east to west would draw, just as the western Allies looking from west to east need not be prodded into seeing the strategic value of a frontier along the Rhine and looping east of the Ruhr. A frontier which one power deems reasonable and just is rarely seen in that light by the power on the yonder side. Russia's European frontiers will not be those Great Britain and the United States would have drawn for her. Russia may choose to rectify some of her Asiatic frontiers. But the world will not go to war over frontier changes Russia may deem to her interest in eastern Europe, southwestern Asia, Turkestan, and Mongolia. On that score the American people, for one, will not fight the Soviet Union. Hence the question of war and peace during the next decades lies not exclusively in Russian power politics—which is neither simple nor enigmatic but as forthright as national self-interest suggests. It lies also in what the Great Powers of the West may do or leave undone.

The power and ideological self-confidence of Russia have been immensely strengthened by victory. While the rehabilitation of her devastated areas will require a vast effort, Russia will be able to count on the export capacity of the United States and the manpower reserves and productive capacity of a large part of Europe. Busy as she may be at home, Russia will not look conveniently the other way when her ideological pull asserts itself beyond her territorial borders.

The ideological truce between the Soviet Union and the Western democracies was imposed by the exigencies of coalition warfare. It is based on military expediency. It is emphatically not based on agreement in political philosophy. Russia does not accord the individual the liberties upon which political democracy rests. Whether the Russian system proves more beneficent to mankind in general and to the backward peoples in particular than political democracy thus far managed remains to be seen. The Russian system promises to resolve the massive contradiction between new powers of production and the traditional economic mores. It does not promise political liberties. The Western democracies may seek to evade the issue of the ideological conflict by themselves accepting the basic formulas of socialism. This in effect is the solution proposed by those who stake future collaboration between the Soviet Union and the Western democracies on a gradual approximation of the two systems. This view evidently dismisses as relics of an unhappy past such facts as the Soviet Union's distrust of Western designs and the historical, almost ecologically conditioned, foreign policies of Russia. It also ignores the fact that the ideological conflict between communism and democracy is fundamental—while that between communism and other totalitarian doctrines is not. But these are not the most compelling reasons why a policy of "approximation" must fail. Unless Russia is to launch upon an unprecedented movement away from dictatorship and toward representative government, she must regard socialist gradualism in the West as her most dangerous enemy, a counterrevolutionary movement against her own system.

Western democracy dreads another war, Russian communism dreads another ideological schism. "Gradualism" flouts the revolutionary orthodoxy of Moscow no less flagrantly than does the Trotzkyite heresy. Some of the tactical successes of Russian diplomacy were won at a heavy cost to the Communist parties in Europe and America. The Russian leaders cannot long continue to jeopardize their hold on their following abroad by prolonging a truce sanctified by one imperative only: defense of the homeland of socialism. When the example of representative government in Great Britain, the United States, and France excited other nations to emulate it, these were not advised by London, Washington, and Paris to desist from dabbling in democratic experiments. Russia will not restrain the devotees of her official ideology. Russia will not jump across her own shadow.

The communist parties abroad are model organizations. In the long run their political power will be as great as the internal tensions they will be able to exploit. These tensions cannot be manufactured by a small group of professional party workers or vicarious intellectuals. All men carry in their systems certain dangerous germs and still enjoy good health. General debility brought on by fatigue or malnutrition may stimulate these germs into virulent action. In the politically mature countries of the West, communism, like all other revolutionary doctrines, is an endogenous phenomenon. Its history as a political movement is in the West one generation older than in Russia. In Asia its cult is of an age no more venerable than that of other Western importations. Everywhere it will be a second choice should the Western powers fail to solve their own social and economic problems. Then the pull of the ideological pole Moscow will become irresistible—not because the Soviet Union has solved these same problems better but because the division of the world along one single line of ideological cleavage offers no other alternative. It is here that we grasp the crucial problem of the balance of power and world peace. To resolve it is to overcome the moral crisis of the age. That crisis does not arise from the nature of democracy but from the promises which have been made in its name.

The promises which have been made to peoples engaged in fighting a destructive war have aroused vast expectations. No one at present has a precise notion how they are to be fulfilled. The road to peace is still littered with the broken promises of World War I. The Napoleonic Wars and World War I were followed by protracted political disturbances and widespread impoverishment. It would be a most unusual occurrence should this, the most costly war in history, have been waged at a profit. Statements noble in purpose have been minted down to undertakings to be fulfilled in the near future. It may have been thought necessary to publicize these pledges in order to obtain for military purposes that degree of collective effort which modern society appears to attain only in the face of considerable reluctance. This policy somehow takes for granted that the average man is incapable of understanding the fundamental issues the war is being fought about, and that democracy can meet the supreme test only by delegating intelligence as well as power. Were this indeed the case, then democracy would be a fiction not only in war but also in peace. For the problems of the impending peace will be no whit less complicated than those of war.

Foreign commitments entered into by representatives of democratic states are binding when and as long as their peoples choose to back them up. Thus unredeemed promises in foreign policy are promises broken by a whole people. Conversely, cynicism aroused by the breach of promises a democratic government has made to its own people filters into foreign policy. In foreign policy the United States and Britain are pledged to respect the sovereign rights of all nations styled peace-loving, and to restore and safeguard the independence of those nations which fell victim to aggressors. The independence and freedom of association of the smaller powers, it has been argued in these pages, are essential features of a world system adaptable enough to allow for change. "Not the least contribution [of the small nations]," Arnold Wolfers writes, "consists in the self-restraint their existence imposes on mightier nations." It is just this exercise of self-restraint which must permeate the humdrum routine of keeping the peace. And self-restraint is the leaven of international collaboration just as it is of a free society.

That the keeping of the peace depends in the main on the actions of the Great Powers is not a new discovery. The dullest diplomat of the seventeenth, eighteenth, and nineteenth centuries knew as much, and the truism does not become more impressive by repetition. Peace is indivisible, and as long as the Great Powers do not delegate their sovereign rights to a higher authority, the problem of sovereignty, be it that of a Great or of a Small Power, remains the problem of the peace. Despite the stampede from President Wilson's declared principles into *Realpolitik,* the prestige of the United States is fatefully involved in the issue of the rights of small nations. That issue obviously does not mean in the semantics of American politics what it means in that of the Soviet Union. Both points of view may be taken as rooted in profound convictions. The policy of the Soviet Union with regard to small neighboring powers is undoubtedly considered as sound and successful by most Russians. It is not the kind of policy with which the United States has been associated historically. This poses a difficult problem in the "art of the possible." The United States, too, cannot jump across its own shadow.

The primary objective to which the United States is committed is the survival and reinvigoration of Western civilization. It may be irrational to state this as an objective. These pages have attempted to analyze factors of power. But power is a means to an end. That end is the preservation of individual lives and a harmonious community. If we believe that mankind should progress farther on the path of knowledge, wealth, and Christian ethics, that the individual, his rights and freedom, is the ultimate goal of politics, and that gradual adaptation is preferable to violent change, then we are pledged to bear with Western civilization together with its many and conspicuous shortcomings. The present war was fought in Europe over the balance of power. But it was also fought against one of the prominent members of Western civilization who violated its basic tenets. It was thus not only a power war but also a civil war. The war against Japan is not fraught with this dual implication.

The reconstruction of Europe must be begun by the powers who fought Germany. It cannot be completed without ultimately leading the German people back into the community against which they have revolted. That task cannot be completed by a fragmented Europe awaiting salvation from without.

The peace settlement cannot satisfy all claimants. The number of chips is limited and not all players can be winners. Even a defeated Germany may have political alternatives. The strategic area between the Atlantic littoral, the Rhine, the Alps, and the Baltic plains will continue to produce a vigorous and speculative race driven by the inscrutable urge to gain power and influence. In the interwar period the fissures of the international structure afforded Germany a hold by which she lifted herself back into the arena of world politics. A vanquished Germany may be able to fuse anew the rancors of political and racial minorities the world over into a phalanx of rebellion. World War I, which began as a simple conflict of powers, released revolutionary forces transcending political frontiers. World War II is a climax, not the culmination, of a world upheaval.

From the outset the issues of the mere struggle for national survival have been immensely complicated by social, economic, and racial conflicts. All the continents are fertile soil for revolutionary ideologies. For more than a hundred years Germany has been a pressure house of political ideas which have triggered diverse and most contradictory political movements. German society has been torn up by its roots; German cities have been reduced to rubble. The philosophical nihilism affected by the intellectual precursors of National Socialism may sweep the German masses—an ideology to end all ideologies. Not only in Germany but virtually in all of continental Europe the violence of the struggle has snapped the strands of historical continuity. Everywhere, races dispossessed and steeped in doctrines of stark expediency are ready to push that which is falling. Policies which rely on the divisive force of national antagonisms may prove to have misjudged fatally the true direction whence Germany may renew her bid for European hegemony. Policies which seek to freeze the political divisions of Europe and do not promote the formation of new and orderly supranational groupings large enough to function as modern economic units, invite the spread of a new and revolutionary supranational ideology.

The formation of larger power units—a federation of those peoples of western Europe who share with the United States a political tradition and outlook—appears a logical step toward the creation of a viable European order. By dealing unilaterally with the states of western Europe the United States can assure itself a preponderance in the affairs of a region which, were it united politically, might prove less amenable to whatever the United States may suggest. But would these states be stronger allies in the hour of need were they to remain disunited? The experience of two World Wars and technological changes in modern warfare speak against this assumption. The trend toward regionalism is a comparatively recent phenomenon. It is consistent with economic and technological developments. Its unfolding will be a slow process. That it has found any popular support at all, and it has found a surprisingly broad backing, is the only truly new phenomenon which has appeared on an international stage which for more than a century has been dominated by nationalism.

The term "region" should not be confused with such vague, all-inclusive, and not too candid terms as "orbit," "bloc," or "zone"—euphemisms for domination plain and simple. The regional affinities of western Europe lie in its economic interdependence, Atlantic outlook, and cultural experience, a distinctive blend of geographical and historical characteristics. Despite political antagonisms, the peoples of the Danubian basin and the Arab lands of the Middle East are each drawn together by a common or similar geographical environment and shared historical experience. The accent may lie on this or that unifying factor. The fact is that among these races the idea of regional unity has sturdily survived long periods of fragmentation and foreign domination.

The integration of western Europe would restore the political equilibrium of Europe and amalgamate several interdependent national economies into a balanced whole. Despite these patent advantages the scheme is fraught with dangers. Every new development involves risks. Two main objections can be advanced against this scheme. The first is that any federation or confederation of European states may fall under the sway of Germany. Such a danger could only arise were all of Europe to be united into one political unit. And it will be precisely the foremost concern of a Western federation to prevent such European unifaction under the leadership of Germany or any other power—for it is against this same threat that Britain and France took up arms in 1914 and 1939.

The other objection is that regionalism tends to foster economic self-sufficiency and thus conflicts with the ideal of free trade. Indeed it is but a compromise between free trade and economic nationalism. It is not a perfect solution but a step toward world integration. The lifting *now* of bars to the free movement of men and goods within a limited area is preferable to waiting for their problematic disappearance under the aegis of an international authority. The development of techniques of transportation and manufacture of substitutes makes possible a high degree of economic self-sufficiency within large units. Since, however, autarchy involves certain sacrifices and political dangers, international agreements should be expected to be the norm rather than the exception under a regional system. A west European federation, least of all, would seek to replace its international connections by economic isolation. The volume of trade within that region can be expected to increase spectacularly. And can the most fervent advocates of free world trade deny that a greater volume of intraregional trade raises the level of employment and well-being and hence ultimately redounds to the benefit of all trading nations?

But far more pressing than economic considerations is the political urgency. A federation of the west European powers must by necessity arrive at a compromise with the Soviet Union in the Balkans and the Middle East. The power potential of this new combination would be large enough to meet all foreseeable contingencies, though not overpowering enough to overawe the Soviet Union. The military commitments of the United States in Europe and the Middle East would thus be reduced to a minimum. Conversely, for the United States the only alternative to such a restoration of the balance of power is a system of tight military alliances which, in the last resort, will be centered on a permanent Anglo-American coalition. These pages have dealt with probabilities, not blueprints for a world order. Its shape will depend on factors which the future alone can reveal. But it is plain that Western civilization, to remain a living thing, must evolve new political forms adapted to a new political situation and its power-political instruments.

The concept of the West is not an exclusive concept. Somber invocations of Western solidarity against the hordes of Asia are apt to produce a psychosis in which fear is the strongest element. Were it to dominate the policy of the United States in the Far East, no rational solutions to problems of American security in the Pacific could be found. The concept of west European unity is that of a new political formation which possesses genuine power of its own yet serves as a bridge between the world powers, the Anglo-Saxon, Latin, and Slavic peoples. Western integration and world integration are not mutually exclusive goals.

The General International Security Organization chartered at San Francisco provides for many likely (and many unlikely) contingencies in international relations—but not for the substitution of a world government for the existing system of sovereign states. Since "the organization is based on the principle of the sovereign equality of all peace loving states," the

275

concept of world state, *civitas humana,* does not find its organic law in the charter of this organization. The power granted to the mightiest states to curb small ones deemed guilty of aggression endows with legal sanction power differentials which exist and have always existed between sovereign states. It does not infringe upon the principle of sovereignty. The solution does not change the basic pattern of world politics.

The alternatives remain the same: the perpetuation of the present system with its characteristic conflicts; the ascendancy of one power to world domination; or the creation of a world federation. The first has been explored uninterruptedly for fifty generations. The second is the world picture projected by *Geopolitik,* the final stage in geopolitical evolution. In this prodigious simplification of history, the emergence of huge power blocs is the phase before the last, to wit, the final struggle for world imperium. The third is federation by consent. It is the American solution.

An American foreign policy which nurtures federalism of regional as well as global dimensions is consistent with American interests and traditional concepts. The solution is not protected by copyright. It can be, and has been, borrowed by other powers professing various ideologies. Its practical application may become the transcendent issue of coming decades. If this is the right reading of the future, then the question before the makers of United States foreign policy is this: Shall the United States lead in a world-wide movement nourished by its own historic experience? This, to be sure, is not the only question. But the verdict of history-still-to-be-written may turn on the answer to that question.

NOTES

CHAPTER 1

1. "That is why I think that the decisions of the Dumbarton Oaks conference should be regarded as one of the clear indications of the stability of the front against Germany. . . .

"To win the war against Germany means to accomplish a great, historic task. But to win the war does not yet mean security to the peoples of the world in the future. The task is not only to win the war against Germany but also to make impossible the outbreak of new aggression and a new war, if not forever, at least for the duration of a considerable period. . . .

"What means are there for averting new aggression by Germany and, if war arises in spite of that, stifling it at its very beginning and not allowing it to develop into large scale war? . . .

"There are such means for this purpose. Apart from complete disarmament of the aggressive nations there is only one means, namely, to create a special organization to defend peace and insure security, composed of representatives of the freedom-loving nations, to put at the disposal of the leading organ of such an organization the essential amount of armed force required to avert aggression, and to make it the duty of this organization, in case of necessity, to apply without delay these armed forces to avert or liquidate aggression, and to punish those guilty of aggression. . . .

"Can one reckon on the fact that the activity of this international organization will be sufficiently effective? . . .

"It will be effective if the Great Powers, which have borne on their shoulders the main burden of the war against Germany, will act in future also in the spirit of unanimity and concord. It will not be effective if these essential conditions are violated."
—Premier Stalin's Address in Moscow on the eve of the 27th anniversary of the Revolution, as quoted by the *New York Times*, November 7, 1944.

2. Because clarity on this point is essential, the understanding of other powers as to the purpose and functions of a general system of security "like that sketched at Dumbarton Oaks" bears

close reading. The newspaper *l'Aube,* formerly edited by M. Georges Bidault, French Foreign Minister, discussed, a few days after the signing of the Franco-Russian military alliance, the "different conceptions" of an international security system:

"Two general conceptions are in latent conflict. . . . Russia believes that if the unanimity rule is paralyzing, on the other hand the unanimity rule for the great powers is the only one that takes account of experience and geography. . . .

"At the other extreme, what is called Senatorial opinion in United States distrusts all two-power pacts and regional security organizations. . . .

"France perfectly understands the Russian doctrine that embodies this truth: the international organization cannot and ought not to be conceived except in relation to the German menace and the Japanese menace—since Stalin has now classified Japan as aggressor. Such an organization could not in any case act against one of its members, who, by preventive action, should destroy the aggressive power of a future Reich. This is the idea of all the invaded peoples."—M. Schumann, *l'Aube,* Paris, January 12, 1945, as quoted in the *New York Times.*

3. "At the Moscow conference the Soviet delegation . . . announced with sufficient clarity that premature attachment of small states to theoretically conceived groupings would be fraught with danger to these very states as well as to the future peaceful development of Europe. . . .

"Especially is it important to emphasize that the Soviet point of view firmly opposes efforts to resurrect the policy of the *cordon sanitaire* against the Soviet Union, whatever the form under which it masquerades."—Unsigned article in *Izvestia,* Moscow, November 8, 1943, as quoted in the *New York Herald Tribune.*

4. President Roosevelt stressed the attainment of the practically possible, not the theoretically perfect as the aim of his foreign policy.

"President Roosevelt, analyzing the Dumbarton Oaks security agreements at a news conference today, declared that the proposal might not achieve peace forever, but that it could certainly serve to safeguard peace for our time."—Lansing Warren, reporting on White House news conference, in the *New York Times*, October 17, 1944.

"Perfectionism no less than isolationism or imperialism or power politics may obstruct the paths to international peace. Let us not forget that the retreat to isolationism a quarter of a century ago was started not by a direct attack against international cooperation, but against the alleged imperfections of the peace."—President Roosevelt's Message on the State of the Nation, January 6, 1945.

5. "Now, I am not so impractical as to expect any country to act on any final motive other than self-interest. I know of no reason why it should. That is what nations are for. I certainly intend that intelligent and loyal American self-interest shall be just as vigilantly and vigorously guarded as is amply obvious, from time to time, in their own behalf by the actions of our allies. The real question always becomes just this—where does real self-interest lie?

"Here we reach the core of the immediate problem. Without remotely wanting to be invidious, I use one of many available examples. I would not presume to use it except that it ultimately involves us. Russia's unilateral plan appears to contemplate the engulfment, directly or indirectly of a surrounding circle of buffer states, contrary to our conception of what we thought we were fighting for in respect to the rights of small nations and a just peace. Russia's announced reason is her insistent purpose never again to be at the mercy of another German tyranny. That is a perfectly understandable reason. The alternative is collective security. . . .

"Well—at that point, Russia, or others like her, in equally honest candor, has a perfect right to reply and say this to us—'where is there any such alternative reliance until we know what the United States will do? How can you expect us to rely on an enigma?'

"Now we are getting somewhere: Fear of reborn German aggression in years to come is at the base of most of our contemporary frictions. It is a perfectly human and understandable fear on the part of all neighboring nations which German militarism has twice driven to the Valley of the Shadow within one generation.

"Fear of reborn German aggression in years to come is the cause assigned to unilateral plans for Russian post-war expansion. Fear of reborn German aggression is the reason assigned to the proposed partition of Poland. Fear of reborn German aggression gave birth to the Anglo-Soviet agreement of 1942; the Soviet-Czechoslovak agreement of 1943; the Franco-Soviet agreement of 1944, and similar unilateral and bilateral actions inevitably yet to come. Fear of reborn German aggression is our apple of discord. . . .

"Whether we Americans do, or do not, agree upon all the powers that shall reside in an ultimate international council to call upon us for joint military action in behalf of collective security, surely we can agree that we do not want an instant's hesitation or any instant's doubt about our military cooperation in the peremptory use of force, if needed, to keep Germany and Japan permanently de-militarized. Such a crisis would be the lengthened shadow of the present war. It would be a direct epilogue of the present war. It should be handled as this present war is handled.

"There should be no need to refer any such action back to Congress any more than Congress would expect to pass upon battle plans today. The Commander in Chief should have instant power to act, and he should act. I know of no reason why a hard-and-fast treaty between the major Allies should not be signed today to achieve this dependable end. We need not await the determination of our other post-war relationships. . . .

"Then, in honest candor, Mr. President, I think we have the duty and the right to demand that whatever immediate unilateral decisions have to be made in consequence of military need, and there will be such even in civil affairs, they shall all be temporary, and subject to final revision in the objective light of the post-war world and the post-war peace league as they shall ultimately develop. . . .

". . . If Dumbarton Oaks should specifically authorize the ultimate international organization to review protested injustices in the peace itself, it would at least partially nullify the argument that we are to be asked to put a blank-check warrant behind a future status quo which is unknown to us, and which we might be unwilling to defend."—Senator Vandenberg's speech in the Senate, January 10, 1945, as reported by the *New York Times*.

CHAPTER 2

1. Guglielmo Ferrero emphasized that the decline of population was one of the fundamental causes of the decline of Rome.

He asserted that "excessive urbanization . . . was in fact . . . the disease which killed the Roman Empire. . . . Neither the attacks of barbarism from outside nor those of Christianity from within would have prevailed against its might and its massive weight if the strength of the colossus had not been already undermined by this internal cancer. . . . The empire covered itself with cities great and small rivaling each other in splendor and wealth: and into these cities, at the expense of depopulating the countryside where nobody was willing any longer to live, were attracted the peasantry, the village artisans and the yeomanry. From the Third Century onward the excessive urbanization in the Roman Empire which had been the cause of the splendor and apparent wealth of the preceding century began to change into a dissolving force . . . Agriculture was little by little ground down by ever increasing burdens . . . In the fields, which were expected to feed all these men who had crowded into the cities to work or to idle, there was a dearth of peasants to cultivate the land. Also with the disappearance of the rural population the problem of recruiting the army which drew its soldiers then as always from the country became increasingly serious. While the cities tricked themselves out with magnificent monuments the Empire was threatened with a dearth of bread and of soldiers."—*Ancient Rome and Modern America, A Comparative Study of Morals and Manners*, New York, 1914, pp. 78-83.

CHAPTER 4

1. The population of the United States accounts for one-half of the total. Estimates place the population of the Argentine (13.1 million in 1940) at less than 16 million in 1970, provided immigration is maintained at the 1930-1938 level. Weakness in numbers no less than a location remote from the great political centers and trade routes of the globe will frustrate the grandiose ambitions of the Argentine nationalists, even were the anachronisms of the social system and the overwhelming reality of U.S. power not to doom beforehand Argentinian hopes for Latin American dominion. Moreover, among the three competitors for Latin American leadership, Brazil, Mexico, Argentina, Argentina runs a poor third in numerical strength. Brazil, with 44 million people in 1941, will in 1970 count 56 million inhabitants; Mexico will have increased from 19.4 to 28 million. Among the Latin American countries the most backward are slated for the

largest increases, exactly as in the low-standard-of-living belt of the Asiatic monsoon lands.

2.

PREDICTED NUMBERS OF MALES OF AGES 20-34 IN VARIOUS COUNTRIES
(in millions)

	1940	1950	1960	1970
United States	16.11	17.14	17.98	18.63
France	4.60	4.57	4.48	4.33
Germany	8.45	8.61	8.58	8.36
Italy	5.29	5.77	6.17	6.50
Great Britain	5.68	5.79	5.80	5.73
India	51.48*	59.98	72.23	87.42
Russia	21.03	23.46	25.85	28.24
Japan	8.22†	11.59	14.70	18.49

* Census of 1941
† Census of 1935

United States: Least Squares Parabola fitted to 1890, 1900, 1910, 1920, 1930, and 1940 censuses. Larger interval was chosen to counteract effect of immigration.

France: Least Squares Parabola fitted to 1911, 1921, 1926, and 1931 censuses and 1940 estimate.

Germany: Least Squares Parabola fitted to 1910, 1925, and 1933 censuses and 1940 estimate. It was assumed that in 1933 half of 30-39 group were in 30-34 range.

Italy: Least Squares Parabola fitted to 1911, 1921, and 1931 censuses and 1940 estimate.

Great Britain: Least Squares Parabola fitted to 1891, 1901, 1911, 1921, and 1931 censuses and 1940 estimate. In 1891 and 1901 North Ireland is not included. In 1921 and 1931, the 1926 figure for North Ireland is used.

India: Least Squares Parabola fitted to 1911, 1921, and 1931 censuses. A fourth point is used, assuming for this purpose an 11 per cent increase between 1931 and 1941. This increase is based on data for part of the country.

Russia: Least Squares Line fitted to 1897 and 1926 censuses and 1940 estimate.

Japan: Least Squares Parabola fitted to 1913, 1925, 1930, and 1935 censuses. It was assumed that in 1913 half of the 30-39 group were in the 30-34 range.

CHAPTER 12

1. ". . . Wars are fought primarily with weapons which were developed before the fighting began. . . . During war a nation has time only to improve and adapt weapons the fundamentals of which were evolved during the preceding years of peace. . . .

"The two most spectacular new weapons used in this war are rockets and radar. Both of them prove that, if a weapon is to be employed during a war, the fundamental research underlying it must have been conducted over a protracted period before the war.

"Rockets, of course, are a very old military weapon. . . . Work on what might be called a modern rocket engine dates back at least to the 1920's. Every year since 1925, the Navy Department has made an annual contribution to research on rocket engines. . . .

"Both among our Allies and our enemies, modern rocket development has a similar history, having been under way in Germany, according to recent reports for some twenty years.

"Radar surely will stand as the most effective new weapon in this war. . . . All of these innovations stem back to basic research which began in 1922. In September of that year, two scientists at the Naval Aircraft Radio Laboratory at Anacostia, D.C., made the first observations which led to the development of radar. Throughout the next eighteen years, they and their associates conducted the time-consuming basic research which today makes possible our amazing and varied uses of radar—an art in which we are far ahead of our enemies."—*Annual Report, Fiscal Year 1944, of Secretary of the Navy James Forrestal, to the President of the United States,* released to newspapers February 21, 1945.

2. See E. R. Stettinius, Jr., *Lend-Lease, Weapon for Victory,* New York, 1944, pp. 250-253, for the great variety of items furnished to Soviet industry. "Even though the Nazis failed to reach the major Soviet oil fields in the Caucasus during the 1942 fighting, gasoline and oil have bulked large in Lend-Lease shipments to the Soviet since the very beginning because Russia has been so short of refinery capacity, particularly for aviation gasoline . . . the older factories are producing at least as much as before with the help of new machine tools made in Russia, the United States or Britain. Where there were three plants before, there are now six, and the combined output has more than

doubled. The factory superintendents and foremen took great pains to point out the machine tools that came from the United States as they took General Burns down the production lines. The bulk of the tools were plainly Russian-made, but American Lend-Lease tools were working beside them to make possible all-out production." (Quoted by permission of Macmillan Company, publishers.)

See also *Eighteenth Report to Congress on Lend-Lease Operations,* for the Period Ended December 31, 1944, U.S. Government Printing Office, Washington, 1945, pp. 19-21. "We have . . . sent 12,000 airplanes to the Soviet, more than to any other ally under the lend-lease program . . .

"The Soviet armies that have covered such great distances in such a short time have required hundreds of thousands of motor vehicles and railroad cars, as well as vast quantities of communication equipment to support their overland advances. Lend-lease has played an important rôle in furnishing these to the Soviet armies.

"Up to December 1, 1944, we had sent to the Soviet Union under lend-lease, 362,000 motor vehicles, including 46,000 jeeps and 29,000 motorcycles. One hundred and forty-four thousand of these were sent during the first 11 months of 1944 in preparation for the Soviet Army's great winter offensive. On some parts of the Eastern Front these American vehicles are carrying more than one-half the supplies moving up to the Soviet troops.

". . . To provide electric power for war industries in liberated areas, we developed in this country a power train. It consists of a complete steam generating unit mounted on railroad flat cars, which can be moved from city to city or industry to industry as the need demands. As soon as the local utilities are functioning again, the power train moves on to 'spark' the industries in another district. Up to December 1, 1944 we had sent 60 of these trains and the Soviets had already put some of them to good use in the Donets Basin."

3.   It has been estimated that in the United States at least 3 to 4 per cent of the labor force must be available as a mobile reserve to keep the economy "flexible in the joints." A solution of the problem of maintaining a mobile reserve of labor in a manner compatible with the welfare, dignity, and freedom of the individual is suggested by an editorial of the *Times,* London, March 4, 1943. "Would it not be possible to introduce a scheme

by which the State itself should become a third party to contracts of employment and carry the employee through intervals of unemployment at full pay? He would then be in the position of a soldier waiting at his depot for posting orders, and not of one flung out of the service. . . . Such a scheme would have to be optional, since as a *quid pro quo* for the security provided, the worker would have to be willing, as occasion required, to change his trade and even the place of his home. . . . The worker clamours for more security; the community needs more mobility. Both needs can be met if we give one as the price of the other."

The proposal visualizes the task of occupational training as lying within the province of popular education and social security, pre-empted by all modern governments. Workers "waiting for posting orders" will thus be helped in learning new skills. The scheme is based on *voluntary* adaptation.

"Mobility of labour does not mean perpetual motion. Mobility of labour means merely that labour should be capable of moving and ready to move if necessary. Organized mobility means that men do not move if movement is futile and do move rapidly and directly to the job when there is a job." Sir W. Beveridge, *Full Employment in a Free Society,* W. W. Norton and Co., New York, 1945, p. 175.

CHAPTER 14 ·

1. For a contrary opinion see John Fischer, "India's Insoluble Hunger," *Harper's Magazine,* No. 1139, April, 1945, pp. 438-45.

"Indian Nationalists are fond of pointing to the Russian example, and in many respects the Bombay Plan is modeled frankly after the Soviet Five Year Plans. Like them, it calls for a massive investment of labor and material in heavy industrial plant—steel mills, machine tool factories, chemical and power projects—within a very brief period. The Indians, however, are apt to gloss over the methods Russia had to use. The Soviets carried through their Five Year Plans by cutting sharply the consumption of the people and throwing the resources thus saved into a rapid building up of capital equipment. That entailed a ruthless and efficient dictatorship, willing to plunge ahead regardless of the cost in suffering and human life . . . In Russia, even after the devastation of World War I and the Revolution, the people as a whole had a standard of living considerably above the subsistence level. There was some fat on the economy, which could be shaved off and diverted to the building of industrial plant. In India there is no such margin. Present living standards cannot be hammered much lower—for whatever worthy purpose—without causing wholesale starvation. . . . There is little prospect that a Free India would have a government strong enough to impose great sacrifices on its people, even if they had anything much to sacrifice."

A sceptical observer could, in 1865, have marshaled arguments as plausible as the above against the liklihood that Japan could ever rival the industrial development of any major European power.

CHAPTER 16

1. The naval tonnage of the Great Powers at the outbreak of war is given by *Brassey's Naval Annual 1942* as follows:

Germany	Sept. 1939	205,111
France	Sept. 1939	518,730
Italy	Jan. 1941	535,156
USSR	Oct. 1941	279,092
Great Britain	Sept. 1939	1,356,674
Japan	Oct. 1941	1,049,148
Total		3,953,911

CHAPTER 17

1. Field Marshal Jan Smuts stated in an article contributed to *Life:*

"Such a change, involving decentralization so far as the Mother Country is concerned and centralization with large powers so far as the colonies are concerned, would be a welcome advance in the direction of colonial freedom and responsibility, which is the general trend of colonial development.

"As a further stimulus to the development of such an enlarged colonial unit, its general development policy should be entrusted to a council on which would sit not only the British Government as the parent State, but also the unit itself and any interested neighbouring States of the British Commonwealth—such as Canada, Australia, New Zealand and South Africa—that could prove beneficial to the advance of their less developed neighbours.

"There should be a system of regional grouping of colonies. . . . While the mother countries would be exclusively responsible for the administration of their policies, the ultimate control of the general or common policy would come under a regional commission or council, on which would be represented not only the mother countries but also others regionally interested for security or economic reasons."

See also Julian Huxley, "West African Possibilities," *Yale Review,* Vol. 34, No. 2, Winter, 1945; Lord Hailey, *Great Britain, India, and the Colonial Dependencies in the Post-War World,* the University of Toronto Press, 1943, p. 30; and K. M. Panikkar, *op. cit.,* pp. 19-21.

2. It is a historic fact that British diplomacy labored to bring about the consolidation of an independent federated eastern Europe. November 18, 1943, may be said to have been the official date marking the demise of that British policy. *Izvestia,* the mouthpiece of the Soviet government, published a vigorously worded reply to suggestions in two British periodicals, the *New Statesman and Nation* and the *Economist,* that the Moscow declaration on Austria carried with it at least implied Soviet approval of a central or eastern Europe federation of small states. Of the reasons advanced for the Soviet attitude three deserve particular emphasis. The first, according to *Izvestia,* was the uncertainty of social and political conditions in the small states. "Important acts like federation with other lands and people, renunciation of possible sovereignty, are permissible only as free and well-reasoned expression of the people's will." Secondly, *Izvestia* pointed to the injustice of permitting "some states which became Germany's satellites" to become "members of this or that federation . . . thus being accorded an equal place with countries which have been subjected to invasion and occupation." But far more important is the third reason, namely, "That the Soviet point of view firmly opposes efforts to resurrect the policy of the *cordon sanitaire* against the Soviet Union, whatever the form under which it masquerades." The phrase *cordon sanitaire* had not made its appearance in the Russian press for many years, and for that matter, had not occurred for many years in British writings. The forthright rejection of the scheme for an east European federation by Soviet Russia marks the beginning of a profound reversal of British foreign policy.

INDEX

295